BECOMING AN ACCREDITED GENEALOGIST

Plus 100 Tips to Ensure Your Success!

by Karen Clifford, AG
President, Genealogy Research Associates

Ancestry

Library of Congress Cataloging-in-Publication Data

Clifford, Karen.
    Becoming an accredited genealogist : plus 100 tips to ensure your success! / by
Karen Clifford.
        p.   cm.
    Includes bibliographical references.
    ISBN 0-916489-81-7
    1. Genealogists—Certification.   2. Genealogy—Examinations, questions, etc.
I. Title.
CS14.C55 1998
929'.1--dc21   97-51543

Published by Ancestry Incorporated
P.O. Box 990
Orem, UT 84059

Printed in the United States of America

10 9 8 7 6 5 4

Contents

Figures

Dedication

This book is dedicated to those who had the vision to create credentialing programs and to those who continue to maintain and enhance them. They have elevated the discipline of genealogy, made it a true profession, and given us a standard against which to measure our competence.

Acknowledgments

The Church of Jesus Christ of Latter-day Saints discontinued their sponsorship of the professional Accreditation Program as of 31 August 2000. They negotiated with the Utah Genealogical Association (UGA) to continue this long-standing and highly-respected Accreditation Program under a newly organized International Commission for the Accreditation of Professional Genealogists. ICapGen, as it is called, was transferred both the proprietary use of the AG initials as well as the current written official examinations. ICapGen will continue to provide closely monitored and timed tests, with a verbal examination as part of the accreditation process, much as the former Accreditation program tests were handled. This process of proctored exams is comparable to other professional examinations.

Much of the expenses to start this new organization are being underwritten by UGA until the new commission is fully implemented. "We believe it is essential to the integrity of the profession to have two testing and credentialing bodies which offer vastly different approaches to determining the competency of professional genealogists," stated Jimmy Parker, former Managing Director of the Family History Library, and current Interim Director of this new commission. Jimmy was also on the original team which set up the Accreditation Program in 1964.

Other executive members of the Interim Commission include Ray Clifford who has professional experience with national and regional accreditation processes and has served as a Consultant for the California Commission on Teacher Credentialing. Dr. Clifford is an internationally recognized expert in testing and assessment. His combination of skills will help in the standardization of assessment procedures and in the expansion of the Accreditation options to cover more areas of the world. Jill N. Crandell, an Accredited Genealogist and Director of the Salt Lake Institute of Genealogy, and the current treasurer of UGA adds her financial expertise to putting the commission on firm financial footing.

Advisors to ICapGen included representatives from the Family History Library, librarians, university professors, private researchers, and genealogy corporations as they met in September, 2000 in an all-day session with existing Accredited Genealogists to establish their set of bylaws and to set up the multi-member, multi-national, multi-backgrounded group of approximately 9 to 11 individuals who will eventually be known as the Commission. Information on the new organization is being continually updated on the UGA website: <www.infouga.org>.

UGA is proud to be a supporting sponsor in the creation of ICapGen. "We recognize the high standards required of Accredited Genealogists throughout the world, and want those standards to be maintained free from outside influences. Therefore, ICapGen will function as an independent credentialing commission." By mid-October, the Family History Library will have completed most of the transfer of its materials to the new commission. If you have questions about the new sponsorship of the Accreditation Program, contact UGA at 1-888-463-6842 or email: info@infouga.org.

My gratitude is extended to Jimmy B. Parker, AG, Interim Director of ICapGen for reviewing this text for its third printing. He stated, "The principles presented herein are still true and important for the researcher to know. I see no need to make drastic, time-consuming changes at this point." However, within the next few years there will be several important changes in this exceptional program as the new commission is established. Until that time, however, what is found in these pages will assist the candidate for Accreditation in his or her preparations.

I also wish to thank Paul F. Smart, AG, MA, FGS, Former Coordinator of the Accreditation Committee at the Family History Library, for reading the original manuscript and suggesting improvements, additions, and corrections involving the accreditation process. Also I wish to thank Elizabeth Shown Mills, CG, CGL, FASG, past president of the Board for Certification of Genealogists, for her professional courtesy in providing information on the certification process.

My great appreciation is extended to my co-laborers at Genealogy Research Associates (partners in a vision) who have allowed me to give freely of my time to serve as former President of UGA and toward preservation of the Accreditation credential.

 # Why This Book Was Written

The Need for Credentials

Tip 1: If you are planning to become a professional genealogist, credentials are important. The credentialing examinations not only help to maintain quality and public confidence in the field of genealogy, but also help gauge personal preparation and qualifications.

Interest in genealogical research is expanding rapidly both in the United States and abroad. This heightened interest is due mainly to the inexplicable pleasure we find in tracing our personal family history. While some people desire to leave behind tangible evidence of their existence in the form of a family history, others seek their past in an attempt to be whole again and perhaps feel less alone after being adopted, abandoned, or torn apart by war or other disasters.

Discussions in the newspapers, on television, and in magazines about hereditary diseases and the value of being aware of personal health risks have convinced many people of the health benefits that can be gleaned from genealogy research.

Also, people are living longer and accumulating more wealth, and they sometimes leave this wealth to be divided among unknown heirs. As a result, genealogy has become big business for those whose job it is to locate rightful heirs.

With this increased demand has come an increased need to set standards for the profession. Out of a desire to protect the consumer, two examination processes for obtaining a professional genealogy or family history credential have developed. One process originated with a group of concerned genealogists and is called certification, while the other originated with a genealogical institution and is known as accreditation.

Institutions Granting Credentials

The two major independent organizations that test genealogists are the International Commission for the Accreditation of Professional Genealogists, known as ICapGen, which grants accreditation, and the Board for Certification of Genealogists (BCG) in Washington, D.C., which grants certification. Other genealogy credentials are granted by colleges which provide a certificate of completion (Monterey Peninsula College and Hartnell College in California are two in this category), and universities which grant a degree in Family History (Brigham Young University is the largest). Each of these programs has different assessment procedures, different requirements, and different ways of defining areas of specialization within the genealogical field. However, all require the same basic abilities.

Tip 2: Universities and colleges provide degrees of learning and certificates of accomplishment which focus on preparation for taking one of the two major exams.

These programs have created a much-needed service that tests the competence of genealogists and provides assurance to those who want to hire a professional in the field. Even though each program has some unique features, each was created in response to the same general need.

Although some differences will certainly be noted, the emphasis in this book is not on the differences between the processes but how their foundations are similar. After both processes are examined, the applicant can make an educated decision as to which credential is appropriate based on personal career goals, income, location, abilities, and clientele. Figure 1.1 summarizes the features of various credentialing programs.

There is a difference between a professional, or credentialed, genealogist and a paid researcher. Anyone can collect money for doing research and be called a paid researcher, but the knowledge, training, ethics, honesty, integrity, and efficiency of credentialed genealogists set them apart. Many researchers accept payment before they have received any formal or complete training. Often, such researchers have not developed the skills to locate quickly the best possible record to solve a client problem but will often use a "hit-or-miss" routine of searching whatever record happens to be most accessible. Even more alarming is a paid researcher who incorrectly evaluates a record for the client because of lack of sufficient training.

Tip 3: As long as paid researchers do not misrepresent themselves nor charge inappropriately for their on-the-job self-training, their service can be valuable. In fact, they are gaining experience.

When Laverne Galeener-Moore referred to paid genealogists in her book, *Collecting Dead Relatives* (Baltimore: Genealogical Publishing Co., 1986), as genealogy mercenaries, I was the first to compliment her on her wit and acumen. Now, concerned that some may take her quips seriously, I want to point out that the many paid researchers and credentialed genealogists I know are not avaricious, money-grubbing hirelings (as the term "mercenaries" portrays). Rather, the vast majority:

1. generously lend their efforts to volunteer projects such as indexing resources,

2. serve on many boards to encourage the preservation and promotion of genealogical records,

3. and freely give more than they are paid for.

I would rather call these unselfish genealogists, whether paid researchers or credentialed genealogists, "angels in training." Although the public in general may equate anyone "paid to do genealogy" with a "professional genealogist," in this book the term "professional" means a genealogist with the training, knowledge, testing, efficiency, integrity, and business expertise to serve the industry well. The suggested readings at the end of this chapter explain some of the contributions qualified genealogists make to society and show the clear contrast with researchers of whom to be wary.

Tip 4: Every person is so important to everyone else in his sphere of influence that if one of us fails, those who have been held in our orbit by attraction may lose their balance as well. Likewise, when someone becomes successful, they take with them their associates. At the same time we are having an effect on others, others are having an effect upon us. Be sure to associate with those who are positive about your goal to become a professional genealogist.

Still, there is often an adverse public reaction toward professional genealogists; many have the mistaken idea that genealogy is "easy." Why, then, would anyone want to be a professional? What is expected of a credentialed genealogist, anyway? And should you wish to become a professional, which program would best suit your particular needs and interests? How prepared are you for a credentialing examination?

After outlining the benefits of genealogical credentials, this book describes the knowledge and basic research skills expected of a professional. Then it examines broadly the experiences, testing procedures, and application processes specifically needed to apply for credentials, and finally it focuses on the accreditation process.

Self-assessment, tests, and assignments are provided to help you evaluate your own readiness. Finally, appropriate addresses will help those who are serious about entering the professional arena to start the application process. Suggestions on how to prepare *now* for your business, such as how to put together personal study guides, will help you prepare for your exams and prepare for your career, as well.

Figure 1.1 summarizes some unique features and benefits of the various credentialing processes. Note in Figure 1.1 the post-testing support, for example. Little support is given by the accreditation program to enhance the genealogical skills of individuals once they pass the exam. However, Brigham Young University's continual educational support for family history and the UGA Salt Lake Institue of Genealogy's intensive program for professional development make up for this deficiency.

Figure 1.1   Unique Features of Various Genealogy Credentialing Programs

	Accreditation	Certification	College/University
Research Aspects	Generally focuses on the ability to trace ancestral lines back in time, while researching the entire family—not limiting research to main line only.	Some levels include the ability to trace ancestral as well as descendant genealogy. The CG exam focuses on whole family reconstruction.	Prepares students for both ancestral and descendant genealogy.
Sources	Tests regional competence in using U.S., Canadian, or International sources.	Tests competence in using local and regional sources of a national and international interest as they pertain to U.S. research.	Tests competence in basic and specialized regional sources.
Foreign Emphasis	Tests research ability in the use of records of the British Isles, Scandinavia, Continental Europe, Canada, the Pacific Area, or Latin America, as well as regions of the United States. Includes the ability to read foreign languages, understand foreign customs as they relate to research, and interpret foreign records.	Tests those who live outside the continental U.S. on their regional research abilities that relate to U.S. genealogy. Also tests foreign language skills or the capability of understanding foreign customs as they relate to research. Please write to BCG for specifics (see appendix page 213).	BYU prepares students to pass foreign credentialing exams; other colleges currently do not.
Record Types	Ensures the researcher is both knowledgeable about, and can use records in the collection of the Family History Library (FHL) as they pertain to his/her region of specialization as well as other research tools which are available for the area of specialty outside the FHL.	Ensures the researcher is knowledgeable about the area, specialty record types, and research processes in the specific certification level for which they apply.	Prepares students to use the resources of the FHL and other major repositories of genealogical significance.

	Accreditation	**Certification**	**College/University**
Testing Procedures	Requires submission of a four-generation pedigree prior to 1875 with associated research reports, documentation, transcriptions, and abstracts as well as an evaluation of the research findings. Also evaluates one's knowledge and abilities through a formal set of proctored test batteries that include objective and short-answer tests, case studies, document recognition, written sample reports, and an oral defense of one's work. It also includes a timed research exam, with report of an actual problem provided by ICapGen.	Requires submission of a portfolio that includes sample research reports, document transcriptions and abstracts; evidence analysis and work plans, essays discussing resources relating to the applicant's specialty; and variously completed genealogies (for CG and CAILS), lineage applications (for CALS), taped lectures (for CGL), and lesson plans and taped lessons (for CGI). While the CALS and CAILS are tested on the ability to trace forward and backwards in time, the CGRS is tested on neither. (Levels explained in appendix A.)	Involved in preparing students to take either the accreditation or certification exams. Certificate or degree implies a basic knowledge of sources but does not test experience to the extent of the other two credentialing programs.
Fees	There is no charge, but applicants must travel to Salt Lake City to take the exam. ICapGen will request samples of your recent reports as part of a renewal of your accreditation every five years. You'll not need to travel back to Salt Lake City.	There is a $25 preliminary application fee and a $150 final application fee payable upon submission of the portfolio. A renewal application and fee are required every five years and changing categories requires a new application.	No special fee for the examinations, but, fees of several hundred to thousands of dollars are spent for tuition.
Post Testing Support	Lists of accredited genealogists are distributed at no cost as inquiries are received.	A roster of certified genealogists is published biannually and supplied free of charge to major institutions. Lists are distributed at no cost at major conferences and on the Board's web page. Certified persons are expected to maintain a subscription to the Board's newsletter which provides additional support.	No advertising. Students are encouraged to attend BYU Family History Conference, the UGA Institute, and later NGS and FGS national conferences.

Benefits

Tip 5: If you plan on becoming a paid credentialed genealogist, start now to think of a business name. You may wish to register it in several states.

Let's discuss other specific benefits available for those who obtain a professional genealogy credential:

Advertising. Unless you request not to be listed, your name will be placed on a list with other credentialed researchers. Thousands of copies are circulated each year to potential clients.

Advancement. Becoming an accredited, certified, or degree-holding genealogist can be a stepping stone to becoming a staff worker in a genealogy library, a college genealogy instructor, a professional genealogy researcher, or a business owner. It also prepares you to be more effective in related careers: family history author/publisher, surname periodical publisher, heraldry consultant, missing-heir investigator, adoption researcher, hereditary society lineage specialist, Native American researcher, genealogy data base developer or programmer, lecturer, or even a writer of historical novels.

Certificate. Of course, when you obtain a genealogy credential, you receive a certificate to hang on your wall. You will also receive a wallet-sized card which identifies you as a professional researcher and gives you access to record collections not always available to the general public.

Tip 6: Get your business license and federal ID number early so you are not delayed when you're ready to start your genealogy business.

Confidence. Obtaining professional credentials is a great confidence booster, since you know you have met the professional standards established to separate credentialed genealogists from well-intentioned hobbyists and paid para-professionals.

Contributions. Knowledge gained and shared as you earn your credentials contributes to the larger body of knowledge available to the field.

Tip 7: Compare prices on business cards, stationery, and checks.

Credentials. If you are awarded one of these credentials, you are authorized to use one or more of the following designations, depending on your specialization: AG for Accredited Genealogist, B.A., B.S., M.A., or Ph.D. as university degrees if in genealogy or family history, CGRS for Certified Genealogical Record Specialist, CALS for Certified American Lineage Specialist, CAILS for Certified American Indian Lineage Specialist, CG for Certified Genealogist, CGL for Certified Genealogical Lecturer, or CGI for Certified Genealogical Instructor.

Tip 8: Obtain your own business checking account.

Earnings. Earnings are usually higher for those who have documented their abilities through accreditation, certification, or by obtaining a degree. Genealogical record specialists, para-professionals, and data-input specialists usually start out at minimum wage and move up to $10-$15/hour, depending on their location.

Accredited or certified genealogical specialists charge anywhere from $15-$75 per hour plus expenses for professional research. Degree-holding individuals earn from $35-$80 per hour.

Ethics

Tip 9: The genealogist's code of ethics sets a standard which we should apply and encourage in all ways. Having a framed copy in your office encourages clients to deal with you.

The genealogical profession, like other professions, has had its share of charlatans waiting to make an easy profit from unwary clients. To prevent this from occurring, to detect those who may be committing fraud, and to improve the overall level of competence in the field, both ICapGen and the Board for Certification of Genealogists hold members to a strict code of ethics—whether or not the individual is being paid for his/her work. Figure 1.2 is the agreement by the genealogist with the International Commission for the Accreditation of Professional Genealogists as a condition to accreditation and Figure 1.3 is the Code of Ethics used by the Commission. This standard of ethics and code of honor has helped to increase the credibility of the profession for all genealogists.

Something for Everyone

In every class I teach I am asked, "What do I need to do to become a professional genealogist?" Or, "What kind of experience is required if I would like to do what you do for a living?" Requirements for credentialing become a road map to the beginning genealogist to help chart professional development.

Whether you are a volunteer librarian, a compiler of genealogical data, or a personal user of genealogical collections, understanding the basic credentialing requirements of a professional researcher will aid you in accomplishing your personal goals.

Tip 10: It doesn't matter where you are on the road to becoming a genealogist as long as you are facing the right direction.

This book can be used by reference librarians and certified genealogists to help them understand the accreditation process. It can be used by advanced researchers to prepare to pass credentialing exams. It can be used by beginning and intermediate researchers who desire to get a head start on their professional careers in genealogy. As this happens, the entire profession will benefit, because more people will become better genealogists earlier in their careers; thus they will have more time to make contributions to the field. The book can also be used by volunteer and amateur researchers as a way to judge acceptable genealogical research and to identify researchers best qualified to help them with their particular research problems.

Figure 1.2 Agreement by the Genealogist with the International Commission for the Accreditation of Professional Genealogists as a Condition to Accreditation

As a genealogist accredited by the International Commission for the Accreditation of Professional Genealogists, I agree to—

1. **Reply promptly to all letters received which concern my employment as a genealogist.**

2. **Clearly inform my patrons of:**
   a. **Fees charged;**
   b. **Deposits required;**
   c. **Use of other agents (for whose work and use of funds I accept full responsibility);**
   d. **Methods of reporting;**
   e. **Specific areas of my accreditation. (It is recommended that you refer to yourself not only as being accredited by the International Commission for the Accreditation of Professional Genealogists but also state the geographical area of accreditation.)**

3. **Make regular written reports to my patrons explaining:**
   a. **Research steps taken;**
   b. **Results found (or reasons for step if results are negative);**
   c. **Basis for accepting any pedigree connections;**
   d. **Reasons for delay if six months have elapsed since the last report of initial deposit;**
   e. **Recommendations for future research;**

4. **Maintain an adequate accounting system to fully protect any funds deposited by any patron until fully earned by myself, and I will not use these funds for personal use until fully earned (NOTE: Full protection of a patron's funds is best ensured by opening a separate bank account for the funds. If you open an account as a trust account for the patron, these funds will be protected from your personal creditors until you have earned them and withdrawn them from the account.)**

5. **Reply promptly by correspondence to the International Commission for the Accreditation of Professional Genealogists, to any inquiry regarding my conduct as an accredited genealogist.**

6. **Adhere to "Board for Certification of Genealogist Code of Ethics" as prepared by the Board for Certification of Genealogists, P.O. Box 14291, Washington D.C., 20044 (see page 9).**

7. **Be subject to the policy of the International Commission for the Accreditation of Professional Genealogists which states in part "that the ICapGen reserves the right to deny or withdraw genealogical accreditation status to any person(s) at its sole discretion."**

_____   _____
Date   **Accredited Genealogist**

Figure 1.3   Board for Certification of Genealogists Code of Ethics as Used by
ICapGen

As a practicing genealogist, mindful of my responsibilities to the public, the genealogist consumer, and my fellow practitioners, I do hereby pledge to strive for the highest level of truth and accuracy in all phases of my work; to work in my client's best interests and protect my client's privacy, exclusive access, and proprietary rights in any work done for hire; to act honorably toward other genealogists and the profession as a whole; and to adhere to the Board for Certification of Genealogists Standards of Conduct.

Standards of Conduct

To the public:

- I will delineate my fees, abilities, and/or publications in a true and realistic fashion.

- I will not publish or publicize as facts anything I know to be false, doubtful, or unproven; nor will I be a party directly or indirectly to such action by others.

- I will quote documents precisely and cite as sources only those documents I have personally used.

- I will present the purpose, practice, scope, and possibilities of genealogical research within a realistic framework.

To the individual consumer:

- I will furnish only facts that I can substantiate with adequate documentation; and I will not withhold any data necessary for the consumer's purpose.

- I will keep confidential any personal or genealogical information given me by the consumer, unless I receive written consent to the contrary.

- I will reveal to the consumer any personal or financial interests which might compromise my professional obligations.

- I will undertake paid research commissions only with explicit consent from the consumer as to scope and fee. Any payment in excess of the contract will be returned.

Figure 1.3   Board for Certification of Genealogists Code of Ethics as Used by the FHL (continued)

- I will seek from the consumer all prior information and documentation related to the research commission and will not knowingly repeat the work without explanation as to good cause.

- I will seek from the client the goals and scope of the research question and, to the best of my abilities, address the research, and report to that question.

- If I cannot resolve a research problem within the limitations of time or budget established by contract, I will explain the reasons why; and if other feasible avenues are available, I will suggest them.

- I will embark on research only within the client's authorization until receiving permission to continue; I agree not to misrepresent the possibilities of additional research.

- If the research question addressed involves analysis of data in order to provide proof of a genealogical relationship or identity, I will advise the client that the conclusions are based on the preponderance of the evidence available and that absolute proof is usually impossible.

- I will not publish nor circulate research or reports to which the consumer has a proprietary right without prior written consent of the consumer -- whether payment was made directly, or to an employer or agent.

To the profession:

- I will act, speak and write in a manner which I believe to be in the best interests of the profession.

- I will participate in exposing genealogical charlatans but will not knowingly injure or attempt to injure, with demonstrable justification, the professional reputation, prospects, or practice of another genealogist.

- I will not attempt to supplant another genealogist already employed by a client or agency.   I will substitute for another researcher only with specific written instructions provided by the client or agency.

- I will not represent as my own the work of another. This includes works that are copyrighted, in the public domain, or unpublished. This pledge includes reports, lecture handouts, or audio/visual tapes. In citing another's work, I will give proper credit; and before using another's materials, I will obtain permission. 21 June 1995

Suggested Reading

Benedict, Sheila, Kathleen W. Hinckley, and James W. Warren. "Working with the Client: A Panel Discussion on the Relationship Between Professional Researchers and Their Clients." *From Sea to Shining Sea; Federation of Genealogical Societies and Seattle Genealogical Society, 20-23 September 1995; Seattle, Washington,* S-122. (May be ordered from Repeat Performance, 2911 Crabapple Lane, Hobart, IN 46342, session S-122.)

Greenwood, Val D. "Understanding Genealogical Research," *The Researcher's Guide to American Genealogy,* 3d ed., Baltimore: Genealogical Publishing Co., 2000, 3-18.

Hinchliff, Helen. "Fraud, Fortune Hunters, and Falsified Pedigrees!" *A Place to Explore; National Genealogical Society and San Diego Genealogical Society,* 3-6 May 1995; San Diego, Calif., 5-7. (May be ordered from Repeat Performance, 2911 Crabapple Lane, Hobart, IN 46342, session W-2.)

Milner, Paul. "A New Location: Procedural Steps for Methodically Getting Started." *Meet Me in St. Louis; Federation of Genealogical Societies and St. Louis Genealogical Society, 11-14 August 1999;* St. Louis, Missouri, T-53. (May be ordered from Repeat Performance, 2911 Crabapple Lane, Hobart, IN 46342, session T-53.)

Slater-Putt, Dawne. "Organizing Genealogy Materials." *Meet Me in St. Louis; Federation of Genealogical Societies and St. Louis Genealogical Society, 11-14 August 1999;* St. Louis, Missouri, T-54. (May be ordered from Repeat Performance, 2911 Crabapple Lane, Hobart, IN 46342, session T-54.)

British Isles Research
Chapman, Colin. *Tracing Your British Ancestors.* Baltimore: Genealogical Publishing Co., repr 1996.

Falley, Margaret D. *Irish and Scotch-Irish Ancestral* Research. Baltimore: Genealogical Publishing Co., repr 1998.

Herber, Mark D. *The Complete Guide to British Genealogy and Family History.* Baltimore: Genealogical Publishing Co., 1998.

Grenham, John. *Tracing Your Irish Ancestors.* Baltimore: Genealogical Publishing Co., repr 1998.

Irvine, Sherry. *Your English Ancestry: A Guide for North Americans.* Orem, Utah: Ancestry, revised ed. 1999.

Canadian Research

Merriman, Brenda Dougall. *Genealogy in Ontario: Searching the Records*. Revised. Toronto: Ontario Genealogical Society, 1988.

Punch, Terrence M.. *Genealogist's Handbook for Atlantic Canada Research*. Boston: New England Historic Genealogical Society, 1989.

Continental Europe Research

Baxter, Angus. *In Search of Your European Roots: A Complete Guide to Tracing Your Ancestors in Every Country in Europe*. 2nd ed. Baltimore: Genealogical Publishing Company, repr 1996.

Baxter, Angus. *In Search of Your German Roots: A Complete Guide to Tracing Your Ancestors in the Germanic Areas of Europe*. 3rd ed. Baltimore: Genealogical Publishing Company, 1999.

Cole, Trafford R. *Italian Genealogical Records: How to Use Italian Civil Ecclesiastical, and Other Records in Family History Research*. Orem, Utah: Ancestry, Inc., 1998.

Colletta, John Philip. *Finding Italian Roots: The Complete Guide for Americans*. Baltimore: Genealogical Publishing Company, repr 1998.

Hispanic Research

Platt, Lyman D. *Genealogical Historical Guide to Latin America*. Detroit: Gale Research Co., 1978.

Platt, Lyman D. *Hispanic Surnames and Family History*. Baltimore: Genealogical Publishing Co., repr. 1997.

LDS Research

Jaussi, Laureen R. and Gloria D. Chaston. *Genealogical Records of Utah*. Salt Lake City: Deseret Book Co., 1974.

Native American Research

Gormley, Myra Vanderpool. *Cherokee Connections*. Baltimore: Genealogical Publishing Company, repr 1999.

Hill, Edward E. *Guide to Records in the National Archives Relating to American Indians*. Washington, D.C.: National Archives, 1981.

Prevost, Toni Jollay. *The Delaware and Shawnee Admitted to Cherokee Citizenship and the Related Wyandotte and Moravian Delaware*. Bowie, Md.: Heritage Books, 1993.

Scandinavian Research

Johansson, Carl-Erik. *Cradled in Sweden*. Logan, Utah: Everton Publishers, Inc., 1995.

Public Expectations of a Professional Genealogist

Tip 11: Learning to quickly evaluate problems and develop efficient research strategies are skills learned most effectively by practice. To develop these skills, volunteer as a society researcher, as a Family History Center (FHC) staff member, or as a contributor to your local society newsletter.

Professional genealogists must be accountable to their clients. Clients expect researchers to use their experience and professional judgment to determine which records to search, where to obtain them, and how to search them quickly and efficiently. Once records are obtained, they expect the genealogist to be able to read them, which may entail a knowledge of ancient paleography and/or foreign languages.

Professional genealogists must also be thoroughly versed in the principles of evidence used to evaluate research hypotheses and be able to develop efficient research strategies. Anyone can take a shotgun approach to genealogy research, randomly checking one record after another, but a professional genealogist focuses on those records most likely to contain the information needed to meet the client's research objectives.

Basic Knowledge

Tip 12: Learn to ask questions, such as "What would determine a movement pattern (mountains, Indians, swamps, etc.)?"

Credentialing tests the candidate's abilities in the above stated areas. Professional genealogists are also expected to have:

● Knowledge of the topography and land forms of the area of specialization in order to understand migration, jurisdiction of records, and neighborhood connections.

● Knowledge of the history of the area, which may lead to new, unexplored sources of information.

Tip 13: History provides clues to events which generated records, i.e. a war generates military records; a fire results in loss or movement of records, etc.

● Knowledge of the history of the records themselves—why they were kept, who created them, who has jurisdiction over them today, and how these factors affect the accuracy of those records.

Tip 14: The knowledge of why records were kept comes from federal, state, & local histories.

Tip 15: To discover where original records are kept, use union catalogs to manuscripts and archive collections.

Tip 16: The book, Albion's Seed *is a helpful resource concerning customs in the U.S.*

Tip 17: Language guides are available from the Distribution Center of The Church of Jesus Christ of Latter-day Saints.

- Knowledge of prevailing customs—needed to interpret records accurately and thus prevent drawing the wrong conclusions.

- Knowledge of the period's languages, calendar changes, and writing styles to better interpret original records.

- Knowledge of paleography (the ability to read the language as it was then written) coupled with a knowledge of the language and writing styles—needed to assess the value of a document, form proper hypotheses, and discover solutions to family lineage problems.

- Knowledge of the sources available in a specific region, so you don't waste time seeking nonexistent records.

- Knowledge of various methods for obtaining and using available sources. It is not enough to know a source exists; it is necessary to know the optimal order to search the sources to most efficiently find the answers you need.

- Knowledge of how to draw on all of the above skills to reach and defend a conclusion.

Thoroughness

Tip 18: Research suggestions on calendar changes are available on the British and International floors of the FHL.

Tip 19: The only way to read the old handwriting efficiently is by practice, practice, practice. Although you can learn on your own, a good class on paleography can speed up the process considerably.

Tip 20: The most noteworthy sources are listed in the Research Guidance and Research Helps areas *(in the Search section) of the FamilySearch™ Web site (www.familysearch.org). Other sources are also available from genealogical publishers.*

All candidates for accreditation or certification must demonstrate their ability to conduct a genealogical search and to provide credible proof to support their conclusions. They also must be able to produce a clearly written report of their findings, which should show proof that the research was thorough.

Primary Records. The research should include evidence that the search was conducted in primary records as well as published sources.

All Reasonable Sources. Evidence should show that the search covered all records that could reasonably be searched.

A Broad Range of Records. The search should not be limited to a few sources such as censuses and wills, but should include a broad range of records such as estate packets, deeds, local histories, tax records, court records, city directories, voting lists, and records of local, state, colonial, and national governmental units.

Adjoining Jurisdictions. The search should include adjoining jurisdictions and areas where children, siblings, or parents settled, as well as the geographic area from which the family moved.

Collateral Relations. The search should not be limited to a single surname, generation, or generational link. Rather, records of collateral relations of the same or different surnames and of neighbors and associates should be included in the researcher's search strategy.

Tip 21: Knowing the proper order to search sources comes from a thorough knowledge of all the major record groups.

Searching a complete array of available records eliminates the possibility of "same name" families being confused. For example, all censuses, tax lists, or city directories should be searched, as should all deeds, land grants, mortgages, etc. Several (often many) years of court records that might include additional information should be investigated. Then one should ask, was *all* pertinent information in *each* record considered?

Clearly Convincing Evidence

Tip 22: Working as a record searcher first, provides invaluable experience. One day I did 60 New York passenger list index searches and discovered a whole new & faster way to approach that tedious task.

Sometimes no sources exist that definitely prove the relationship, event, or date you are seeking. In that case, you must know how to present the evidence to support your conclusions. Proof by clear and convincing evidence shows that you've weighed all the evidence in terms of its reliability and consistency with applicable laws, social customs, historical developments, and other pertinent background information.

Tip 23: Writing genealogical articles helps you to draw on your other skills and defend your conclusions.

In order to reach valid conclusions and support those conclusions, professional researchers must be able to differentiate various classes of evidence, know the weight to be given each, select the best evidence, properly evaluate the quality of any printed work that is used, and draw logical conclusions from this material.

Tip 24: Lecturing at local societies and volunteering to give presentations also helps you draw conclusions and defend a position.

Therefore, one of the things both credentialing processes require is that you be able to show, based on your own research, the ability to properly evaluate all available evidence. This involves describing the problem, analyzing both the information which supports your conclusions and that which contradicts them, and adequately rebutting all factors that could negate your conclusions. Each fact mentioned in the discussion must carry its own separate source citation presented in an acceptable format.

Professional Development

Tip 25: Avoid developing an "I can't be wrong" attitude. Being defensive will make people suspicious of the quality of your work. Since record keepers made errors, your conclusion may be wrong. Be humble! We all eat our words at one time or another.

Although not an expectation of the general public, continual development should be a goal for any professional. Professional organizations provide development for their members, set standards for their discipline, and provide opportunities for members to share their expertise. The professional organization for genealogists is the Association of Professional Genealogists (APG). You can write the Association at: Association of Professional Genealogists, 3421 M Street, N.W., Suite 236, Washington, DC 20007. This membership organization, which publishes the *Association of Professional Genealogists Quarterly* and the *Directory of Professional Genealogists*, is composed of potential professionals, full-time volunteers, retired professionals, and active professionals. Whether you want to learn how to bill a client or to use the Internet for

Tip 26: *Lectures at national conferences provide knowledge on a broad range of sources. National conferences include those sponsored by the Federation of Genealogical Societies, the National Genealogical Society, and the Utah Genealogical Association.*

research, information will be available in the *APG Quarterly*. The biennial *Directory* of its more than 800 members, with research specialties listed, is available from APG for a nominal fee. The *APG Quarterly* covers topics ranging from what fees to charge to how to deal with difficult clients. Opportunities are provided to share your own experiences as well as learn from others.

Report Writing

Tip 27: Animap *is a computer program on U.S. regions that helps you visualize adjoining jurisdictions.*

The role of report writing for the professional genealogist should not be underestimated—it is so important that a full chapter is devoted to that topic. What good does it do to have the answers if you cannot communicate those results to others? Some sources to aid in the development of competent writing skills are provided in the suggested reading at the end of this chapter.

It is important that genealogists learn and implement an accepted method of documentation, although no universal documentation standards exist. Doing so not only makes it easier to work with clients, but can prevent complaints by fellow genealogists.

Summary

Tip 28: Ancestry's Red Book: American State, County and Town Sources, *edited by Alice Eicholtz,* The Handybook for Genealogists, *published by The Everton Publishers, Inc., and the* Map Guide to the U.S. Federal Censuses, 1790-1920, *by Thorndale and Dollarhide, published by GPC, are excellent printed sources for government jurisdictions. For German research,* Meyers Orts-und Verkehrs-Lexikon des Deutschen Reichs and Müllers Großes Deutsches Ortsbuch *is a must. For England, the* Atlas and Index of Parish Registers *by Cecil R Humphrey-Smith is the best.*

A good professional genealogist must demonstrate a knowledge of topography, geography, history, customs, language, and sources. He or she must know how to obtain those sources, the best methods of using those sources, and how to draw on these items to reach a defendable conclusion.

Both credentialing processes require an ability to follow instructions; competency in planning and executing a program of research; precision and cogency of reasoning and writing; competency in the use of the English language (grammar, punctuation, sentence structure, and spelling); and knowledge of bibliography, resources, and research methodology. As you can see, the expectations for a professional genealogist are high.

The following chapters will provide more detail on the requirements for accreditation, how skills are evaluated, and how you can prepare to pass the exam. An understanding of these requirements should also help you to better plan your genealogical career.

Suggested Reading

Chicago Manual of Style. 14th Ed. Chicago: University of Chicago Press, 1993. On the Web, you can access http://msoe.edu/gen_st/stylguid.html for guidelines which follow the CMS.

Clifford, Karen. *The Complete Beginner's Guide to Genealogy, the Internet, and Your Genealogy Computer.* Baltimore: Genealogical Publishing Company, 2000.

Costello, Margaret F. and Jane Fletcher Fiske. *Guidelines for Genealogical Writing.* Boston: The New England Historic Genealogical Society, 1990.

Curran, Joan F. "Writing Your Family History: It's Not As Hard As You Think." Audio tape of lecture presented at the National Genealogical Society 1991 Conference in the States, Portland, Oreg. Hobart, Ind.: Repeat Performance, 1991.

Curran, Joan F. *Numbering Your Genealogy: Sound and Simple Systems.* Arlington, Va.: National Genealogical Society Publications, 1992.

Gardner, Loni. "Tracing Medical Pedigrees: A Practical Application of Genealogy." Audio tape of lecture presented at the National Genealogical Society 1995 Conference in the States, San Diego, California. Hobart, Ind.: Repeat Performance, 1995.

Jones, Thomas W. "Compilation Technique: Evaluating Our Evidence in Light of the Genealogical Proof Standard." *Meet Me In St. Louis; Federation of Genealogical Societies and St. Louis Genealogical Society, 11-14 August 1999*; St. Louis, Missouri, S-137. (May be ordered from Repeat Performance, 2911 Crabapple Lane, Hobart, IN 46342, session S-137.)

Lackey, Richard S. *Cite Your Sources.* New Orleans: Polyanthos, 1980.

Leary, Helen F. M.. "The Oft-Overlooked Technique: Keeping Track of What We Collect." *Meet Me In St. Louis; Federation of Genealogical Societies and St. Louis Genealogical Society, 11-14 August 1999*; St. Louis, Missouri, S-159. (May be ordered from Repeat Performance, 2911 Crabapple Lane, Hobart, IN 46342, session S-159.)

Mills, Elizabeth Shown. "Your Research Report." *On Board: Newsletter of the Board for Certification of Genealogists*, 1 May 1996: 9-13.

Mills, Elizabeth Shown. "The Preponderance of the Evidence Principle: How to Build a Case to 'Prove Your Point'." Tape # AZ-92. Hobart, Ind.: Repeat Performance, 1992.

Tip 29: The FHLC (Surname Catalog), the Ancestral File on CDs, Genealogies in the Library of Congress, The World Family Tree CDs, www.MyFamily.com; www.Genealogy.com; www.Kindred konnections.com; and www.FamilySearch.com all provide compiled pedigrees which may contain your family.

Tip 30: The term "clear and convincing evidence" is replacing the phrase "preponderance of the evidence."

Tip 31: Studying articles in the NGS Quarterly, the NEHGS Register, the American Genealogist, and the UGA Journal help you see how researchers have used clear and convincing evidence to reach conclusions.

Tip 32: Compare examples of endnotes, footnotes, and paragraph citation inserts to find a style that you enjoy writing. Remember if you hope to have your work published in a particular journal, you will need to submit your materials in that journal's format.

Tip 33: APG originated in Salt Lake City, Utah, but today has reached national proportions.

Mills, Elizabeth Shown. *Evidence!* Baltimore: Genealogical Publishing Company, 1997.

Reisinger, Joy. "Being Professional No Matter What Genealogical Hat You're Wearing." *Traveling Historic Trails; National Geneal-ogical Society and Middle Tennessee Genealogical Society*, 8-11 May 1996; Nashville, Tenn., S-150. (May be ordered from Repeat Performance, 2911 Crabapple Lane, Hobart, IN 46342, session S-150.)

Roman, Kenneth and Joel Raphaelson. *Writing That Works: How to Improve Your Memos, Letters, Reports, Speeches, Resumes, Plans, and Other Business Papers.* New York: Harper Collins, 1992.

Rose, Christine. "The Basic Technique: Considering Ethics in Our Collection, Use and Documentation of Genealogical Data." *Meet Me In St. Louis; Federation of Genealogical Societies and St. Louis Genealogical Society, 11-14 August 1999*; St. Louis, Missouri, T-41. (May be ordered from Repeat Performance, 2911 Crabapple Lane, Hobart, IN 46342, session T-41.)

Stevenson, Noel C. *Genealogical Evidence: A Guide to the Standard of Proof Relating to Pedigrees, Ancestry, Heirship, and Family History.* Laguna Hills, Calif.: Aegean Park Press, 1979.

Warren, Paula Stuart. "The Professional Genealogist's Tools: Beyond the Usual." *On to Richmond: Four Centuries of Family History; Federation of Genealogical Societies and Virginia Genealogical Society*, 12-15 October 1994; Richmond, Va., 111-114.

Tip 34: Good reports are the bread and butter of a good professional. Although there is no universal report style, they all express the objectives, explain the evidence, defend the position, give a conclusion, and suggest options for further extension of knowledge.

Tip 35: High expecta-tions do not exist to dis-courage you with a downcast stance but to encourage vision and an upward glance.

Tip 36: Documentation styles vary according to medium (pen, typed, computer), projected final project (inclusion in a database, sent to a publication, report to a family), and time allowed.

Tip 37: All documenta-tion should enhance the project and provide enough information to guide other researchers to the exact sources being referenced. This would include name and address of repository or possessor of informa-tion, unique identifying numbers or call num-bers, if any, page or folio numbers, title, and authors, if any.

The Accreditation Process

Tip 38: You do not have to be a member of the LDS church to apply for accreditation. Most of my students who have obtained their accreditation were not LDS.

The Family History Library of The Church of Jesus Christ of Latter-day Saints (LDS church), the largest genealogical library in the world, originally sponsored the Accreditation Program for individuals who wanted to become professional genealogists. The program began in 1964. Under the new ICapGen sponsorship, the process will continue to improve as accreditation in new areas of the world is offered. This chapter describes the skills you should have before applying for accreditation, what the testing procedures are, and how to complete your accreditation application.

Overview of the Accreditation Process

Tip 39: Summer months find the FHL full most days. Winter months are better for taking the exam.

The examination is given at the Family History Library in Salt Lake City, Utah. At the time an appointment is scheduled with the Accreditation Section (at least a month ahead), the candidate must submit the four-generation project and research report as explained more fully below. If the four-generation project and research report are of acceptable quality, an appointment will be set up for the accreditation exam. Exceptions to this scheduling process are rarely made.

Tip 40: Salt Lake City is 5,000 feet above sea level. If from out of state, allow yourself a day or two to adjust. You'll be winded and thirsty at first. You may find it easier to spread the exam across more than the two day minimum.

As an accreditation candidate, you will be assigned an examination supervisor who works in the library. He or she distributes the various timed examination papers in the appropriate sequence and at the scheduled times. There are several subtests: (1) document recognition, (2) document transcription, (3) case studies, (4) a written examination on a regional area, and (5) interviews in which you may be asked to explain and defend the research you did on the case studies and answer any questions the accreditation committee

19

Tip 41: Part of your submitted case study will remain as a sample of your work. It is not used by ICapGen for any other purpose than to study your research abilities. It is appropriate for you to submit and share your personal work with others.

may have regarding your submitted four-generation research project and report.

Completing the written examinations and the case studies takes eight hours, and the length of the oral examination is dependent on what is discovered in the written examination. Since the examinations must be graded before the interviews begin, the testing process takes at least two days.

There is no fee for taking the examination or for maintaining the credential, but those who pass the examination must sign and abide by a code of ethics to receive their accreditation.

Prerequisites

Tip 42: Start recording your research hours today. You'll be surprised how quickly they add up but also how prone you are to use the tools you are most familiar with to solve different problems. Branch out and experiment with other repositories and other sources.

Research Experience. One prerequisite that you must meet before applying for the accreditation exam is to have at least 1,000 hours of research experience in the regional or subject area in which you wish to be accredited. This 1,000 hours should include experience in specific records of the geographic area of choice as well as in general records pertaining to the area.

For example, research in any of the U.S. regions would require a knowledge of general United States or federal records applying to that area of specialization and the use of automated resources such as those of the FamilySearch® program developed by The Church of Jesus Christ of Latter-day Saints (hereafter referred to as LDS or Mormon). You will be asked to specify the personal research experience you have had in original and microfilmed records and/or the time you have spent corresponding with field researchers. For U.S. accreditation, this experience must be itemized state-by-state on the application.

Tip 43: FamilySearch® *is composed of the* Ancestral File, *the* International Genealogical Index *(and Ordinance Index),* The Family History Library Catalog, *the* Social Security Death Index, Military Records and the Scottish Old Parochial Parish Register Index. *Can you use them all? Do you know the six passes possible to search the IGI? How do you trace a batch number? What is the* Parish and Vital Record Index?

Paleography. Your ability to read the older handwriting of particular records in the selected area of specialization will be tested in two ways: first, by your ability to identify numerous documents once they have been shown to you; and second, by your ability to transcribe documents presented to you (and to translate those in a foreign language). The documents you will be tested on will be representative of those records found in your specialty area.

Ability to Evaluate Pedigree Problems. You will be asked to evaluate several pedigree problems. As a sample problem is presented, you will be asked what sources you would search, what order you would search them, and what you expect to obtain from those sources. You will then be expected to solve that particular problem within a specified period of time.

Tip 44: Researching with objectives elevates you beyond the obstacles.

Knowledge of Available Records. Your knowledge of records must include (1) what records are available, (2) where the records are located, and (3) how to use the records. You can acquire this knowledge through personal study and research, home-study classes or college courses, workshops and institutes, volunteer training, and working as an apprentice for another professional genealogist.

What records would provide proof of birth for someone born in America in 1889? If the person was alive in the early 1900s, the 1900 federal census would provide a month and year of birth. But what if the person didn't come to America until 1907? The 1910 census could help you establish an approximate year of birth in either time period. However, other records may need to be used because the 1910 census may not be indexed for the state in which the person lived. A city directory can be used to guide a researcher to an approximate address in 1910, but where would the directory be found? Is the street guide to the major cities and enumeration districts of 1910 available at a local repository? What other records could be used? Learning to use *all* available records is very important.

The Application

Directions. Contact the Accreditation Committee for an application form (figure 3.7). It is important to know in advance the area in which you have the most experience (at least 1,000 hours) and where your interests lie, because applicants are asked to specify an area of interest.

Code of Ethics. Each applicant is asked to read and sign a code of ethics. (See figure 1.3 in chapter 1.) Notice how the AG program supports the BCG code.

Statement of Goals. Each applicant is asked to specify the purpose for requesting accreditation. The main purpose for most applicants is to become a paid professional.

Education and Training. Past experiences may satisfy basic prerequisites necessary to pass the accreditation examination. Although no specific college or university courses are required of anyone taking the examination, such courses or training at genealogical institutes could significantly help you in gaining accreditation. Anything that helps you become a better genealogist will help you with the accreditation process; conversely anything you do to prepare for accreditation should help you be a better genealogist.

The Utah Genealogical Association (UGA) provides an annual Salt Lake Institute of Genealogy during the month of January to help

Tip 49: Write to Salt Lake Institute of Genealogy, P.O. Box 1144, Salt Lake City, UT 84110 to obtain information on the Institute.

Tip 50: By apprenticing with a genealogist or a genealogy company, you learn discipline, record group analysis, and much more. Be willing to sign on for a period of time to make their training more valuable to you and to make yourself more valuable to those hiring you. Why should a company spend time training you if you merely plan to leave them and become a competitor. You may be asked to sign a non-compete, non-disclosure agreement.

Tip 51: Computer, language, writing, business, paleography, and financial classes all help the professional be better prepared.

serious genealogists develop their skills while using the resources of the Family History Library and other repositories. Brigham Young University (BYU) offers a week-long Genealogy and Family History Conference the first week in August. The instructors include reference specialists who work in the Family History Library, university professors, college instructors, and other professionals well known in the field of genealogy. This four-day long conference has various classes for the beginner, intermediate, and advanced researcher.

National conferences such as those held by the National Genealogical Society (NGS) and the Federation of Genealogical Societies (FGS) offer excellent classes for the serious genealogist as well (see more in chapter 8). Courses, institutes, and mini-classes all fill an educational need for researchers.

Hands-on Experience. Tracing your own family genealogy is an excellent way to gain hands-on experience. I have encouraged my students from the first day of class to keep track of their hours as they research their own family histories. They are asked to record not only the hours they spend but also the localities in which they are doing research and the repositories they are using. A form similar to the one in figure 3.1 will help record the repositories, dates, surnames, and locations, as well as the record types with which you have had experience.

The accreditation form (see figure 3.7) does not require you to list every hour that you spent or to name each library where you've worked. However, listing your own experiences on a time chart will help you pinpoint your strengths or weaknesses. The records you may research for one family seldom cover every jurisdiction and type of record found in even one accreditation area, and you will need to branch out.

Your time chart can be used as a supportive document or you can summarize the information on it to respond to the questions on the application. The time chart will also help you establish the habit of keeping track of your time—an organizational skill essential to a professional. More time charts are available in appendix C.

Areas of Accreditation

Accreditation is currently offered for the following twenty-seven areas: New England States, Eastern States, Southern States, Midwestern States, England, Scotland, Ireland, Wales, Norway, Sweden, Denmark, Finland, Belgium, France, Italy, Germany, Netherlands, Czech Republic, Switzerland, Poland, Slovak, French Canada, Canada (general), Polynesian, Mexico, Records of The Church of Jesus Christ of Latter-day Saints, and American Indians. Other areas are being pre-

Figure 3.1   Research Experience Record

Research Experience Record

GENEALOGY
RESEARCH
ASSOCIATES

Researchers name _____

Date	Repository	Surname	Locality searched	Record type	Time spent

Tip 52: What do I want to see on my students' time charts or those who work for my company? If they are trying to be accredited in the Midwest, I want to see references to work done in the Allen County Public Library, the federal archives, at least some of the midwestern state libraries, correspondence with local midwestern courthouses and archives, and other repositories holding midwestern records. A British researcher should indicate experience using British repositories.

Tip 53: Accreditation originated out of a need to help others use the records of the FHL. You may have noticed there is no Accreditation for the Western States. In the past there were few Western States records in the library. I believe that, in the near future, accreditation will be offered in other foreign and U.S. regions because more records are now available in the FHL to do an adequate job of research.

pared. A separate examination is given for each area. Those areas marked below with an asterisk (*) require a working knowledge of another language.

United States

New England States:

Connecticut	Rhode Island	New Hampshire
Massachusetts	Maine	Vermont

Eastern States:

Delaware	New York
New Jersey	Pennsylvania

Southern States:

Alabama	Louisiana	South Carolina
Arkansas	Maryland	Tennessee
Florida	Mississippi	Texas
Georgia	Oklahoma	Virginia
Kentucky	North Carolina	West Virginia

Midwestern States:

Illinois	Michigan	Ohio
Indiana	Minnesota	Wisconsin
Iowa	Missouri	

British Isles

England	Wales
Scotland	Ireland
Isle of Man	

Scandinavia

Norway*	Denmark*
Sweden*	Finland*

Continental Europe

Belgium*	Netherlands*	France*
Czech Republic*	Italy*	Switzerland*
Germany*	Poland*	Slovakia*

Canada

French Canada	Canada (general)

Figure 3.2   Map of Areas Covered by Accreditation

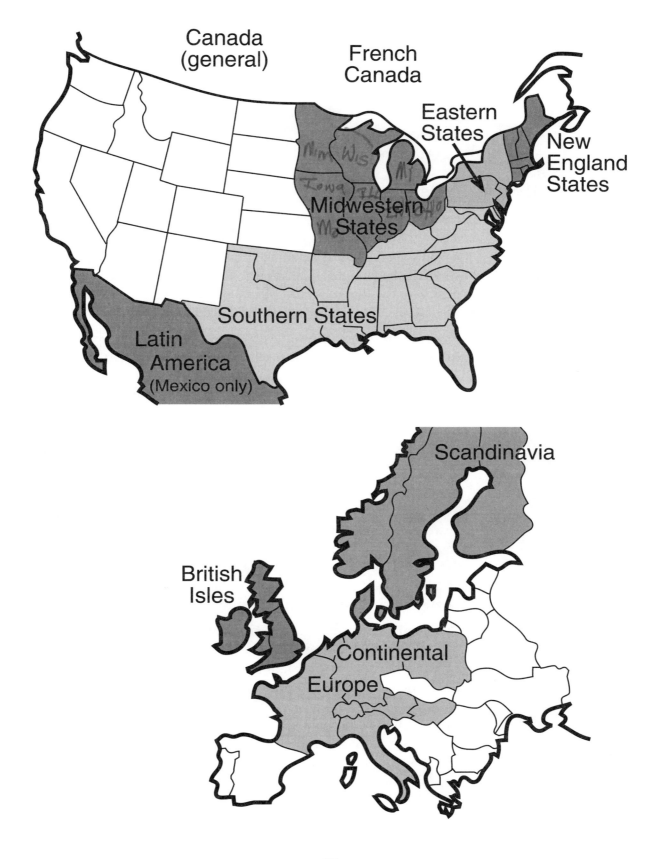

Pacific Area

Polynesian* (non-English speaking)

Latin America

Mexico*

Subject Areas of Testing

Records of The Church of Jesus Christ of Latter-day Saints
American Indians

Demonstration of Skills

Tip 54: Latin terms are used in many legal documents and church records. The FHL provides a Latin word list to help you understand these terms (see SourceGuide™ page 28).

Tip 55: There are excellent articles in The Genealogical Journal *of the Utah Genealogical Association which provide needed background information on foreign record collections. Many of the conference lectures are available on tape (see the lists of suggested readings in this book) or on microform through your local Family History Center.*

Tip 56: Much of research is interpreted, judged, and guided by reason of experience.

Other Languages. Accreditation offers a credential in foreign areas as well as United States specializations. Those wishing to become accredited in a country outside of the United States need to know the language of that country. For example, if you wish to specialize in the Quebec area, you must learn French; if you wish to specialize in Mexican research, you need to know Spanish.

Language skills are helpful even in the United States. My familiarity with German has helped me in Pennsylvania, North Carolina, and Ohio; my limited Scandinavian background in Minnesota and Wisconsin; my Spanish classes in the Deep South and California. Knowledge of French would help in the Midwest and some Southern states, and Latin phrases are the basis of many early church records.

Those who have acquired language skills through experience in the military, in business, or as a foreign missionary or public servant for a group such as the Peace Corps, may assume that applying for accreditation in a Spanish-speaking area, for example, would be easier than applying in a U.S. area. Don't be lulled into that reasoning. The same record types will be tested as in any U.S. areas, such as land, probate, compiled sources, and church records because any or all may be needed to extend family history research for a client.

Practical Experience. Experience comes in many forms. Have you volunteered for lineage societies, at family history centers, with county societies, or with family organizations? Do you publish a newsletter, edit a paper, enter accessions, file cards, help others with research, or act as a searcher for a professional genealogist? These activities provide valuable experience, and should be listed on your application.

Demonstration of Knowledge

Tip 57: Take computer classes. Trying to do genealogical research efficiently and speedily without a computer is almost impossible today. As a minimum, you'll need the skills to use a word processor, enter data into data bases, and make backup copies of computer files. Also, increasing your speed at keyboarding is valuable.

Universal Records

No matter what area of specialization you wish to pursue, you'll have to develop expertise in using records which cover comprehensive, general, or universal areas. For example, general United States records may be local in nature but cataloged on a national level. Bible records, biographical records, and railroad retirement papers may be created locally but cataloged as national collections. This classification process is true for every country.

Federal Records are an example of general records involving all U.S. research regions. There are similar records created in other countries by their central government. Universal records most often used by genealogists include civil registrations, land, and immigration records.

LDS Compiled Sources

The Family History Library has assembled all research outlines onto a CD compilation known as *Family History SourceGuide™*, which lists all the major record groups by the location in which they are found. The research outline for the United States provides a brief overview of all the major categories. This research outline should be well studied by students in any of the United States accreditation areas. You can use the CD compilation on the Internet for no charge or order your own copy of the CD at www.familysearch.org.

Tip 58: Courses dealing with Library Science can make you more efficient in using automated library services such as OCLC (On-Line Computer Library Catalog, which is the largest world-wide bibliographical catalog data base) or RLN (Research Libraries Network, predominantly used by academic libraries). Knowing how to access these same records using the Internet is extremely valuable. For example, it is possible to search the Library of Congress Card Catalog on the Internet and then order the sources on interlibrary loan or request a paid searcher to obtain information for you.

In addition to information on the United States, *SourceGuide* contains research outlines of brief, informative summaries of each area included in Accreditation, how the records can be accessed, and in what order to use the sources to best answer your questions. Explanations of terms and procedures for finding sources are invaluable.

The Church of Jesus Christ of Latter-day Saints (LDS) has compiled the world's largest collection of local, national, and international genealogical records. Candidates for every area covered by Accreditation must know how to use these compiled sources and how to trace the record back to their original sources.

A major component of the collection involves *FamilySearch*, which is a complex computer program which operates and manages several large data bases of information. It includes the *Ancestral File*, the *International Genealogical Index*, the *Social Security Death Index*, the *Military Index*, and the *Scottish Parochial Index*. Others can be added as they are developed. This program is available at the Family History Library, the Joseph Smith Memorial Building, local Family History Centers, and many large public and college libraries.

Information on how to use the *FamilySearch* program and its various components are contained on the SourceGuide CD (see figure 3.3) or on the www.familysearch.org Web site. The Internet site

Figure 3.3 *SourceGuide*™ produced by The Family History Library

---

***SourceGuide*™ contains all:**

How-to Guides (e.g., U.S. Military Records, 1881 British Census Index, etc.)

Research Outlines (e.g., U.S. General, Massachusetts Research Outline, Latin America Research Outline, etc.)

Word Lists (e.g., Latin, German, Spanish, Scandinavian, etc.)

Maps (e.g., England, Wales, Scotland, etc.)

Research Support (e.g., addresses of Family History Centers, How-to-Use a Family History Center, etc.)

For more information on *SourceGuide*™

Where to write-	Family History Department
	attn: Family History Support
	50 East North Temple Street
	Salt Lake City, UT 84150-3400
Internet-	www.familysearch.org

---

also allows Internet access to *FamilySearch* itself, but the Internet features are different than those available in the CD versions. You should know how to use the FamilySearch™ Web site and all its features for obtaining information.

The International Genealogical Index (IGI®)

Started in 1969 this index now contains over 600 million names on the computer FamilySearch program. It is arranged by surname and locality. Millions have been "extracted" by volunteers who copy information from original documents (birth, christening, marriage records, etc.) onto computer cards. Using this index can help you locate an elusive ancestor, find others searching your lines, locate primary sources, and pinpoint localities for an unusual surname. Because many original church records are included in this data base, it is considered the largest church file in the world representing most major denominations in the United States.

You should know how to locate, and be able to explain how to locate, original sources in the IGI. You should then be able to use another component of FamilySearch, the Family History Library Catalog, to locate those sources. More detailed explanations may be found in the book *The Complete Beginner's Guide to Genealogy, the Internet and Your Genealogy Computer Program* by Karen Clifford (Baltimore: Genealogical Publishing Company, 2001).

Tip 59: Highlight every source suggested in the U.S. outline and try to use each one.

Tip 60: Highlight every paragraph of explanation and see if you understand it.

Tip 61: The IGI has been called the largest electronic database in the world for church records covering most denominations.

Tip 62: If you are not familiar with the use of FamilySearch®, you should study the research outlines on the International Genealogical Index (IGI), Ancestral File ™, Military Index, the U.S. Social Security Death Index (SSDI, also known as Social Security Death Benefits Records), the Scottish Church Records, TempleReady™ and the Family History Library Catalog, or find explanations and full copies of each, reproduced in the SourceGuide™.

Tip 63: One of the fastest and most accurate ways of copying information from the FHLC is by printing to disk in ASCII format to be read by your word processor. After retrieval you may type a line indicating what you hope to get from the source and who you are looking for.

Tip 64: The only way to truly experience the LDS archives collections is to use them. They are especially strong in New England and English pedigrees.

Ancestral File

In 1980 LDS Church members submitted four generations of their families which became the foundation of the *Ancestral File*. Many LDS members are unaware that they may need to correct or resubmit some information to bring their records up to date. Non-LDS Church members also submit their genealogical data. This was the largest lineage-linked data base of family names in the world before the Internet. Today new submissions are being put into *Pedigree Resource File* formats on CDs which allows for inclusion of any notes and documentation collected by the person submitting the information. You should know how to find the original submitter of the information as well as how to make corrections to the *Ancestral File*. Full descriptions of this process are found in *The Complete Beginner's Guide to Genealogy, the Internet and Your Genealogy Computer Program* by Karen Clifford (Baltimore: Genealogical Publishing Company, 2000).

Family History Library Catalog

The *Family History Library Catalog (FHLC)* is a data base of the Family History Library collection in Salt Lake City. It is the key to treasures held in the library. Unless you know how to turn the key, however, most of the treasures of this collection will remain locked away.

One way to use this resource is to learn the major category headings so you will be able to find the sources you are seeking. *The Complete Beginner's Guide to Genealogy, the Internet and Your Genealogy Computer Program* provides a list of those categories and many pages of explanation on how to use this resource. The program can then quickly lead you to original records on microform, published histories and collections, and numerous reference books. You should also be able to use the "browse" feature to locate towns and counties which are often misspelled. For example, a client wanted a place in Finland she had spelled, "Tareaharve." Using the locality browse feature, I quickly located Terajarve, Finland, the correct spelling.

Besides helping you to locate records from all areas of the world, the *FHLC* will permit you to search the data base by surname. If the surname is a common one yielding several hundred or several thousand books, key-word searches, such as a location or collateral surname, may be added to the search to concentrate it and yield better results. This resource is available on the Internet site provided previously, at local Family History Centers, at several major repositories, and soon on CD. You should be able to locate records using film numbers, authors, titles, subjects, and localities.

Tip 65: Successful research strategies are developed by studying fine ideas which are reinforced by great examples from a multitude of sources which are then applied to our own problems.

Family Group Records Collection

The Family Group Records Collection is also known as the LDS Archives. These records have been filed with the LDS Church since 1942. They are filed alphabetically by surname, then by the name of the father of the submitting family. These records can be used to identify previous research done on an LDS line. The sources for the information often came from the personal knowledge of people or their family records pre-dating vital records for the people under investigation. Relationships are often accurate but localities and dates are sometimes erroneous. For more information on this record group use the Research Outline LDS Records found under the state of Utah in *SourceGuide*. The records are found in the Joseph Smith Memorial Building and they have also been microfilmed.

LDS Research Accreditation

While it is important for all person's seeking Accreditation to know how to use the sources listed above, there are many others listed on the Research Outline covering LDS Records that are not required for anyone but those receiving an Accreditation in LDS Research. LDS records are stored in numerous repositories throughout the United States as well as in Utah. Candidates for Accreditation in this area should know about all the major collections and how to use them.

How to Prepare for Accreditation

Tip 66: If we are willing to learn, the opportunities are everywhere.
–John Gardner

Aids. The International Commission for the Accreditation of Professional Genealogists suggests studying the sources suggested under the Guidance options available for each locality at teh FamilySearch™ Web site, or obtain a copy of the *SourceGuide* CD by clicking on the Site Map option and then Order/Download products. There you may find the Research Outlines, CDs, and programs. Many other resource items are also suggested in this book.

The Family History Library originally prepared a handout entitled *Hiring a Professional Genealogist*, which is in the *SourceGuide*. This booklet is included as appendix B in this book because the "Professional Methods" portion is a succinct outline of what an accredited genealogist should be doing for those with whom they contract.

Tip 67: A mediocre idea well written is often more effective than a better idea poorly expressed.

Genealogy Training Courses. Although genealogy courses are not required for accreditation, they provide exposure to a range of experiences broader than those you'll have in your own personal research. Genealogy courses are an excellent way to gain insights into many problem-solving approaches—insights that can be worth their weight in gold. Of course, what you learn from a course is dependent not only on the instructor but also on what you put into the class. On your application form, when you list classes you've taken, indicate whether they were taken for credit or audit, what institution sponsored them, and who the instructors were. See chapter 8 for more educational opportunities.

Grammar and/or Composition Courses. A professional genealogist will need to write reports. Courses in grammar and composition are most helpful. Most college and university general education requirements include at least one or two years of English grammar or composition. When filling out your application, look at your college transcripts and record relevant information on your sample application form. Did you attend any workshops or summer classes in these areas? If you did not attend a college or university, what grammar or composition classes did you take in high school?

History Courses. History classes or historical video series which focus on your specialty give you a feel for the events of the times and provide evidence of events which might have been recorded by some private or public agency. Thus, history is our clue to sources. Printed guides (such as *The Almanac of American History* by Arthur Schlesinger Jr. published by The Putnam Publishing Group, New York) as well as automated sources (such as *The CD Sourcebook of American History*, available through Western Standard Publishing [Orem, Utah]), can be useful references, but nothing is as important as studying the actual area in which you specialize.

Sources. To obtain accreditation, you'll need to become familiar with the different sources and techniques applicable to your area of specialization. Information regarding sources and techniques can come from genealogy classes, seminars and workshops, conferences and institutes, personal research, and problem-solving sessions. The following books and CDs are also useful resources for finding area-specific sources.

√ American Society of Genealogists. *Genealogical Research: Methods and Sources*. Vol. I, rev. ed. Edited by Milton Rubincam, Washington, D.C.: The Society, 1980. [State-wide techniques.]

√ American Society of Genealogists. *Genealogical Research: Methods and Sources*. Vol. II, rev. ed. Edited by Kenn Stryker-Rodda. Washington, D.C.: The Society, 1983. [State-wide techniques]

√ *Ancestry Reference Library on CD-ROM for Windows and Macintosh*. Contains *The Source, Ancestry's Red Book, The Library of Congress, The Archives,* and *The Library*. Ancestry, 1-800-ANCESTRY(262-3787) [General U.S. and state references.]

Tip 68: Budding genealogists receive pleasure in improving themselves day by day by learning something new.

Tip 69: One's judgment is never superior to one's information. We must know what produces success before we can produce it ourselves—thus the power of good sources.

√ Clifford, Karen. *The Complete Beginner's Guide to Genealogy, the Internet and Your Genealogy Computer Program.* Baltimore: Genealogical Publishing Co., 2001.]

√ Clifford, Karen. *Genealogy and Computers for the Determined Researcher.* Baltimore: Clearfield Co., 1995. [Migration, handwriting, research methodology, sources, land, military, immigration, and naturalization records.]

√ Clifford, Karen. *Genealogy and Computers for the Advanced Researcher: Pulling It All Together.* Baltimore: Clearfield Co. 1995. [Oral histories, evaluating original documents, contracting out research, overseas research, foreign paleography, compiling family health histories, and preparing a video family history.]

√ Szucs, Loretto Dennis and Sandra Hargreaves Luebking. *The Source: A Guidebook of American Genealogy.* Rev. ed. Salt Lake City: Ancestry, 1997. [How to use sources.]

√ Family History Library, *Family History SourceGuide.* CD-ROM. Salt Lake City: Church of Jesus Christ of Latter-day Saints, 1998.

Written Components. As mentioned earlier, the accreditation examining process consists of a pre-submitted four-generation case study with supportive documentation and an open-book, approximately eight-hour written test. Generally only one candidate is tested at a time. For the United States, different tests are given for New England, the mid-Atlantic states, the South, and the Midwest. You can take the tests in as many areas as you like, but you will need a new case study and should have performed the 1,000 hours of research in each of those specialty areas.

The written exam includes an examination covering general questions and answers pertaining to the history and records of your chosen area and how that history affects your research. It also includes document recognition, transcription, and various case study problems. The applicant will actually work on one case study, or pedigree problem, in the Family History Library during a time period of approximately three hours. The oral exam is given after the written exam has been graded, usually two days later. Oral exams are scheduled only if a grade of 90% or better was achieved on the written exam. This oral exam can last approximately two hours.

If you fail to pass the written examination, you can retake the test, but you will be asked to wait three months before reapplying. You should also be prepared to demonstrate to the Accreditation Committee that sufficient measures have been taken to overcome the weaknesses apparent in the previous examination.

Tip 70: Most professional genealogists use a computer for writing their reports, organizing their genealogical data, and producing unique pedigree charts and graphs that are requested by their clients. There are several computer programs available that either organize the family history data or produce simple or multi-leveled reports. There are also programs available that do both or do various combinations of the two. Other examples of report writing can be found in Genealogy and Computers for the Advanced Researcher: Pulling It All Together *by Karen Clifford.*

Tip 71: Imagination is a fantastic picturing power whereby we can take the individual elements of successful techniques from others and put them together in new combinations.

Those taking the exam are allowed to use their own materials (this is one reason I have included a chapter on preparing research notebooks); they may also use a computer to aid them in the report writing section.

The Oral Exam. During the oral exam, you will be asked to defend your research. If your written exam or written report was not self-explanatory, you will be asked to explain your research strategies. This exercise helps to review areas in which you are weak on the written exam. (Questions to clarify any parts of the written exam may be included.)

Your written report—a four-generation case study—will be judged on (1) the accuracy of your research, (2) your ability to evaluate records, and (3) your knowledge of records. This report should be submitted at the time you schedule the written exam.

The testing committee, usually three individuals, will go over the pedigree you've submitted. This should be a four-generation case study prior to 1875 from the geographical area in which you wish to specialize. It should be submitted in report form and include well-documented Family Group Record forms for each family on the pedigree. Assume, for example, that you are specializing in the Midwest. Try to calculate the family which follows to see if it would qualify for a Midwestern states problem.

Figure 3.4   Pedigree Analysis

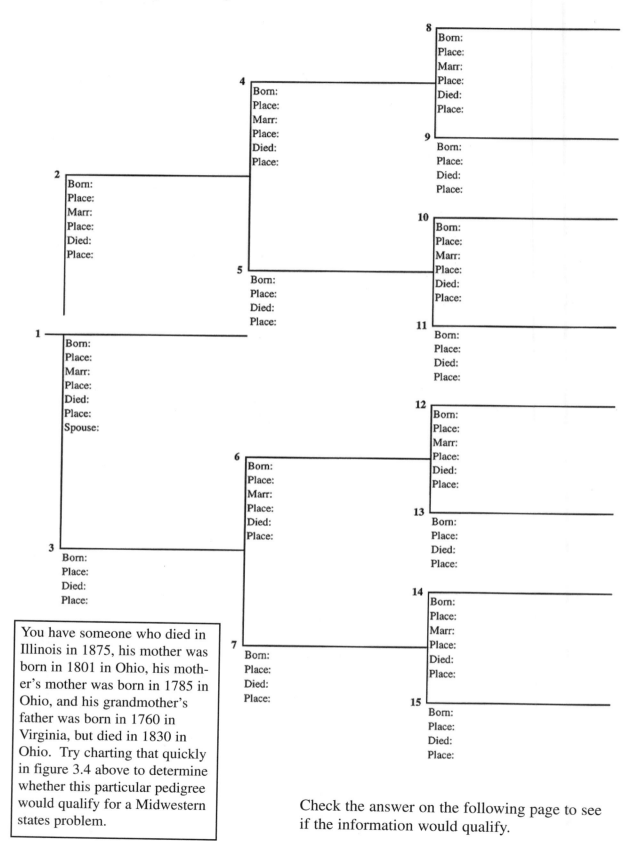

You have someone who died in Illinois in 1875, his mother was born in 1801 in Ohio, his mother's mother was born in 1785 in Ohio, and his grandmother's father was born in 1760 in Virginia, but died in 1830 in Ohio. Try charting that quickly in figure 3.4 above to determine whether this particular pedigree would qualify for a Midwestern states problem.

Check the answer on the following page to see if the information would qualify.

Figure 3.5 Pedigree Analysis Answer

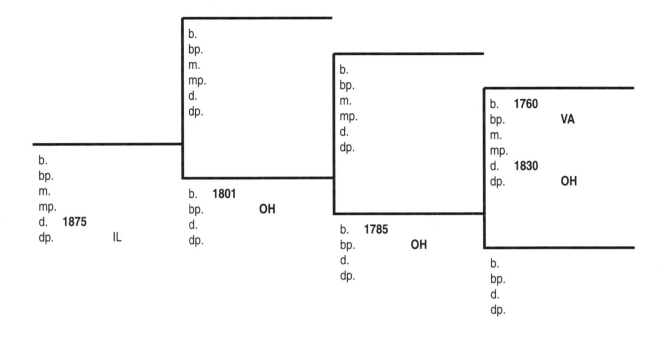

Yes, as you can see, this pedigree would qualify as a four-generation Midwestern states project.

Although there is no standard format given for reporting your genealogical research conclusions as part of the accreditation application, it is assumed that your research report will be neat and well organized, with few, if any, grammatical errors. If you plan to work for clients (which is the primary reason for accreditation), your report should always:

1. Reflect an understanding of the problem under consideration,

2. Demonstrate a proper use of the sources by listing the sources searched in a research planner (a sample research planner is included in figure 3.6), a research planner (where items to be searched in the future, as well as items presently searched are listed), or in a report showing both successful and unsuccessful searches,

3. Illustrate the effectiveness of your research as well as its limitations (usually by including in a report each step taken to solve the problem and why it was taken),

4. Include recommendations for future research and state the probability of success if those searches are carried out,

5. Present a professional image.

Figure 3.6 Research Planner

Research Planner

GENEALOGY
RESEARCH
ASSOCIATES

Remember to only have one goal per Research Planner.

Goal _____

_____

Surname/Subject _____ Researcher _____

Area _____ Client _____

Source Location		Description of Source	Object	Time	Remarks		
Date source searched	Library or repository & call #	(State, county, type of record, and time period of record)	(Person's name or what is sought)	(Person's age or date of event)	Comment or ID # of family	Index	File

Self-Analysis

Perhaps you will have more or less experience than indicated above. Remember: quantity of experience in one small area or record type will never make up for the breadth of experience needed in the regional accreditation process. Preparing for accreditation in one of the foreign specialties or in the LDS area requires the same background as stated above but includes an added emphasis on specific record collections, how to read them, use them, and interpret them for others. Specific research outlines are available in the *SourceGuide*™ to help those individuals who are new to a particular locality (see pages 27 and 28). Foreign language word lists that are specific to these areas are also available at the FamilySearch™ Web site by clicking on the Site Map option and looking down the list.

If you know how to do the things outlined in this chapter, and you wish to become an accredited genealogist in one of the regions listed previously, then continue below and proceed to chapter 4.

If on the other hand, you feel you would like more information on the certification program at this time, skip to appendix A, which introduces you to the certification process.

Applying for Accreditation

There are no fees or charges for any of the examinations, but apply four weeks before you wish the examination to be scheduled. Send your application and attachments to:

> International Commission for the
> Accreditation of Professional Genealogists
> P.O. Box 1144
> Salt Lake City, UT 84110-1144

You will then be contacted by the Commission. Or you may e-mail the commission through the administrative secretary at UGA at info@infouga.org.

Every five years accredited individuals must demonstrate continued proficiency and an awareness of any new developments in their specialty by submitting a copy of a current client report as well as a variety of other documents, case studies and reports. And, if necessary, they must answer specific questions.

Suggested Reading

Meyerink, Kory L. "IGI Bibliography" *Genealogical Journal* 24, no. 3 (1996): 139-141.

Nichols, Elizabeth L. "Family Group Records Collections and Related Records of the Family History Library." *Genealogical Journal* 24, no. 1 (1996): 11-21. (May be ordered from the Utah

Genealogical Association, P.O. Box 1144, Salt Lake City, UT 84110.)

Nichols, Elizabeth. *Genealogy in the Computer Age: Understanding FamilySearch.* 2 vols. Salt Lake City: Family History Educators, 1994, 1997.

Assignment

Up to this point, I've merely suggested articles to augment your studies. Starting in this chapter, I will give you assignments to help focus and direct your preparations for accreditation.

Assignment 1: Sample Accreditation Application

Now that you have an overview of what is expected before you apply for accreditation, fill out the sample Accreditation Test Application (Figure 3.7).

1. Write down on a separate page the various repositories you have personally visited, e.g. a National Archives branch; Sutro Library in San Francisco, California; the Family History Library; Allen County Public Library in Fort Wayne, Indiana; the Library of Congress; any courthouses; any public libraries; any family history centers; any state archives; the DAR Library in Washington, D.C.; the BYU genealogy library; etc.

2. Now circle those which apply to your area of specialization.

3. Next consider the family you will be submitting as your four-generation problem. Could more research be done on that project to increase your hours and your experience in those records? Do you feel you need more experience in your area of specialization?

4. Consider your English grammar and/or composition courses. Check your college transcripts and record applicable classes. If you did not attend a college or university, what classes did you take in high school which developed your writing skills? Have you attended any report-writing workshops?

5. How many hours of experience have you had using basic LDS record groups such as the *IGI* (with its corresponding sources), the *FamilySearch* Internet program including the *Family History Library Catalog, IGI, Ancestral File*, and *Social Security Index*? Find your weaknesses and make a plan to strengthen your abilities in those areas.

6. List your education and training in genealogical research. When you list your classes, indicate if they were taken for credit or audit, what institution sponsored them, and who the instructors were.

7. Under "Other items of interest and/or genealogical experience," write down your volunteer service in lineage societies, at family history centers, with county societies, and with family organizations. Include experience publishing a newsletter, editing a paper, entering accessions data, filing cards, helping others with research, acting as a searcher for a professional genealogist, etc.

Figure 3.7 Sample Accreditation Test Application

To be submitted with a pedigree which you have extended at least four generations prior to 1875. This pedigree should be from the geographical area in which you wish to be accredited. It should be presented in report form and included well-documented Family Group Record forms for each family shown on the pedigree. This report should also indicate each research step taken and explain why it was taken.

General Information

Name				Sex	Age		Phone

Address	Area of accreditation interest (Circle)
	Midwestern, New England, Eastern, Southern, Other (state)

Purpose for requesting accreditation

Education and Training

Training courses in genealogical research theory (Do not include church classes or workshops.)	Where held	Instructor

Academic degrees obtained (indicate major & degree)	University or College	Date

English grammar and/or composition courses taken

Indicate research experience in the use and analysis of original and microfilmed records and/or time spent in correspondence with field researchers. For U.S. accreditation itemize by state. (Use back if desired)

Experience	Year	Number of hours
	Total Hrs	
Number of hours experience using L.D.S. Church Records	from above	

Indicate language ability for non-English accreditation

Other items of interest and/or genealogical experience

Signature	Date

Figure 3.8 Genealogy Computer Programs

DOS and Windows Varieties (only a small portion are listed here)

Organizes Data in DOS	Organize Data in Windows	Converts Family Data to Reports	Photos, Footnotes, Endnotes	Import Report & Change in Word Processor	Charts and Graphs of Various Types, Other
PAF 2.31 PAF 3.0	Personal Ancestral File (PAF) 4.0	PAF 4.0	PAF 4.0	PAF 4.0 with PAFCompanion 2	PAF 4.0 with PAFCompanion 2 (does calendars)
Roots	Ultimate Family Tree (UFT)	UFT	UFT		UFT (good sourcing)
	Family Tree Maker (FTM)	FTM 7.0	FTM 4.0 and up		FTM 7.0 (timelines and map migrations)
TMG	The Master Genealogist (TMG)	TMG	TMG	TMG	TMG (good sourcing)
	Family Origins (FO)	FO	FO		FO
	Legacy (LG)	LG	LG		LG (good LDS data transfers)

Macintosh Genealogy Computer Program Varieties

Organizes Data	Converts Family Data to Reports	Add Ons: Photos Footnotes, etc.	Charts and Graphs	Other
PAF for Mac	GED companion		GED companion	
Family Roots	MAC GenBook			
Reunion	Reunion 4.0	Reunion	Reunion	
Family Tree Maker (FTM)	Family Tree Maker	Family Tree Maker	Family Tree Maker	Family Tree Maker

Some Genealogy Programs Providing Research Assistance Rather Than Data

Name of Program	Research Assistance Offered
Animap	U.S. State and county formation maps by each year. Has longitude and latitude site finder, allows for marking and writing information
Clooz	Organizes data by fields, good for organizing photos.
Deedmapper	Analysis of land records, provides visual picture of land records.
FamilyTreeMaker 7.0	Provides research suggestions, family calendar, time line of event, public record office address and links to Internet site for more information
Genelines	More sophisticated time lines of events to merge with your GEDCOM for reporting to clients.
Vital Record Assistant	Keeps track of, composes, and formulates amounts on correspondence to Vital Record Offices.

Are You Ready to Apply for Accreditation?

Evaluating Your Skills

Perhaps you are a little nervous or unsure about your abilities. This chapter has been prepared to allow you to test your abilities and prepare for the accreditation examination. See how many of these questions and tasks you can complete, then evaluate yourself.

Assignments

The assignments for Chapter 4 are divided into four sections and follow the Suggested Reading:

√   Pre-Test

√   Preparation of a Report

√   Case Studies

√   Summarizing Research Results

Suggested Reading

Major United States Research Guides

Greenwood, Val D. *The Researcher's Guide to American Genealogy.* 3d ed. Baltimore: Genealogical Publishing Co., 2000.

Meyerink, Kory. *Printed Sources: A Guide to Published Genealogical Records.* Orem, Utah: Ancestry, 1998.

Pfeiffer, Laura Szucs. *Hidden Sources: Family History in Unlikely Places.* Orem, Utah: Ancestry, 1999.

Szucs, Loretto Dennis, and Sandra Hargreaves Luebking. *The Source: A Guidebook of American Genealogy*. Rev. ed. Salt Lake City: Ancestry, 1997.

Wright, Raymond S., III. *The Genealogist's Handbook: Modern Methods for Researching Family History*. Chicago: American Library Association, 1995.

Documentation

Holsclaw, Birdie Monk. "How to Cite Your Sources With Any Genealogical Software." *Traveling Historic Trails; National Genealogical Society and the Middle Tennessee Genealogical Society,* 8-11 May 1996; Nashville, Tenn., S 169. (May be ordered from Repeat Performance, 2911 Crabapple Lane, Hobart, IN 46342, session S-169.)

Lackey, Richard S. *Cite Your Sources.* New Orleans: Polyanthos, 1980.

Mills, Elizabeth Shown. *Evidence!* Baltimore: Genealogical Publishing Company, 1997.

University of Chicago Press. *The Chicago Manual of Style.* 14th ed. Chicago: University of Chicago Press, 1993.

Paleography

Hill, Ronald A. "Interpreting the Symbols and Abbreviations in 16th and 17th Century English Documents." *On to Richmond: Four Centuries of Family History; Federation of Genealogical Societies and Virginia Genealogical Society,* 12-15 October 1994; Richmond, Va., 162-165, T-61. (May be ordered from Repeat Performance, 2911 Crabapple Lane, Hobart, IN 46342, session T 61.)

_____. "Interpreting the Symbols and Abbreviations in 16th and 17th Century English Documents." *Genealogical Journal* 21, no. 1-2 (1993): 1-13. (May be ordered from the Utah Genealogical Association, P.O. Box 1144, Salt Lake City, Utah 84110.)

Hunter, Dean J. "Handwriting Workshop--Reading British Documents." *From Sea to Shining Sea; Federation of Genealogical Societies and Seattle Genealogical Society,* 20-23 September 1995; Seattle, Wash., T-60. (May be ordered from Repeat Performance, 2911 Crabapple Lane, Hobart, IN 46342, session T 60.)

Kirkham, E. Kay. *The Handwriting of American Records for a Period of 300 Years*. Logan, Utah: Everton Publishers, 1973.

Maness, Ruth Ellen. "This Record is Fraktured!! or The Chicken Walked Here!! Learning to Read the Gothic Script: Principles and Procedures." *From Sea to Shining Sea; Federation of Genealogical Societies and Seattle Genealogical Society*, 20-23 September 1995;

Seattle, Wash., T-61. (May be ordered from Repeat Performance, 2911 Crabapple Lane, Hobart, IN 46342, session T 61.)

Mirick, Zella Weaver. "Reading German Script." *Meet Me In St. Louis; Federation of Genealogical Societies and St. Louis Genealogical Society, 11-14 August 1999*; St. Louis, Missouri, T-42. (May be ordered from Repeat Performance, 2911 Crabapple Lane, Hobart, IN 46342, session T-42.)

Sperry, Kip. *Reading Early American Handwriting*. Baltimore: Genealogical Publishing Co., repr. 1999.

Wright, Raymond S. "Latin for Genealogists." *A Place to Explore; National Genealogical Society and San Diego Genealogical Society*, 3-6 May 1995; San Diego, Calif., 193-196. (May be ordered from Repeat Performance, 2911 Crabapple Lane, Hobart, IN 46342, session T-56.)

Report Writing

Mills, Elizabeth Shown. "Your Research Report." *On Board: Newsletter of the Board for Certification of Genealogists,* 1 May 1996: 9-13.

Mills, Elizabeth Shown. "The Research Report." *Traveling Historic Trails; National Genealogical Society and Middle Tennessee Genealogical Society*, 8-11 May 1996; Nashville, Tenn., F-102. (May be ordered from Repeat Performance, 2911 Crabapple Lane, Hobart, IN 46342, session F-102.)

Roman, Kenneth and Joel Raphaelson. *Writing That Works: How to Improve Your Memos, Letters, Reports, Speeches, Resumes, Plans, and Other Business Papers*. New York: Harper Collins, 1992.

Pedigree Analysis

Cerny, Johni and Arlene Eakle. *Ancestry's Guide to Research: Case Studies in American Genealogy*. Salt Lake City: Ancestry, 1985.

Rising, Marsha Hoffman. "Problem Analysis and Strategy Planning." *Traveling Historic Trails; National Genealogical Society and Middle Tennessee Genealogical Society,* 8-11 May 1996; Nashville, Tenn., W-2. (May be ordered from Repeat Performance, 2911 Crabapple Lane, Hobart, IN 46342, session W-2.)

Watson, Larry. "Native American Research." *A Place to Explore; National Genealogical Society and San Diego Genealogical Society*, 3-6 May 1995; San Diego, Calif., 197-200. (May be ordered from Repeat Performance, 2911 Crabapple Lane, Hobart, IN 46342, session T-57.)

Wilson, Shirley. "Conway Twitty's Roots--Methodology Used in Tracking a Sharecropper in a Burned County." *A Place to Explore; National Genealogical Society and San Diego Genealogical Society*, 3-6 May 1995; San Diego, Calif., 432-434. (May be ordered from Repeat Performance, 2911 Crabapple Lane, Hobart, IN 46342, session F-118.)

Major Sources- Land

Hone, E. Wade. *Land & Property Research in the United States*. Orem, Utah: Ancestry, Inc., 1997.

Major Sources- Military Records

Neagles, James C. *U. S. Military Records: A Guide to Federal and State Sources*, Colonial America to the Present. Salt Lake City: Ancestry, 1994.

Major Sources- Immigration

Roberts, Jayare. "Ellis Island." *Genealogical Journal* 23, no. 2 & 3 (1995): Special Double Issue; "Ellis Island Bibliography." *Genealogical Journal* 23, no. 4 (1995): 147-175; "Ellis Island Update." *Genealogical Journal* 23, no. 4 (1995): 176-185. " (May be ordered from the Utah Genealogical Association, P.O. Box 1144, Salt Lake City, UT 84110.)

Haslam, Gerald M.. "Scandinavian Emigration History and Sources." *Genealogical Journal* 27, nos. 3-4 (1999). (May be ordered from the Utah Genealogical Association, P.O. Box 1144, Salt Lake City, UT 84110.)

Major Sources- Native Americans

Carnahan, Sharon and NaDine Timothy. "American Indian Material, Pacific Northwest." *Genealogical Journal* 22, no. 1 (1994): 9-11. (May be ordered from the Utah Genealogical Association, P.O. Box 1144, Salt Lake City, UT 84110.)

Major Sources- Newspapers

Roberts, Jayare. "Using U.S. Newspapers for Family and Local History." *Genealogical Journal* 23, no. 1 (1995): 3-11. (May be ordered from the Utah Genealogical Association, P.O. Box 1144, Salt Lake City, UT 84110.)

Major Sources- Periodicals

Adkins, Wilma. "Periodical Source Index (PERSI)." *Genealogical Journal* 22, no. 1 (1994): 12-17. (May be ordered from the Utah

Genealogical Association, P.O. Box 1144, Salt Lake City, UT 84110.)

British Isles Major Source

Baxter, Angus. *In Search of Your British and Irish Roots*. 4th ed. Baltimore: Genealogical Publishing Co., 1999.

Cory, Kathleen B. *Tracing Your Scottish Ancestry*. Baltimore: Genealogical Publishing Co., repr 1999.

Rowlands, John. Welsh Family History. *A Guide to Research*. Baltimore: Genealogical Publishing Co., repr 1997.

Canadian Major Sources

Baxter, Angus. *In Search of Your Canadian Roots*. Baltimore: Genealogical Publishing Co., 1989.

Boudreau, Dennis M.. *Beginning Franco-American Genealogy*. Pawtucket, R.I.: American-French Genealogical Society, 1986.

Continental Europe Major Sources

"Research Outline France," "Research Outline Germany." *Family History SourceGuide*. CD-ROM. Salt Lake City: Church of Jesus Christ of Latter day Saints, 1998.

Hispanic Major Source

Ryskamp, George R. *Finding Your Hispanic Roots*. Baltimore: Genealogical Publishing Co., 1997.

LDS Research Major Source

Jaussi, Laureen R. *Genealogy Fundamentals*. Orem, Utah: Jaussi Publications, 1994.

Native American Major Source

"Research Outline United States-Native Races." *Family History SourceGuide*. CD-ROM. Salt Lake City: Church of Jesus Christ of Latter day Saints, 1998.

Scandinavian Major Source

"Research Outline Denmark," "Research Outline Finland," "Research Outline Iceland," "Research Outline Norway," "Research Outline Sweden." *Family History SourceGuide*. CD-ROM. Salt Lake City: Church of Jesus Christ of Latter-day Saints, 1998.

Assignment 1: Pre-Test

1. Name the major repositories for research in your area of specialization, and indicate their locations.

   Allen Co.

   I   Chicago

   I

2. What relationship do geography and history have to genealogical research?

3. If you are doing U.S. research, indicate which states in your specialty area had state censuses, and what years they covered.

4. Indicate any special indexes available in your area of specialization that cover an entire state or an entire province, district, etc.

5. If you are doing U.S. reseasrch, list at least one statewide periodical for each state in your area of specialization. If you are doing a foreign or LDS speciality, name one periodical covering a province or smaller area than the entire field.

6. Name at least four major periodicals covering United States family history research for your entire region in general (if you are specializing in the United States), or if in a foreign area, list at least two periodicals covering your specific area. Name at least one ethnic periodical in your specialty area.

7. Name a federal or national archive repository or branch in your specialty area.

8. List the types of records that are available at the federal or national level in your specialty area.

9. Describe the land records available in your specialty area. Which land records exist at each government level? How should these land records be used?

10. Describe the various types of probate records. List at least five types of probate records.

11. Why must one be cautious when using probate records?

12. Which federal census was the first to show family relationships in the United States, or which national census in your speciality area was the first to show family relationships?

1850

13. For U. S. research, which federal census is the first to list every member of the house hold? Which federal census provides both the month and year of birth? Which federal census provides the year of immigration?Which federal census records prior to 1850 indicate a foreign birth?

1850)   1900

14. What are mortality schedules in U. S. census research?

15. Give the Soundex code for each of these surnames:

   a) Oppenheimer

   b) Lukaschowsky

   c) Cook

   d) Allricht

   e) Eberhard

   f) O'Brian

   g) Hanselmann

    h) Greenwood

    i)   Quinney

    j)   Nebeker

    k) Ferguson

16. Name the two major categories of military records most often used by genealogists and explain what they might contain in the way of primary evidence.

17. What kinds of genealogy information might be available in court records?

18. For each of the states or provinces in your area of specialization, indicate the major migration routes used prior to 1880.

19. Explain the differences between primary and secondary sources, between direct or circumstantial evidence, and between internal and external evidence.

20. What is the *International Genealogical Index*, the *Ancestral File*, and *FamilySearch*? What kinds of data do they contain?

21. List the major church denominations in each state or province in your area of specialization prior to 1875 and their record repositories.

22. List the unique characteristics of records in your area of specialization. What research techniques work best with these records?

23. List any major genealogical collections in your specialty areas and indicate what states or regions they cover and which repositories have them.

24. List any major genealogical collections in your specialty areas and indicate what states or regions they cover and which repositories have them (continued).

25. If applying for accreditation in the British Isles, draft a letter as though you were going to order a birth or marriage certificate from a country in the United Kingdom.

26. If applying for accreditation in the British Isles, indicate sources for English muster rolls and indicate their value to a genealogist.

27. What do the following terms mean?

a) transcribe:

we write exactly

b) translate:

One Language to another

c) abstract:

d) extract:

Well, how did you do? A pre-test is always a useful exercise. To make it even more of a learning experience, I'm not going to give you the answers. Instead, here is a study guide of references that correspond to the numbers of the test questions. Focus especially on questions you felt you could not answer readily. The references were chosen because they are readily available and use the resources of the Family History Library. This study guide uses short titles. Complete citations are given at the end of these answers.

1. a) *State Research Outline* (see the category "Archives and Libraries").
   b) Greenwood, pages 70-73.
   c) GERMS (look under states of specialty).
   d) Bentley

2. a) Clifford, *Determined*, pages 111, 127-151, 326.
   b) Clifford, *Advanced*, pages 101, 105-106.

3. a) *State Research Outline* (for each state in your specialty area, see the category "Census").

4. a) *State Research Outline* (for each state in your specialty area, see all the major categories).
   b) Clifford, *Advanced*, "CD-ROM Indexes."

5. *State Research Outline* (for each state in your specialty area, see the category "Periodicals").

6. a) *State Research Outline* (for each state in your specialty area, see the category "Periodicals").
   b) *U.S. Research Outline* (see the category "Periodicals").

7. a) *State Research Outline* (for each state in your specialty area, see the category "Archives and Libraries").
   b) Archives.

8. a) *U.S. Research Outline* (under each category).
   b) Clifford, *Determined*, pages 13-35; 173-200; 203-209; 215-229; and 241-250.
   c) Archives.

9. a) *State Research Outline* (for each state in your specialty area, see the category "Land and Property").
   b) Clifford, *Determined*, pages 159-201.
   c) Greenwood, pages 321-378.
   d) *U.S. Research Outline* (see the category "Land and Property").

10. a) *U.S. Research Outline* (see the category "Probate").
    b) Clifford, *Determined*, pages 59-78.
    c) Greenwood, pages 255-320.

11. a) *U.S. Research Outline* (see the category "Probate").
    b) Clifford, *Determined*, pages 59-78.
    c) Greenwood, pages 255-320.

12. a) Clifford, *Beginner*, pages 14-1 to 14-26.
    b) Greenwood, pages 181-254.
    c) *U.S. Research Outline* (see the category "Census").

13. a) Clifford, *Beginner*, pages 14-1 to 14-26.
    b) Greenwood, pages 181-254.
    c) *U.S. Research Outline* (see the category "Census").

14. a) Clifford, *Beginner*, pages 131-159.
    b) Greenwood, pages 181-254.
    c) *U.S. Research Outline* (see the category "Census").

15. Soundex Coding.
    a) Oppenheimer   O155
    b) Lukaschowsky   L222
    c) Cook   C200
    d) Allricht   A462
    e) Eberhard   E166
    f) O'Brian   O165
    g) Hanselmann   H524
    h) Greenwood   G653
    i) Quinney   Q500
    j) Nebeker   N126
    k) Ferguson   F625

16. a) *U.S. Research Outline* (see the category "Military").
    b) Clifford, *Determined*, pages 281-294.
    c) Greenwood, pages 485-544.

17. a) *U.S. Research Outline* (see the category "Court Records").
    b) Greenwood, pages 397-422.

18. a) *State Research Outline* (for each state in your specialty area, see the categories of "Emigration and Immigration" and "History").
    b) Clifford, *Determined Researcher*, pages 99-158.
    c) GERMS (Look under states of specialty).

19. Greenwood, pages 61-68.

20. a) Family History Library. *FamilySearch*: International Genealogical Index (on compact disc), available from the Salt Lake Distribution Center, 1999 West 1700 South, Salt Lake City, UT 84104-4233 or by FAX 1-801-240-3685.
    b) Family History Library. *FamilySearch: Using Ancestral File*, in the *SourceGuide*™.
    c) Clifford, *Beginner*, pages 11-1 to 11-19

21. a) *State Research Outline* (for each state in your specialty area, see the category "Church Records").

    b) *U.S. Research Outline* (see the category "Church Records").

22. a) *State Research Outline* (for each state in your specialty area, see under all categories).

    b) Clifford, *Determined*, pages 295-329.

    c) GERMS (look under states of specialty).

23. Same as 21 above.

24. Personal choice.

25. See the Research Outlines for the countries of the British Isles for reference books and how to obtain these records. This is an example of a source not available in the Family History Library, but one in which an accredited genealogist should be familiar.

26. transcribe: to make an exact written copy; to make a copy in longhand; to make a copy on a typewriter or by any mechanical or electronic means; to write down.

    translate: to turn something written or spoken from one language to another, or to transfer or turn one set of symbols into another.

    abstract: to summarize or abridge by using essential facts only.

    extract: to take out of another source or to copy, usually signifying that the material or item being copied is copied in its entirety from a larger work; a selection from a writing or discourse; to select and copy out, or cite.

Answer Bibliography

Short Title	Complete Citation
State Research Outline	Family History Library. *State Research Outline* (for each state or country in your specialty area), in the *SourceGuide*™ (see pages 27 and 28).
U.S. Research Outline	Family History Library. *United States Research Outline*, available in the *SourceGuide*™ (see pages 27 and 28).
Greenwood	Greenwood, Val D. *The Researcher's Guide to American Genealogy*. 2d ed. Baltimore, Md.: Genealogical Publishing Co., 1990.
GERMS	American Society of Genealogists. Genealogical Research: *Methods and Sources*. 2 vols, rev. ed. Edited by Milton Rubincam, Washington, D.C.: The Society, 1980, 1983.
Bentley	Bentley, Elizabeth Petty. *The Genealogist's Address Book* 3rd ed. Baltimore Genealogical Publishing Co., 1995.
Clifford, Beginner	Clifford, Karen. *The Complete Beginner's Guide to Genealogy, the Internet, and Your Genealogy Computer Program*. Baltimore: Genealogical Publishing Company, 2000.
Clifford, Determined	*Clifford, Karen. Genealogy and Computers for the Determined Researcher.* Baltimore, Md. Clearfield Company, 1995.
Clifford, Advanced	Clifford, Karen. *Genealogy and Computers for the Advanced Researcher.* Baltimore, Md. Clearfield Company, 1995.
Archives	Szucs, Loretto Dennis & Sandra Hargreaves Luebking. *The Archives: A Guide to the National Archives Field Branches*. Salt Lake City: Ancestry, 1988.

Assignment 2: Preparation of a Report

Prepare a report that includes a pedigree extended at least four generations prior to 1875. This pedigree should be from the geographical area in which you wish to be accredited. The complete report should include the pedigree chart, well-documented family group records for each family shown on the pedigree chart, and a statement indicating not only the research steps taken but why each step was taken to solve the stated problem.

Don't let this assignment overwhelm you. Break it into smaller steps. If you have already taken an intermediate course in genealogy or in report writing, such as described in chapters 7 and 8 in *Genealogy and Computers for the Determined Researcher*, you have already practiced these skills. Review those chapters for more tips.

1. Have you stated your goal? What did the client or credentialing institution ask you to do?

2. Did you prepare research calendars or logs of the sources you searched and the results of those searches?

3. Based on steps 1 and 2, prepare the research report listing the research steps taken, why they were taken, and what was found. Don't forget to include an analysis of the evidence. What does it prove? What does it suggest?

4. Describe the next steps. Are records available at another repository? What should be done next? Have you proven every relationship expected as part of the credentialing application?

5. Find an associate who you feel writes well, and have him or her read your report and offer suggestions. Is everything clear, well organized, self-explanatory? Check the grammar and spelling. Is the report neat, without typographical errors? Check your family group records. If you used the methods explained in *The Complete Beginner's Guide to Genealogy, the Internet, and Your Genealogy Computer Program*, your documentation should be ready to turn in. Check your dates. Are they logical? Are your localities entered correctly and consistently? Does the report look professional?

Assignment 3: Pedigree Analysis

Pedigree analysis tests the ability to evaluate pedigree problems. They are an efficient means of evaluating a candidate's problem-solving abilities. Can the candidate find and point out discrepancies in the record and find what was missing? Did the candidate know which records to search first? If there was no single source, what records used together provided the evidence necessary to solve the problem?

In the samples which follow, determine what is missing. How would you find the missing information? What sources would be searched and why would they be used? In what order would they be searched? Work through the case studies found in figures 4.1 to 4.4. Follow the instructions for each study. List selected sources in the priority order of their use. State why that source was selected and what was expected from that source. (Since each region of the U.S. requires a different approach, case studies are provided for each U.S. accreditation region.)

You may need more space to record your answers. Feel free to use another sheet if necessary. Do not let the size of the form prevent a full explanation of your answers.

Figure 4.1   New England States Pedigree Analysis

Study the pedigree below and indicate which sources you would search and why you would search them. Then number your sources in priority order.

```
                                      ┌─────────────────────┐
                                      │ b.                  │
                                      │ bp.                 │
                                      │ m.   16 Feb 1749    ┌────────────────┐
                                      │ mp. Dedham, Norfolk, MA│ b.          │
                                      │ d.                  │ bp.            │
                                      │ dp.  Sharon, Suffolk, MA│ m.          ┌──────────────┐
                                      │                     │ mp.            │ b.           │
              Samuel White            │                     │ d.             │ bp.          │
                                      │ Mary Little         │ dp.            │ m.           │
     b.    17 June 1756               │                     └────────────────┤ mp.          │
     bp.  Sharon, Suffolk, MA         │ b.                  │                │ d.           │
     m.                               │ bp.                 │                │ dp.          │
     mp.                              │ d.                  │ b.             └──────────────┤
     d.                               │ dp.                 │ bp.            │              │
     dp.                              │ 2nd wife Mary Bowlen │ d.             │ b.           │
                                      │    m. 13 Dec 1750   │ dp.            │ bp.          │
                                                                             │ d.           │
                                                                             │ dp.          │
```

Source	Reasons For Searching (Expectations)

Figure 4.2   Eastern States Pedigree Analysis

Study the pedigree below and indicate which sources you would search and why you would search them. Then number your sources in priority order.

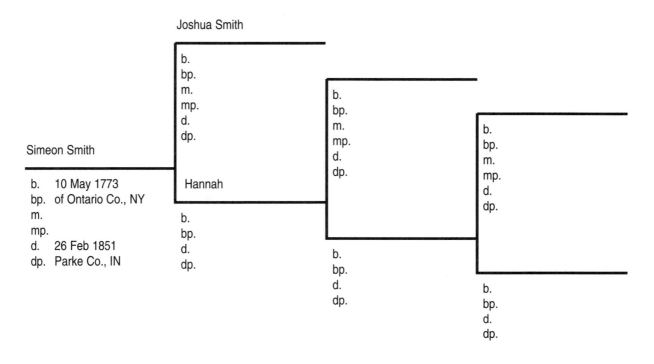

Source	Reasons For Searching (Expectations)

Figure 4.3 Midwestern States Pedigree Analysis

Study the pedigree below and indicate which sources you would search and why you would search them. Then number your sources in priority order.

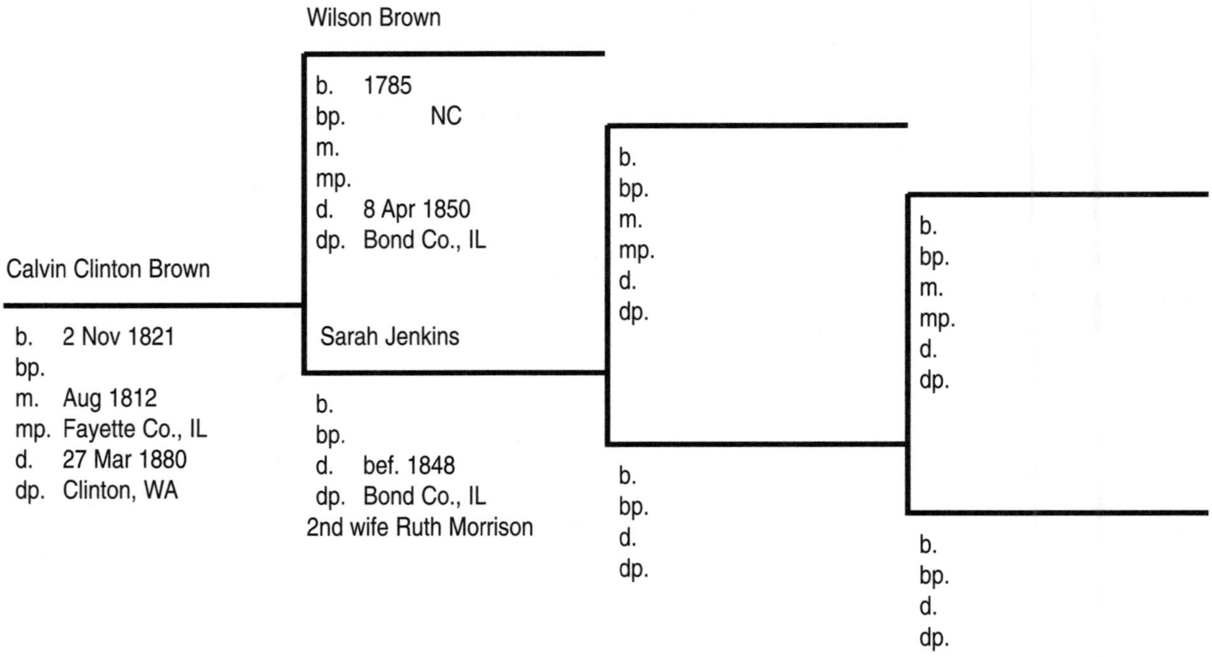

Wilson Brown

```
b.    1785
bp.            NC
m.
mp.
d.    8 Apr 1850
dp.  Bond Co., IL
```

Calvin Clinton Brown

```
b.    2 Nov 1821
bp.
m.    Aug 1812
mp.  Fayette Co., IL
d.    27 Mar 1880
dp.  Clinton, WA
```

Sarah Jenkins

```
b.
bp.
d.    bef. 1848
dp.  Bond Co., IL
2nd wife Ruth Morrison
```

```
b.
bp.
m.
mp.
d.
dp.
```

```
b.
bp.
d.
dp.
```

```
b.
bp.
m.
mp.
d.
dp.
```

```
b.
bp.
d.
dp.
```

Source	Reasons For Searching (Expectations)

Figure 4.4   Southern States Pedigree Analysis

Study the pedigree below and indicate which sources you would search and why you would search them. Then number your sources in priority order.

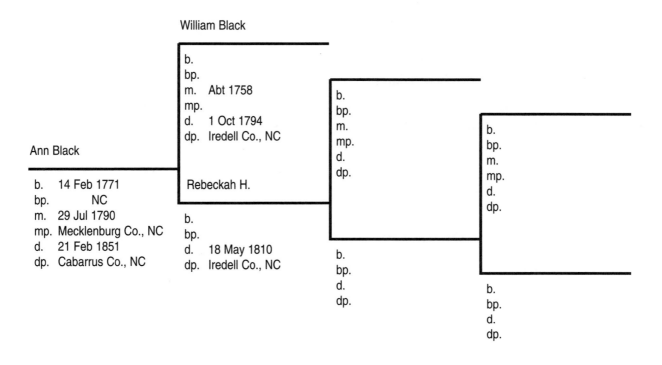

Source	Reasons For Searching (Expectations)

Assignment 4: Summarizing Research Results

Write short, concise reports on each of the four case studies given in figures 4.1 to 4.4 as though you were being paid to do a pedigree consultation. Of course, you are not specialized in all four areas. Indicate which area is your region of specialization, but do the other three assignments for practice. Indicate the following:

1. What sources would you search?

2. In what order would you search those sources?

3. Why would you search those sources?

4. Provide suggestions for further research if you found what you expected in a particular source. In other words, could this new evidence lead you to other records?

# Report Writing

Once the research has been conducted, the preparation of a document is necessary which will both inform and educate the client in the results of the research. Leaving enough time and a good "trail" of research notes to write this document within the time frame allotted by the client is always a challenge. The first reports seem cumbersome and time consuming. In fact, some genealogists recall that this phase of the research process is the most intimidating. Once accomplished, however, the report becomes the showpiece of all your work.

Benefits and Pitfalls

Good researchers who can write good reports are in high demand, especially those who are familiar enough with the sources and methods in their research area to find records efficiently and interpret them correctly. Also valuable is a genealogist who can read records accurately and explain them so effectively that both the benefits and pitfalls of the sources are discussed. This ability to conduct an intelligent search and to prepare a clear, concise summary of the research results is part of the client reporting process.

Tip 75: Prior knowledge of what the client wants makes up part of the "goal."

Clients are often unaware of the relative value of primary and secondary source material. They are often untrained in genealogical sources and methodology, as well. But a good genealogist should demonstrate for the client an ability to find, recognize, and organize records used as evidence in support of each family generation as well as each date and place mentioned. This demonstration takes place as part of the report.

Figure 5.1 Some United States Lineage Societies.

(Many societies have published their own lineage records, pedigrees, and genealogies, and copies are available at major libraries, with many available on interlibrary loan.)

American College of Heraldry
American Order of Pioneers
Ancient and Honorable Artillery Company of Massachusetts
Ancient and Honorable Order of the Jersey Blues
Aryan Order of St. George of the Holy Roman Empire in the Colonies of America
Aztec Club of 1847
Baronial Order of the Magna Charta
Children of the Confederacy
Colonial Dames of America
Colonial Order of the Acorn
Colonial Order of the Crown
Colonial Society of Massachusetts
Colonial Society of Pennsylvania
Dames of the Loyal Legion of the United States
Daughters of the Cincinnati
Daughters of the Republic of Texas
Daughters of the Revolution
Daughters of Union Veterans of the Civil War 1861-1865
Descendants of Founders of New Jersey
Descendants of the Illegitimate Sons and Daughters of the Kings of Britain (Royal Bastards)
Dutch Colonial Society of Delaware
Dutch Settlers Society of Albany
First Families of Ohio
General Society of Colonial Wars
General Society of Mayflower Descendants
General Society of the War of 1812
General Society, Sons of the Revolution
Grand Army of the Republic
Guild of St. Margaret of Scotland
Hereditary Order of Descendants of the Loyalists and Patriots of the American Revolution
Holland Society of New York
Hood's Texas Brigade Association
Huguenot Society of America
Huguenot Society of South Carolina
Huguenot Society of the Founders of Manakin in the Colony of Virginia
International Society of Descendants of Charlemagne
Jamestowne Society
Ladies of the Grand Army of the Republic
Los Pobladores
Louisiana Colonials
Military Order of the Crusades

(Figure 5.1 continued)

Military Order of the Loyal Legion of the United States
National Huguenot Society
National Society, Children of the American Colonists
National Society, Children of the American Revolution
National Society of Americans of Royal Descent
National Society, Daughters of Colonial Wars
National Society, Daughters of the American Colonists
National Society, Daughters of the American Revolution
National Society, Daughters of the Barons of Runnemede
National Society, Daughters of the Revolution of 177
National Society Descendants of Early Quakers
National Society of Andersonville
National Society of Daughters of Founders and Patriots of America
National Society of Magna Charta Dames
National Society of New England Women
National Society of the Old Plymouth Colony Descendants
National Society of the Colonial Dames of America
National Society of the Colonial Dames of the XVII Century
National Society of the Colonial Daughters of the Seventeenth Century
National Society of the Dames of the Court of Honor
National Society of the Daughters of Utah Pioneers
National Society of the Descendants of Lords of the Maryland Manors 1938
National Society of the Sons and Daughters of the Pilgrims
National Society of the Sons of the American Revolution
National Society of the Sons of Utah Pioneers
National Society of the Southern Dames of America
National Society United States Daughters of 1812
National Society Washington Family Descendants
National Society, Women Descendants of the Ancient & Honorable Artillery Company of
     Massachusetts
Naval Order of the United States
Netherlands Society of Philadelphia
Order of Americans of Armorial Ancestry
Order of Colonial Lords of Manors in America
Order of Descendants of Colonial Physicians and Chirurgeons
Order of First Families of Virginia 1607-1624/5
Order of the Crown in America
Order of the Crown of Charlemagne in the United States of America
Order of the First Families of Mississippi 1699-1817
Order of the Founders and Patriots of America
Order of Three Crusades, 1096-1192
Order of Washington
Piscataqua Pioneers
Plantagenet Society
Saint Nicholas Society of the City of New York

(Figure 5.1 continued)

San Jacinto Descendants
Scotch-Irish Foundation
Scotch-Irish Society of the United States of America
Society of American Wars
Society of California Pioneers
Society of Daughters of Holland Dames
Society of Descendants of Knights of the Most Noble Order of the Garter
Society of Indiana Pioneers Society of Kentucky Pioneers
Society of Loyalist Descendants
Society of Montana Pioneers
Society of the Alden Kindred of America
Society of the Ark and the Dove
Society of the Cincinnati
Society of the Descendants of the Colonial Clergy
Society of the Descendants of the Founders of Hartford
Society of the Descendants of Washington's Army at Valley Forge
Society of the Lees of Virginia
Society of the United States Daughters, 1776-1812
Society of the Whiskey Rebellion of 1794
Somerset Chapter Magna Charta Barons
Sons and Daughters of Oregon Pioneers
Sons and Daughters of the First Settlers of Newbury, Massachusetts
Sons of Confederate Veterans
Sons of Delaware
Sons of the Republic of Texas
Sons of Union Veterans of the Civil War
Sovereign Colonial Society Americans of Royal Descent
Swedish Colonial Society
United Confederate Veterans
United Daughters of the Confederacy
United Empire Loyalists Association of Canada
Vermont Society of Colonial Dames
Welcome Society of Pennsylvania
Welsh Society of Philadelphia

Let's use, for example, an individual who is focusing on an American lineage society application as a case study. (Figure 5.1 is a partial listing of societies which require a proven lineage to join them.) The first requirement would be a knowledge of the lineage society requirements. These may be obtained by writing to the society. Many are listed in the *Genealogist's Address Book* published by Genealogy Publishing Company. These requirements should be demonstrated and adhered to in the report. Lineage applications should be organized coherently, with convincing proof of each generational link. Does the report demonstrate an ability to interpret and explain records that contain conflicting information? Was the problem analyzed and the evidence assembled objectively, free of preconceptions? Does the submitted report include complete documentation from predominantly primary sources? Do the research logs reflect good record-keeping practices? Are the items below found in the report?

Items in the Report

Grammar and Spelling. Reports should be neat and orderly in appearance, using standard English grammar and spelling. Discussions and reports must be clear and to the point.

Methods and Sources. A good knowledge of effective genealogical methods and standard sources should be evident, as well as the ability to read the older handwriting. The report should display an understanding of the genealogical significance of primary and secondary records and a good understanding of the difference between an abstract and a transcription. Good quality abstracts or photocopies of documents should be part of the report.

Source Citations. All genealogical statements, whether they are reports about the contents of a record or group of records, or are statements of genealogical fact, should be supported by source citations. Sources in the reports could use standard citation formats from *The Chicago Manual of Style*, 14th ed. (Chicago: University of Chicago Press, 1993) or from other major guides such as Elizabeth Shown Mills, *Evidence! Documentation and Analysis for the Family Historian* (in preparation); or Kate L. Turabian, *A Manual for Writers of Term Papers, Theses, and Dissertations,* 5th ed. (Chicago: University of Chicago Press. 1987).

Although no required format for reporting has been established, the genealogist should be able to demonstrate thorough knowledge and good use of genealogical and citation formats. The genealogist should be able to cite the source (but not necessarily include copies of documents) for every genealogical statement made in all portions of the report.

An excellent summary may be found in Elizabeth Shown Mills, *Evidence!* Baltimore: Genealogical Publishing Company, 1997.

Tip 76: The value of a four-generation pedigree report using pre-1875 records is the exam's ability to show the applicant's use of a variety of records.

Variety of Sources. The report should also demonstrate a thorough knowledge of a wide variety of sources. These sources may also cover a variety of time periods, geographical areas, and government/church jurisdictions in a variety of formats (original, microfilm, published primary, and unpublished secondary).

A checklist of valuable report contents follows. Although every report will not contain every item listed, it can become a succinct reminder of your goals.

A Checklist for the Report Writer

1. Write in coherent, connected sentences and submit a report which reflects effort and thoughtful deliberation.

2. Use different families for various parts of your report: explaining the goal, the preliminary overview of published or compiled genealogies, and the original research.

3. Make complete transcriptions of source documents.

4. Write precise abstracts of relevant supporting documents.

5. Translate documents and alert others of questionable translations of cited sources, if necessary.

6. Provide research goals.

7. Evaluate documents and lay out a plan of action that displays analytical abilities.

8. Demonstrate familiarity with existing records for the time period under specialization.

9. Provide source citations for each reference discussed and support each statement with reliable documentation, using footnotes or endnotes or parenthetical source citations.

10. Include full citations on all photocopies, and full references in the report for each attached photocopy.

11. Demonstrate proper use of acceptable evidence.

12. Use a variety of sources, with an emphasis on primary materials.

13. Use the clues found in published genealogies, but don't consider them to be authoritative sources.

14. Explain that information written years after an event is highly prone to error and needs supportive proof, but such information may be all that is currently available.

15. Make a convincing case, using examples based upon thorough research in all applicable records, without making a premature clear and convincing evidence conclusion.

16. Present your argument in a logical, well-organized sequence.

17. Compile reports that state the research goal, describe the completed research, analyze the results, include all negative searches, and set forth a plan for future research.

18. Supply appropriate family group records and pedigree charts for each generation.

19. Use personal research findings, not those gathered by others, basing your work more on primary sources than secondary sources.

20. Put all the families into their appropriate historical background.

21. Use a standard numbering system.

Practice Report-Writing Skills

Tip 77: In the past years, excellent books have been published such as U.S. Military Records: A Guide to Federal & State Sources *by James C. Neagles (Ancestry, Inc., 1996);* Land & Property Research in the United States *by E. Wade Hone (Ancestry, Inc., 1997); and* Understanding and Using Baptismal Records *by John T. Humphrey (Humphrey Publications, 1996). Genealogists have more sources than ever for learning about the basic record groups.*

To practice your record-keeping abilities you can abstract, transcribe, and give a brief discussion of the genealogical significance of three different documents from three different record groups such as: probate, land, and vital records or church, military, and newspapers. Then develop a research plan based on clues in each document. This analysis allows you to demonstrate your ability not only to do research but to communicate the significance of that research to others.

The above exercises also help you to judge whether you can:

- follow instructions
- abstract and transcribe materials properly
- read early handwriting
- accurately interpret the information according to the historical events and customs of the time

Now, ask a friend to be a "client." Let this "client" request research to be done. Ask yourself the following questions related to this "client's" research project:

- What problem or problems is the investigation intended to solve?
- Are there any limitations imposed by "the client" (such as how much time was to be expended or which records were to be examined)?
- Ask your friend to read your report in light of the requirements laid out and see if all is in order. Correct any deficiencies.

Conclusion

Report writing is vital to a successful genealogy business. Without good reporting skills, your clients are not likely to come back. A good report:

- guides the client to other options he or she has previously been unaware of

- forms the substance of a published family history

- ends one research session and becomes the launching point for

Tip 78: A genealogist is
first of all an educator.
We are constantly edu-
cating others about
records, their value to
the client, and how all
the evidence fits
together.

the next research session because it summarizes what has already been done and what should be done next

- helps others to become aware of missing pieces of a larger "puzzle" in the family history so that suggestions can be forthcoming

- is the jewel in the genealogist's crown. Good reports make or break genealogy businesses.

Figures 5.2 and 5.3 are used in my intermediate classes to focus attention on specific aspects of research and to force that information to be brief. Figure 5.2 begins where all reports should begin, stating the goal, or objective, of this particular research report or research session. The goal can, therefore, be limited to a specific family, in order to report on a segment of the research. The enormity of a four-generation report can overwhelm beginning researchers until they realize that they can break it down into manageable portions.

To use the form, first select one person (usually the person designated by the client) to place into their environment by including facts about the family (items which are documented and proven). Include traditions about the family (items which are not documented or proven) and a summary of the siblings of the person (encouraging the researcher not to overlook the siblings). If sibling names are not available, then include a summary of the person's children so that clues such as naming patterns, customs, movement patterns, etc., may be analyzed.

At this point, indicate whether maps and historical background materials have been gathered, whether customs, folkways, and naming patterns of the time period have been studied, and if neighbors and traveling companions have been analyzed. Finally, list migration trails, common motives for moving to a particular area, and an investigation of other sources possible after the above information has been studied.

Tip 79: There are some
very helpful U.S. migra-
tion maps and early
canal and road maps in
the back of The
Handybook for
Genealogists (The
Everton Publishers,
Logan, Utah, 1999.)

Once you have placed the person in his environment, examine the environment itself for further research possibilities. Study the information regarding historical background thoroughly for information regarding settlement, associations with other travelers, religious affiliations or prominent leaders, and specific ruling governments in order to determine who would have had jurisdiction over any records produced by historical events during the time the individual lived in a particular area.

Once you have filled out these forms, you will have an easier time typing a report draft. You'll see samples of student report preparation forms in figures 5.4 to 5.13. Notice that there are two different forms for each problem, i.e. figure 5.4 and figure 5.5 go together; figure 5.6 and 5.7, etc. These forms are helpful because they:

- focus on one goal at a time
- point out overlooked areas in your research
- guide you to sources previously not considered
- focus your mind toward a conclusion.

Once you have filled out the forms and prepared a rough draft of the report, the next thing to do is to compare the report with the previous checklist for the report writer and make appropriate corrections. Finally, write a concluding statement summarizing the important findings and what can be done in the future, both in the records repository you are currently using and in others.

Assignments will follow which will break the reporting-writing process down into more manageable steps. For example, Assignment 1 will determine your ability to evaluate genealogical information within two documents you select. Since you will be evaluating documents in your reports, this will help you practice that skill. Assignment 2 will allow you to practice transcription and abstraction skills from two documents of your choice.

Since you will not have a choice about which documents to transcribe in the research you perform, I have selected a few genealogical documents for you to transcribe in assignment 3 which are contemporary to the time period of the accreditation process. This assignment also asks you to abstract the information, provide a brief commentary about the genealogical value of the documents included, and to provide a brief research plan based on clues in the documents.

Assignment 4 focuses on your ability to find sources from secondary materials. Select a like-minded genealogist or mentor to help you improve your skills. Assignment 5 is meant to provide practice in appropriately citing sources. Finally, the reading suggestions provide quality articles by expert genealogists regarding the evaluation of evidence. It is important to work with others as we recognize our weaknesses and our strengths. Teaming up with a "buddy" who is also interested in being the best genealogist he or she can be, is an effective way of improving your skills.

Remember, report writing is a very personal skill which can be developed over time. Each of the assignments above can contribute to the overall success of your report writing.

Figure 5.2   The Person Within His Environment

PROBLEM OR OBJECTIVE	
FACTS ABOUT THE FAMILY	
TRADITIONS ABOUT THE FAMILY	
SUMMARY OF SIBLING OR CHILDREN SEARCH CONDUCTED	
HISTORICAL SUMMARY INCLUDING MAPS	
CUSTOMS, FOLKWAYS AND NAMING PATTERNS OF THE TIME PERIOD	
NEIGHBORS AND GROUP CONNECTIONS STUDIED	
MIGRATION TRAILS	
COMMON ENTERPRISES EXAMINED	
WHERE MORE INFORMATION CAN BE OBTAINED	

Figure 5.3   What is Known About the Environment

AREA AND TIME PERIOD SETTLED (List the earliest dates known for this individual and his family in this area.)	
SPECIFIC RULING GOVERNMENT (Was it colonial, territorial, state, county, federal, or foreign?)	
NEIGHBORHOOD SETTLEMENT (Where did the people come from who settled this area in the time period of your family?)	
WHAT WAS HAPPENING IN THIS TIME PERIOD OF SETTLEMENT IN THE REGION?	
WHAT WAS THE RELIGIOUS BACKGROUND OR AFFILIATION OF THE SETTLERS?	
WHO WERE THE PROMINENT LEADERS?	
NEW IDEAS FOR RESEARCH (Based on the information gathered above.)	

Figure 5.4   The Person Within His Environment (sample)

PROBLEM OR OBJECTIVE	Find Clara Florence (Bower) Smedley's paternal immigrant ancestor. (Bower)
FACTS ABOUT THE FAMILY	Florence (b. 1879, Benton Co., Iowa- m. 1910, Benton Co, Iowa, Vernon Smedley, 2 children Vera and Lavonne born in Wayne Co., Ohio- d. 1955, Wayne Co., Ohio) Henry Bowers (b. 1842, Stark Co., Ohio- m. 1867 Holmer Co., Ohio) Sophia Graber (b. 1847, Tusc. Co., Ohio) Christopher Bower (Bauer) chr. 1814, m. 1841, Ohio, to Kristina Kleinschrott, d. 1875, Noble Co., Ind.)
TRADITIONS ABOUT THE FAMILY	Traditional Naming Patterns of Germany
SUMMARY OF SIBLING OR CHILDREN SEARCH CONDUCTED	Henry Samuel (1842, Stark Co., Ohio), John W. (1846), Mary P. (1852), William L. (1858), Ellen., Eliza E. (1861, Tusc., Ohio) (1870 Census Baden/Baveria) (1880 son agreed)
HISTORICAL SUMMARY INCLUDING MAPS	Early maps of county indicate work on the canals
CUSTOMS, FOLKWAYS AND NAMING PATTERNS OF THE TIME PERIOD	
NEIGHBORS AND GROUP CONNECTIONS STUDIED	3 township study of Stark, Tuscarawas, and Holmes co.unties in Ohio, where Christopher Bower lived. Rev. Crouse's history
MIGRATION TRAILS	Canal Great Lakes, Erie, Hudson - Port of N.Y.
COMMON ENTERPRISES EXAMINED	Blacksmith/farmer (1860-1870)
WHERE MORE INFORMATION CAN BE OBTAINED	State census, records if any, tax records, *Germans to America* Resource Book on German Reformed Church, Obituary on Christopher, Pursue Rev Cruise in County History, use National Union Catalog of Manuscript Collections (NUCMC) to locate unpublished German Reformed Church records Study the 1830-1870 German History of Baden

Figure 5.5   What is Known About the Environment (sample)

AREA AND TIME PERIOD SETTLED (List the earliest dates known for this individual and his family in this area.)	1838 Stark Co., Ohio Ohio state history
SPECIFIC RULING GOVERNMENT (Was it colonial, territorial, state, county, federal, or foreign?)	County
NEIGHBORHOOD SETTLEMENT (Where did the people come from who settled this area in the time period of your family?)	German/Canal people
WHAT WAS HAPPENING IN THIS TIME PERIOD OF SET-TLEMENT IN THE REGION?	Building the canals
WHAT WAS THE RELIGIOUS BACKGROUND OR AFFILIA-TION OF THE SETTLERS?	German Lutheran/Reformed
WHO WERE THE PROMINENT LEADERS?	
NEW IDEAS FOR RESEARCH (Based on the information gathered above.)	Ship passenger lists, N.Y. naturalization Determine if other German groups came together to the county.

Figure 5.6   The Person Within His Environment (sample)

PROBLEM OR OBJECTIVE	To find Lizzy Frey. Father's name was Henry Frey. He lived in St. Paul, Minn. Was in the Civil War. He was born in 1825 in Germany.
FACTS ABOUT THE FAMILY	Father lived in St. Paul, Minn. Name was Henry Frey. He was born in Germany in 1825. Lizzy Frey was born 13 June 1864 in St. Paul, Minn.
TRADITIONS ABOUT THE FAMILY	Germans usually had relatives as Godparents. They married in the Diocese of the wife.
SUMMARY OF SIBLING OR CHILDREN SEARCH CONDUCTED	Henry had three daughters: Maria, Theresia (b. 10 Aug 1865), and Lizzy Frey (b. 13 June 1864). One son named Charles Henry Frey. They were born in St. Paul. Baptized at the Assumption Catholic Church. (Note: He was non-Catholic)
HISTORICAL SUMMARY INCLUDING MAPS	Civil War 1861-1865. Lived in Ramsey County. Henry lived with Maria in Wisconsin in 1882. Trimbell, Pierce County. 1st Federal Census of Minn. Terr.
CUSTOMS, FOLKWAYS AND NAMING PATTERNS OF THE TIME PERIOD	Son was a junior. Heard he had a cane and walked with a limp. Lizzy had the funeral director increase the bill so the 2nd wife, Minnie Grant, wouldn't get all his money. Henry came to St. Paul in 1852 per census 1900.
NEIGHBORS AND GROUP CONNECTIONS STUDIED	Valentine Hagg and wife were Maria's Godparents. Were they related? Found their Declaration of Intent Feb 1853-1854.
MIGRATION TRAILS	Henry fought with Colonel Munch of the Munch Bunch in the Minn.1st Light Artillery. Lizzy moved in 1900 to Beadle County, S.D.
COMMON ENTERPRISES EXAMINED	Artificer-Blacksmith
WHERE MORE INFOR-MATION CAN BE OBTAINED	Civil War pension would give me Henry Frey's address, his birth date, town where he lived in Germany, and maybe children's names. Marriage record might give parents, witnesses, and address.

Figure 5.7   What is Known About the Environment (sample)

AREA AND TIME PERIOD SETTLED (List the earliest dates known for this individual and his family in this area.)	Minn. Statehood 1868 1852 for Henry
SPECIFIC RULING GOVERNMENT (Was it colonial, territorial, state, county, federal, or foreign?)	Minn. was part of the Wisc. Terr.
NEIGHBORHOOD SETTLEMENT (Where did the people come from who settled this area in the time period of your family?)	They came from Europe, mainly from Germany and Scandinavia.
WHAT WAS HAPPENING IN THIS TIME PERIOD OF SET-TLEMENT IN THE REGION?	When Lizzy went to S.D., there was land available to homestead. Railroad went there. Gold was in the hills.
WHAT WAS THE RELIGIOUS BACKGROUND OR AFFILIA-TION OF THE SETTLERS?	Lizzy was Catholic. Henry was non-Catholic. Theresa Frey was Catholic.
WHO WERE THE PROMINENT LEADERS?	Minn. Came from the Dakota Indian word "Minisota."
NEW IDEAS FOR RESEARCH (Based on the information gathered above.)	Look at Valentine Hagg in Declaration of Intent to see where they were from. Check divorce records for Ramsey Co. as in 1900 Henry and Theresa were living in separate place in St. Paul. Probably divorced in 1873. Check the 1910 census for Huron, Beadle Co., S.D. Homestead records.

Figure 5.8   The Person Within His Environment (sample)

PROBLEM OR OBJECTIVE	Marriage for Lewis Bowles and Elizabeth Rush (abt. 1840, Illinois)
FACTS ABOUT THE FAMILY	(See below)
TRADITIONS ABOUT THE FAMILY	
SUMMARY OF SIBLING OR CHILDREN SEARCH CONDUCTED	Lewis b. 1810, N.C.. Eliz. Rush b. 1820, Tenn.. 1st child b. in Ill. (1880 census). Bought land in Montgomery C., Ill, 1849. Possible brother, John Bowles, bought land in Mont. Co. at same time next to Lewis. 2 children b. in Madison Co. (Mary: Mad. Co. Hist.; Benjamin: obituary). 6 children total.
HISTORICAL SUMMARY INCLUDING MAPS	Checked neighboring counties- Macoupin, Montgomery (formed 1821), Madison (f. 1812), Bond, Shelby, Fayette for marr. (Indexes)- not there- Checked Marr. Rec. For Montgomery and Madison Counties.
CUSTOMS, FOLKWAYS AND NAMING PATTERNS OF THE TIME PERIOD	
NEIGHBORS AND GROUP CONNECTIONS STUDIED	Poss. Brother, John, living nearby in Mont. Co., Ill.- He first purchased land in 1840
MIGRATION TRAILS	National road
COMMON ENTERPRISES EXAMINED	Farmers- small Baptist group
WHERE MORE INFORMATION CAN BE OBTAINED	Church Records. Family Tree Maker Marriage CDs. 1840 Federal census for Lewis. State Censuses. Military records.

Figure 5.9   What Is Known About the Environment (sample)

AREA AND TIME PERIOD SETTLED (List the earliest dates known for this individual and his family in this area.)	Lewis- 1849 (land) Montgomery Co.
SPECIFIC RULING GOVERNMENT (Was it colonial, territorial, state, county, federal, or foreign?)	County- Most county services state (1818)
NEIGHBORHOOD SETTLEMENT (Where did the people come from who settled this area in the time period of your family?)	Ky., Tenn., N.C., Va., Germany, Md., Pa.
WHAT WAS HAPPENING IN THIS TIME PERIOD OF SETTLEMENT IN THE REGION?	National road being built in Ill. about this time (it reached Vandalia in 1838).
WHAT WAS THE RELIGIOUS BACKGROUND OR AFFILIATION OF THE SETTLERS?	Lewis and Eliz. affiliated with neighboring primitive Baptist Church in Iowa (Wayne Co.)
WHO WERE THE PROMINENT LEADERS?	
NEW IDEAS FOR RESEARCH (Based on the information gathered above.)	Look for father, John Rush, in 1830 Ill. census (also check 1835, 1840 state censuses) Check for any church records in Montgomery/Madison Co.

Figure 5.10   The Person Within His Environment (sample)

PROBLEM OR OBJECTIVE	To more fully document the Dann family in N.Y. and find more info. on Anna and Durham Dann
FACTS ABOUT THE FAMILY	Mariah Dann known to have m. John H. Cooper. Lived and died (Nov 1875) in Spencer, N.Y. Born Albany Co. (N.Y. State census) Rev. War Pension Abijah Danno indicates Mariah.
TRADITIONS ABOUT THE FAMILY	Family said to be shocked that Abijah married a woman much his jr. Abijah and Anna said to have met when he visited her sister who is a Rockwell.
SUMMARY OF SIBLING OR CHILDREN SEARCH CONDUCTED	
HISTORICAL SUMMARY INCLUDING MAPS	
CUSTOMS, FOLKWAYS AND NAMING PATTERNS OF THE TIME PERIOD	
NEIGHBORS AND GROUP CONNECTIONS STUDIED	Some of Abijah's neighbors knew him from Westchester, Green Co., N.Y.- Rockwell living there- m. Rec.
MIGRATION TRAILS	Hudson Ct. to Westchester- much background R- traffic
COMMON ENTERPRISES EXAMINED	
WHERE MORE INFOR- MATION CAN BE OBTAINED	Abijah? Sm. Farmer Francis? Cooper miller Locate Abijah Danno and Durham Dann on 1855 N.Y. State Census.

Figure 5.11   What Is Known About the Environment (sample)

AREA AND TIME PERIOD SETTLED (List the earliest dates known for this individual and his family in this area.)	Dann Westchester 1749 Dunham Green ca 1800 Cooper Renss 1768 Dann Renss?
SPECIFIC RULING GOVERNMENT (Was it colonial, territorial, state, county, federal, or foreign?)	Pre-1775 colonial then N.Y.
NEIGHBORHOOD SETTLEMENT (Where did the people come from who settled this area in the time period of your family?)	
WHAT WAS HAPPENING IN THIS TIME PERIOD OF SET-TLEMENT IN THE REGION?	Need Co. Hist.
WHAT WAS THE RELIGIOUS BACKGROUND OR AFFILIA-TION OF THE SETTLERS?	Cooper Reformed, Presb. Dann - Longr.
WHO WERE THE PROMINENT LEADERS?	
NEW IDEAS FOR RESEARCH (Based on the information gathered above.)	Need to study N.Y. state histories, Green County, N.Y. histories, locate land records on the family, search probate records.

Figure 5.12 The Person Within His Environment (sample)

PROBLEM OR OBJECTIVE	Identify four generation of Inez Wilson's ancestry in the midwest prior to 1875
FACTS ABOUT THE FAMILY	Inez Wilson, b. 1867, Fayette Co., Ill., Parents: Emery W. Wilson, Emily Jennette Morey, m. 1887, Fayette Co., Ill, d. 1895 in Union Co., Ill. - (Additional on back side.)
TRADITIONS ABOUT THE FAMILY	Morey family was from Ohio, previously from Vermont. Lockwood family was from N.Y., previously Vermont. Parents of Adelia Nancy Lockwood were Reuben and Catherine Lockwood Morey.
SUMMARY OF SIBLING OR CHILDREN SEARCH CONDUCTED	Located all children of Emery Wilson, of the children on Henry A, Morey with an additional child living with the family in 1850 whose relationship has not yet been determined, identified three children of Phelbe Lockwood and possible fourth.
HISTORICAL SUMMARY INCLUDING MAPS	Lockwood family moved from Vermont to N.Y. and then to Ill., moved around several counties of Ill.
CUSTOMS, FOLKWAYS AND NAMING PATTERNS OF THE TIME PERIOD	Mostly farmers in this area, very fertile soil, no known naming patterns.
NEIGHBORS AND GROUP CONNECTIONS STUDIED	Methodist Church of Vermont, connection of Elisha Lockwood to Q. P. Alexander, administrator of his will (he was owed money)
MIGRATION TRAILS	National Road (1818-1850) possibly used by Moreys and Lockwoods, Erie Canal (opened 1825) and Ohio and Erie Canal possibly used by Lockwoods
COMMON ENTERPRISES EXAMINED	Farmers, railroad agents
WHERE MORE INFORMATION CAN BE OBTAINED	Methodist Church records for Vermont, Marion, Illinois; Railroad Retirement Board in Washington, D.C.; Warren County, N.Y. land records; Fayette Co., Ill. Cemetery records.

Figure 5.13   What Is Known About the Environment (sample)

AREA AND TIME PERIOD SETTLED (List the earliest dates known for this individual and his family in this area.)	Elisha Lockwood came to Fayette Co., Ill between 1830-1839
SPECIFIC RULING GOVERNMENT (Was it colonial, territorial, state, county, federal, or foreign?)	Wilson family- county records, state gov't certs Morey family- county records, state records Lockwood- town records, county records
NEIGHBORHOOD SETTLEMENT (Where did the people come from who settled this area in the time period of your family?)	N.Y. and New England
WHAT WAS HAPPENING IN THIS TIME PERIOD OF SETTLEMENT IN THE REGION?	Westward expansion, previous settlement in Ill. Has been along waterways of the southern part of the state, the canals and National Road brought settlers to middle of state.
WHAT WAS THE RELIGIOUS BACKGROUND OR AFFILIATION OF THE SETTLERS?	Unknown at this time, later generations were Methodists
WHO WERE THE PROMINENT LEADERS?	John Reynolds, Governor, Ill, 1831-34; Joseph Duncan, Gov., Ill. 1834-38; Frederick Klinge, Kaskaskia Twp. Sup., 1860, 1863-67; James M. Brown. Kaskaskia Twp. Sup., 1861-62
NEW IDEAS FOR RESEARCH (Based on the information gathered above.)	More research needed in the Fayette Co., Ill. records for the Lockwood surname. County records of Wayne Co., N.Y. and Windsor Co., Vermont need to be searched.

Assignment 1: Knowledge of Sources

1. Select two types of sources you frequently examine (e.g., censuses, deeds, vital statistics, or special collections of primary source material).

2. Discuss the genealogical functions of each source you listed. You should include the kinds of information revealed and the accuracy and deficiencies of those sources.

3. Give examples of the advantages and disadvantages of using each type of record.

Assignment 2: Abstracts and Transcripts

Prepare abstracts and transcripts of two primary source documents of your choosing. If you ask someone to review your work, include copies of the original documents.

Assignment 3: Analysis of Primary Sources

For each of the documents on the following pages, prepare the following:

1. A transcript.

2. An abstract containing all relevant details.

3. A brief commentary about the genealogical value of the document that points out items of major significance.

4. A brief research plan outlining the first steps (and the order in which you would take them for continuing the investigation). The plan must be based on clues found in the document, as well as pertinent research methodology. Please do not attempt to project and discuss all variables that might be found in future investigations.

Document 1

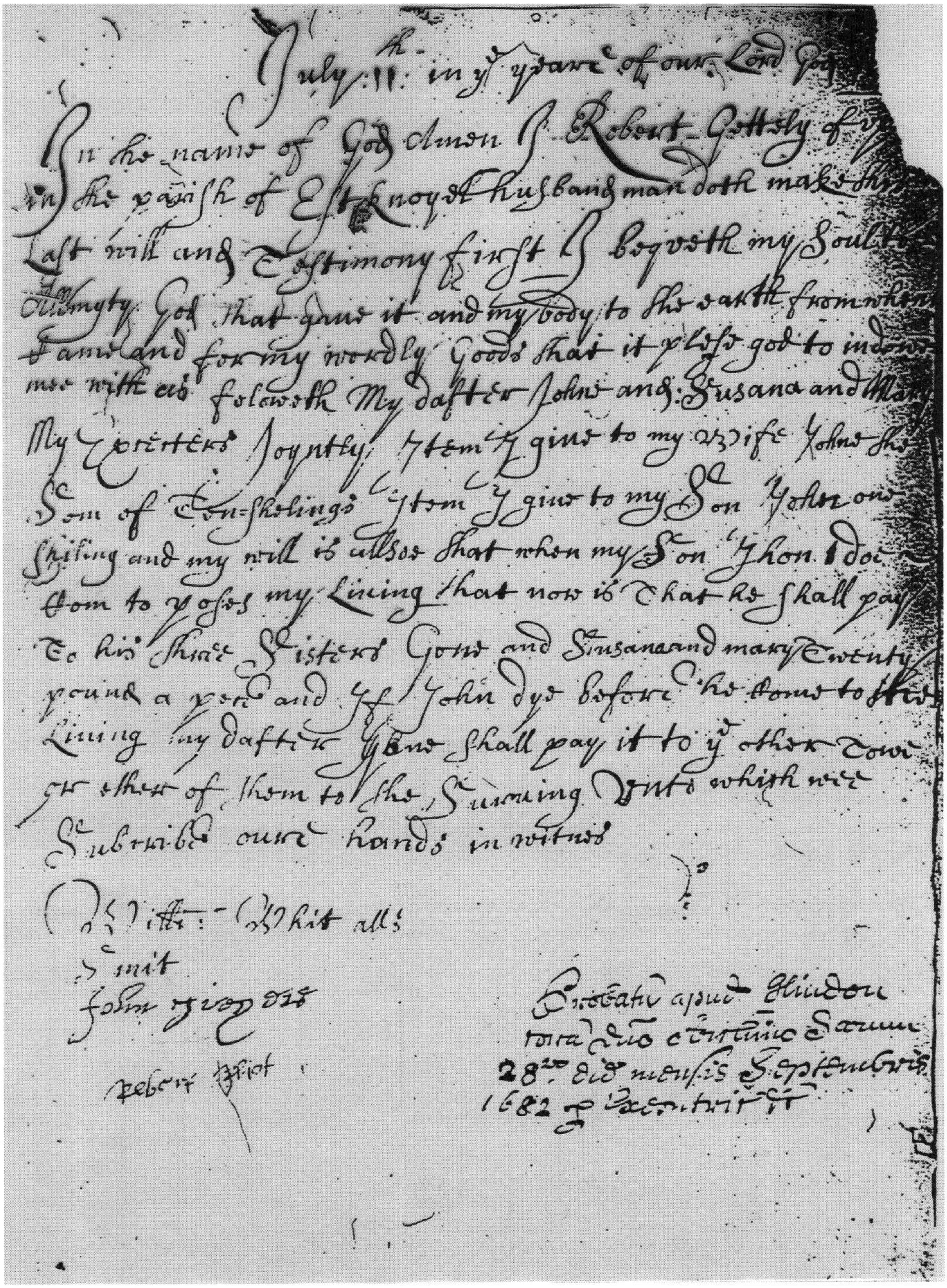

Document 2

The State of Indiana,
Clark County ⟩ Sct.—
Clark Circuit Court November term 1844.
On this sixteenth day of November One thou=
=sand eight hundred and forty four, person=
=ally appeared in open Court William G. Arm=
=strong who being duly sworn doth on his oath
state that the record above attached to this sheet
is in the hand writing of his Father John Arm=
=strong on the first page thereof and to the word
afternoon in the twelfth line of the second page in-
clusive, except the letter G. in the name of Eliza
Armstrong on the first line of the second page which
was inserted by the deponent. That so much of said
record as refers to the marriage of Ann Armstrong
to Joseph Morten and of Catharine Armstrong to
Henry Morten is in the hand writing of Mrs Ann
Morten. And the four last lines of said record
are in the hand writing of this deponent. And
that said family record has been in his possession
more than twenty years

                            Wm G. Armstrong

          Sworn to in open Court. In Testimony whereof
               I. Eli McCalley, Clerk of the
Circuit Court for Clark County in the Second
Judicial circuit of the State of Indiana have
      hereunto subscribed my name and
      affixed the seal of our said court
          at the Courthouse in Charlestown
          this 16th day of November A.D. 1844
          Test.
               Eli McCalley Clerk

Document 3a

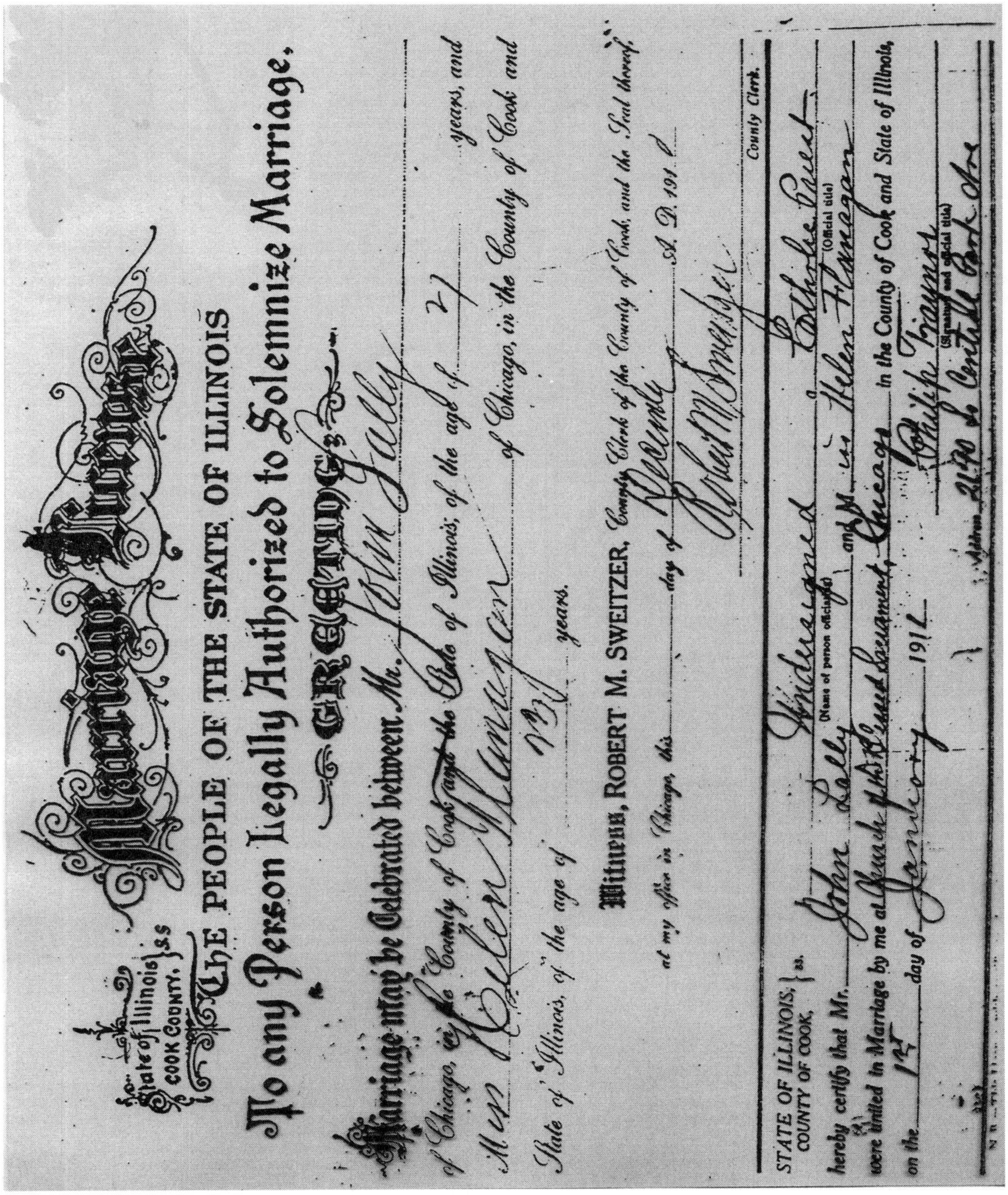

Marriage License

State of Illinois, COOK COUNTY, } S.S.

THE PEOPLE OF THE STATE OF ILLINOIS

To any Person Legally Authorized to Solemnize Marriage,

GREETING:

Marriage may be Celebrated between Mr. John Lally of Chicago, in the County of Cook and the State of Illinois, of the age of 27 years, and Miss Ellen Flanagan of Chicago, in the County of Cook and State of Illinois, of the age of 23 years.

Witness, ROBERT M. SWEITZER, County Clerk of the County of Cook, and the Seal thereof, at my office in Chicago, this ___ day of December A. D. 191_

Robert M. Sweitzer

County Clerk.

STATE OF ILLINOIS, COUNTY OF COOK, } ss. I, Undersigned, Catholic Priest (Official title) hereby certify that Mr. John Lally (Name of person officiating) and Miss Helen Flanagan were united in Marriage by me at Church of the Blessed Sacrament, Chicago in the County of Cook and State of Illinois, on the 1st day of January 1916.

Philip Traynor (Signature and official title)

Address 2140 So Central Park Ave

Document 3b

Registrum Matrimoniorum

Annus 1911

No.	Datum Matrim.	NOMINA ET RESIDENTIAE	SPONSI — DATUM ET LOCUS BAPTISMI	PATRES NOMINA
20	Jan 1st	John Lally	Bapt Turmakeady Mayo Co., Ireland June 22d 1883	Thomas Lally
		Helen Flanagan	Bapt Turmakeady, Mayo Co., Ireland January 1st 1886	Patrick Flanagan
	Jan 4th	John McGrath	Bapt Carrigaholt, Clare Co., Ireland January 30th 1881	Michael McGrath
		Anna Roach	Bapt Carrigaholt, Clare Co., Ireland December 31st 1880	Michael Roach
	Jan 18th	Patrick T Gunning	Bapt St Johns Cathedral Limerick City, Ireland March 7th 1883	Thomas Gunning
		Bridget Divine	Bapt Ballygeary Drommod Co., Limerick Co., Ireland April 23d 1887	Michael Divine

Document 3c

In Ecclesia Blessed Sacrament.

20

SPONSORUM DOMICILIA	TESTES	NOMEN SACERDOTIS	ADNOTATIONES DISPENSATIONES, OBTENTAE LOCUS MATRIMONII, ETC.	NOTITIA MATRIM.	
				Inscripsi Ipse	Misei Notitiam
	Matthew Foely	DELEGATUS Philip Traynor Remitto Se Habere Teator			do
	Mary Doherty	Parochus			
	Frank Covey	DELEGATUS Philip Traynor Rem Ita Se Habere Teator			do
	Nellie Covey	Parochus			
	John J. Hare	DELEGATUS Philip Traynor Rem Ita Se Habere Teator			do
	Elizabeth Devine	Parochus			

Assignment 4: Analysis of Secondary Sources

Choose two books, chapters, articles, finding aids or other examples of secondary material that relate to the region you seek. Briefly discuss their merits and shortcoming (150-300 words for each discussion). Attach selected photocopies to illustrate the points you make in each discussion, but do not submit whole books or lengthy articles.

Assignment 5: Source Citations

1. Source citations should use standard formats. Citation formats for published material can be taken from *The Chicago Manual of Style*. 14th ed. (Chicago: University of Chicago Press, 1993), from Kate L. Turabian, *A Manual for Writers of Term Papers, Theses, and Dissertations*., 5th ed. (Chicago: University of Chicago Press, 1987), from Elizabeth Shown Mills, *Evidence! Citation and Analysis for the Family Historian* (Boston: Genealogical Publishing Co., 1997) or any other citation standard. Prepare ten source citations using an acceptable standard format such as those cited in this chapter and as suggested reading at the end of Chapter 2.

2. Indicate which citation method you used and why you found that one best.

Suggested Reading

Anderson, Robert Charles. "Proving Your Case: Evidentiary Rules for the Genealogist." *A Place to Explore; National Genealogical Society and San Diego Genealogical Society,* 3-6 May 1995; San Diego, California, 12-13. (May be ordered from Repeat Performance, 2911 Crabapple Lane, Hobart, IN 46342, session W-5.)

Hatcher, Patricia Law. "Techniques to Help Good Genealogists Become Even Better." *Traveling Historic Trails; National Genealogical Society and Middle Tennessee Genealogical Society,* 8-11 May 1996; Nashville, Tenn., F-113. (May be ordered from Repeat Performance, 2911 Crabapple Lane, Hobart, IN 46342, session F-113.)

Hatcher, Patricia Law. *Producing a Quality Family History.* Salt Lake City, Utah: Ancestry, 1996.

Mills, Elizabeth Shown. "The Identity Crisis: Right Name, Wrong Person? Wrong Name, Right Person?" *On to Richmond: Four Centuries of Family History; Federation of Genealogical Societies and Virginia Genealogical Society,* 12-15 October 1994; Richmond, Va., 410-411. (May be ordered from Repeat Performance, 2911 Crabapple Lane, Hobart, IN 46342, session S-144.)

Mills, Elizabeth Shown. "Genealogical Principles and Standards." *National Genealogical Society Quarterly* 87, no. 3 (1999): 165-184.

Mills, Elizabeth Shown. "Documentation: Don't Feed Your Family Garbage When They Hunger to Know Themselves!" *Traveling Historic Trails; National Genealogical Society and Middle Tennessee Genealogical Society,* 8-11 May 1996; Nashville, Tenn., T-49. (May be ordered from Repeat Performance, 2911 Crabapple Lane, Hobart, IN 46342, session T-49.)

Mills, Elizabeth Shown. "The Research Report." *Traveling Historic Trails; National Genealogical Society and Middle Tennessee Genealogical Society,* 8-11 May 1996; Nashville, Tenn., F-102. (May be ordered from Repeat Performance, 2911 Crabapple Lane, Hobart, IN 46342, session F-102.)

Practical Exercises in Analysis

Critical Analysis

Learning to look critically at a problem before engaging in research can prevent hours of wasted effort.

Forms, such as that in figure 6.1a, can remind the researcher of items to be examined *before* the research begins. For example, critically examine the pedigree below and see if you can see some problems:

James BROWN

b. 4 Dec 1778
bp. Buffalo, NY
m.
mp. Senecaville, OH
d. 1860
dp. Guernsey, OH

Susan BROWN

b. 31 May 1830
bp.   CA
m.
mp.
d.
dp.

Sally BROWN

b. 30 May 1818
bp. Noble, OH
d. 4 Mar 1865
dp. Hamilton Co., OH

Did you notice that James and Sally Brown were married and died in Ohio but their daughter was born in California one year after their marriage? Possible? Yes. Probable? No. It should be put down as a problem to investigate. Did you notice that Sally was forty years younger than James and twelve years old at the birth of her child, Susan? Possible? Yes. Probable? No. In fact, since the names Sally and Susan were used interchangeably, perhaps there has been a mixup of these two individuals. Maybe Susan was actually born in 1818 and the real wife of James was someone else. Is there a town called Senecaville in Ohio? How far away is Hamilton County from Senecaville? How far away is Guernsey County from Noble County?

As you can see, being analytical and critical can bring up many questions. By asking these questions ahead of time, you can save yourself many hours of unnecessary research. By the way, Susan was actually born in 1850 in the town of California, outside of Cincinnati, Hamilton County, Ohio. The client could not read the old handwriting in the Bible record so had misinterpreted 1830 for 1850. James Brown was born in 1818 but once again the client couldn't read the handwriting. The example on the next page shows you how to use the form to speed up the analysis process:

In this chapter, candidates for the accreditation exam are given opportunities to use substitute vital records, find pedigree problems, and apply pedigree analysis. This chapter also provides exercises requiring knowledge and use of local repositories. In order for candidates to be competent in the genealogical profession, they must be able to utilize the resources at their disposal. These exercises are intended to help researchers become more knowledgeable about their local resources.

Several documents are included to enable you to practice document recognition. After completing these exercises you should be able to judge for yourself whether you have had enough experience in genealogical research to recognize basic genealogical documents when you see them and to apply the information gleaned from those documents to the solving of genealogical problems.

Individual documents alone will not solve all family history enigmas. As mentioned previously, various isolated aspects of our ancestors' lives may provide us with clues that, when put together, provide the evidence to support our hypothesis. One such aspect is that of folkways or customs of the time in which the ancestor lived. I believe that we are often mirrors of our past, in that we desire security, love, and a better world for our offspring, and so did our ancestors. Success in family history is achieved when these common human values connect us to the ancestors who have prepared the way for us today. Unless we are able to place the actions of our

Critical Analysis Example

Item Investigated	Problems & Possible Solutions
Name of individuals	Since the name Sally and Susan are used interchangeably, perhaps there has been a mixup of these two individuals. Is Brown Sally's maiden name? Need to ask client sources of information.
Date of birth of individuals	Sally is forty years younger than James and twelve years old at the birth of her child, Susan. Maybe Susan was actually born in 1818 and the real wife of James was someone else.
Place of birth of individuals	James and Sally Brown were married and died in Ohio but their daughter was born in California one year after their marriage. How far away is Guernsey County from Noble County?
Date of marriage of individuals	James and Sally Brown were married and died in Ohio.
Place of marriage of individuals	Is there a town called Senecaville in Ohio? How far away is Hamilton County from Senecaville? Look at a gazetteer or atlas.
Date of death of individuals	Could James and Sally have died in the Civil War or could Sally have moved because of effects of the Civil War on her family?
Place of death of individuals died, from Noble County,	How far away is Hamilton County where Sally died from Senecaville where she married? How far away is Guernsey County, where her husband died, from Noble County, where his wife was born? Look at a gazetteer or atlas.
Parents of individuals	Maybe Sally is not the mother of Susan at all. Ask the client for the sources of the information.

ancestors within the context of the society in which they lived, we may miss these connections. Or even worse, if we try to apply the standards of the twentieth century to families of the seventeenth century, we will be misled. On the other hand, if we interpret their actions within the societal, economic, and political framework in which they lived, we will be led to sources to solve our research problems.

Substitutes

Often when gathering information for the accreditation examination or for a client report, an original vital record or a single document cannot be located to prove relationship to a parent. In their anxiety over not being able to prove a birth, marriage, or death date, or to find one document to link a child with his/her parents, candidates for accreditation may panic and assume they cannot submit the pedigree they were working on for part of their accreditation project. Here are examples of some sources (and I'm sure you can think of others) which could be used to help build the evidence necessary to prove a birth, marriage, death, or relationship:

1. Sources for Birth Dates

    a. Use "circa" dates from the federal census to approximate birth dates. If completing lineage papers (although this is only a small percentage of total professional research done), make certain that the individual society will accept an estimated birth year.

    b. Use the year an ancestor paid personal or poll taxes for the first time as evidence that he was of legal age. If you can document that the ancestor lived in the county in prior years, then his sudden emergence on the tax rolls may indicate that he had just come of age. However, it is also possible that in prior years he was not taxed because he belonged to an exempt group or had not yet moved in. (In various areas exempt groups could include certain office holders or certain strategic occupations such as medical doctors and militia officers.)

    c. Check deeds, because the law required a seller to be at least twenty-one years old. (However, he could have owned land at an earlier age, and there are, of course, numerous exceptions.)

    d. Check for voter registration.

    e. Check for membership in fraternal organizations (e.g., Masons or Oddfellows).

    f. Check tombstone dates.

    g. Check christening dates.

    h. Check adult baptism records.

    i. Check marriage application records for birth date and place.

    j. Check for age on a death certificate.

    k. Check for age on a passenger list.

    l. Check for birth date and place in a military pension or enlistment paper.

2. Sources for Marriage Dates

    a. Take the birth year of the oldest child and subtract one year, or estimate from a post-1850 federal census by the age of the oldest child. If this is being done for a lineage society, it depends upon the society as to whether or not they will accept this approach.

    b. Look for the wife's signing of dower if she lived in a dower state such as Virginia. This does not constitute proof of the actual date of the marriage but will suggest an estimate by saying: ". . . married prior to 10 March 1789 . . .".

   c. Check the 1900 census, if applicable, for the number of years married.

   d. Check county, town, or land grant records for indication of marriage.

   e. Check for marriage date in military pension records.

   f. Check homestead application or bounty land records for marriage information.

3. Sources for Death Dates

   a. Use the last document showing the person alive such as: (1) his signing a deed, (2) being listed in the census, or (3) paying taxes.

   b. Use probate filing date.

   c. Check for an obituary.

   d. Look for a tombstone.

   e. Look for mention of a second wife or husband in marriage records.

4. Proof of Parentage Sources

   a. Prove a relationship between your person and one of his/her siblings who has already been proven to be a child of the ancestor.

   b. Locate deeds where the heirs sell shares of a deceased parent's property.

   c. Find the will or intestate probate of a sibling who died without heirs and look for property which was divided among other siblings.

Evidence As It Pertains to Genealogy

Often proving facts in our research is quite easy. We are able to find just the perfect document attested to by a reliable witness which proves an event. Many times, however, we are forced to make an hypothesis that something is the case based on a combination of documents. How many documents this takes is not as important as the power of the evidence provided in each document.

What is an hypothesis? First let us examine the definition of the term "hypothesis" according to *Webster's, New World Dictionary, Second College Edition*: "An unproved theory, proposition, supposition, etc. tentatively accepted to explain certain facts or to provide a basis for further investigation."

Each time we obtain a document and evaluate the new evidence it provides in light of our goals, our mind runs through many scenarios. This is because each genealogy problem is unique. This uniqueness is due not only to the availability of evidence necessary to prove a fact, but also due to the environment surrounding an event. This environment consists of applicable law, social customs, historical developments, or other pertinent background information.

Evidence in genealogy comes from objects, photographs, records, documents, testimonies of witnesses, the opinions of experts, the existence of known facts, even circumstances. We have been taught to search out documents which provide primary evidence (that which was recorded by a reliable witness at, or near the time of, an event) or direct evidence (a document which states a fact directly such as "my daughter Eliza Cooper") in order to best establish an event as it actually occurred.

Sometimes, however, indirect evidence (also known as "circumstantial evidence") is also used. For example family relationships are often inferred from an individual's placement on an 1850 U.S. federal census record. If the person's name, age, and birth state are given and someone with the same name and age were found ten year's earlier in a different state, what evidence is there to prove these are the same people?

For the documentation to be sufficient it should include information about each individual which clearly identifies who he or she is and link him or her to the correct family. The least amount of information for identification is that amount needed to continue research into other generations. For example, the individual's given name, surname, and at least one parent, sex, approximate birth year and probable place, and the spouse's name and approximate marriage date, if married, is needed. Without the minimum identification of the name, the date, and the place of an event, it is not possible to continue research.

When we cannot find that one perfect document, our mind seeks for other alternatives and ways to prove a point. Sometimes the proof consists of eliminating all other possibilities. This, however, still leaves room for doubt. Your ability to articulate clearly the problem under consideration is now very important as a researcher. Can you analyze both the information that supports your conclusion as well as those which contradict it? If something comes up to contradict your conclusion, do you have an adequate answer to each item?

To help you put together evidence which is both clear and convincing, ask yourself these questions:

- Did you provide a separate source of information for each fact mentioned in your discussion?

- Is the source presented in an acceptable format?

- Did you initiate a thorough study of the historical background and customs of the localities during the specific time period being researched?

- If you try to eliminate other possibilities, did you first identify several individuals or the entire family group as potential targets rather than one person?

Sometimes secondary evidence may be of greater worth than primary evidence. For example, a researcher who carefully collects information from many sources (such as published abstracts, indexes, lists, family histories, etc.) may prove that the primary evidence was not true.

Clues to consider when you must build a case could include:

- Others in the family are found in the same area as the individual under study.

- Others who were neighbors or associates at another time period in this individual's life, appear in the same documents as the individual in another locality at a different time period.

- Dates recorded in family papers match dates recorded on government papers.

As we have seen, evidence come in a variety of ways. Two types of evidence were not yet mentioned. Collateral Evidence is sometimes found in a source that has nothing to do with that record itself and the purpose for which the record was created. A researcher may find a wife's father on a land record, for example. And Hearsay Evidence is evidence given to a witness by another source rather than his or her personal knowledge. When all we have is hearsay evidence, when can we use it? In law, it is acceptable for proof unless another piece of evidence over-rides it.

- The document is over 30 years old and comes from a natural and reasonable official custody. This is called an "Ancient Document Acception." Only the original copy of a deed or will can be an ancient document, not the recorded copy. A photocopy of an original will or Bible record is an example.

- Records made by trusted public officials such as recorded copies of land records are part of a "Public Records Exception."

- A "Certified Copy Exception" document certified by a proper authority to verify its origin and content (usually photoduplicated copies) such as a certified death certificate.

- And a "Dying Declaration Exception" which are statements made by persons when on a deathbed.

It takes time and experience to learn how to analyze evidence well. We live in a time when others have willingly shared their experience and methods with us. The suggested readings for this chapter cover some of the best articles on the subject. I highly suggest that each one be read.

Using Repositories

Familiarity with local repositories such as field branches of the National Archives, a local family history center, an historical or genealogical society library, a major genealogical library (Allen County Public Library in Ft. Wayne, Indiana, for example), county courthouses, and private manuscript repositories will make you more valuable as a professional genealogist. These repositories may hold valuable resources for many aspects of your work, such as:

1. Background material for reports or published histories

2. Summaries for the states under investigation

3. Special collections listed in *Research Outlines*, society lectures, or teacher handouts

4. Relevant maps

5. Unique resources in which the repository specializes

6. The ability to tie in with other repositories in either an electronic format such as on-line catalogs or via CD-ROM technology

Now turn to the various assignments on the following pages to practice critical analysis, pedigree analysis, repository familiarity, and document recognition. Samples of how other students have approached these projects as well as some of their results are included at the end of the assignments. Finally, assignment 3 includes further approaches to analyzing repositories which could guide you to other sources.

Assignment 1: Pedigree Problems

This assignment has several parts. Various stories are given in the next few pages. They are followed by forms to help make the assignment easier.

  a) Select two stories from your area of specialty.

  b) Using two different critical analysis forms, determine any discrepancies, errors, or omissions in the stories. Record your answers on the forms.

  c) Now look at your own pedigree chart.

  d) Using another critical analysis form, evaluate your own research and record the answers.

NOTE: Record as much information as you think is necessary, adding more paper if the space provided on the forms is inadequate.

Stories

Select any two of the following case studies. The information is given just as it was received from a client. Remember, clients may be in error. Be sure to indicate any discrepancies you notice.

Southern States Problems

1. I am trying to prove the lineage of the original James P. Appleby of St. George Parish, South Carolina. He came to South Carolina about 1785 and he sold property there in 1785 to David Rumph Jr., so he must have either been there earlier to own the property or inherited it. He was a senator for the state, a school teacher, a large planter, a justice of the peace, a Mason and a Methodist, a captain in the state militia in the War of 1812 and had a large family. He came to Colleton County "with a fine horse, a pack mule and a slave." He died in 1849 and was buried in Hagerman's Cemetery near St. George Parish. His wife Mary died in 1852 and was buried in the same place. They had eleven children, all born in that parish starting in 1792. The following deeds were located for this man from the land indexes:

    Deed Book U-6, pp. 187-8: 16 Sep 1787, James Applebrey [sic] to David Rumph Jr.

    Deed Book K-6, pp. 254-255: 7 Jan 1794, David Rumph Jr., of Colleton County, Charleston District, to James P. Applebry [sic] and wife Mary, for good will and affection.

2. A family history found at the Family History Library states that Samuel Henry Nowlin, Sr., was a son of James and Rainey Downey Nowlin and was born about 1780, presumably in Pittsylvania County, Virginia. I believe this is an error because James

was not born until 1772 and his Samuel Henry was not born until 1802 or 1803, but the rest of the information could be correct. Samuel Henry Nowlin is actually the son of Bryan Ward Nowlin and is listed in Bryan Ward Nowlin's will. Anyway, Samuel Henry Nowlin married Frances Clark of the Virginia Clarks. Her great-grandfather was John Clark of Caroline County. He had six sons, five of whom were officers in the Revolutionary War. The sons were Jonathan, John, George Rogers, Richard, Edmond, and William. Edmond had a son John who was the father of Frances who married Samuel Nowlin, according to the history. Frances Clark was born about 1785 and her father, Edmond, was born 25 September 1762. Samuel Henry and Frances had at least eight children. My direct line ancestor, Joseph Clark Nowlin, was born in 1809 in Virginia but he probably died in Tennessee or Illinois when the family moved on. I'd like to know more about the George Rogers Clark connection.

Eastern States Problems

3. I am trying to find the father of Wait Smith, who died in 1753 in Goshen, Orange County, New York. His wife was named Charity, and he had as children Wait, Samuel, Oliver, James, William, Joshua, Solomon, a daughter Elizabeth, and one named Charity Thomson.

4. James Humphreys was born 26 May 1792 in Cumberland, New Jersey. He married Sarah 29 Mar 1814 in Bridgeton, Cumberland, New Jersey, and he died 9 Feb 1879 in Washington Twp, Warren County, Ohio. His father, Lewis Humphreys, was born in 1750 and lived in either New Hampshire or Maryland. He married in 1782, and died 4 Mar 1805 in Greenwich, Cumberland County, New Jersey. The mother of James was Elizabeth, who was born about 1751. I would like to find Elizabeth's maiden name.

Midwestern States Problems

5. My ancestor Samuel Melton was born about 1829 in Harrison County, Indiana and died in 1915 in Red Oak, Iowa. He married Elizabeth Grass (b. 1820 Indiana d. 1894). His son Wilford Melton was born Jan 1861 in Galesburg, Illinois and died in 1952 in Clarkston, Washington. I would like to know more about my Melton ancestry.

6. Emily P. Stokes was born 8 Jun 1806 in Cadiz, Ohio and died 29 Dec 1878 in Mansfield, Ohio. She married William Booth Bradley 3 Dec 1844 in Ohio; he was born in 1795 and died in 1874. I would like to continue the Stokes/Stoakes family research. I believe Emily's father is Thomas Stoakes, who died in 1814 in Cadiz, Harrison County, Ohio, and her mother is Ann, who died in 1827 in Dover, Ohio.

New England States Problems

7. Israel Selden Spencer was born 1 Aug 1762 and lived in Hadlyme, Connecticut. He

married about 1785 and died 5 Mar 1837 at Port Gibson, Mississippi. I would like to know more about the Spencer and Marsh families. Israel's father Israel was born 30 Jan 1731/32 in East Haddam, Massachusetts and died 18 Nov 1813 in the same place. He married about 1760 Elizabeth Marsh, who was born 30 Apr 1729 in Braintree, Massachusetts and died 8 Jul 1801 in Hadlyme, Connecticut.

8. Captain Job Allen was born 27 Aug 1750 in Suffield, Hartford County, Connecticut. He died 16 Mar 1798 in Rockaway, Morris County, New Jersey. His father was also named Job and he was born 20 Nov 1709 in Suffield, Hartford County, Massachusetts. He died 5 Nov 1767 in Rockaway, New Jersey. His wife lived after him. She was Christiana Ward. I would like to know more about Christiana and when she and Job Allen married.

Figure 6.1a   Critical Analysis Form
(Do you see any discrepancies in the pedigree problems provided to you?)

Critical Analysis

GENEALOGY
RESEARCH
ASSOCIATES

Name of Individual _____

Item investigated	Problem
Name	
Date of birth	
Place of birth	
Date of marriage	
Place of marriage	
Date of death	
Place of death	
Parents	

©1997 Genealogy Research Associates, Inc. 2600 Garden Road, Suite 224, Monterey, CA 93940   Tel: 408-373-5206   Fax: 408-373-5208   8/97

Figure 6.1b   Critical Analysis Form

(Do you see any discrepancies in the pedigree problems provided to you?)

Critical Analysis

GENEALOGY RESEARCH ASSOCIATES

Name of Individual _____

Item investigated	Problem
Name	
Date of birth	
Place of birth	
Date of marriage	
Place of marriage	
Date of death	
Place of death	
Parents	

Figure 6.1c   Critical Analysis Form
   (Do you see any discrepancies in the pedigree problems provided to you?)

Critical Analysis

GENEALOGY RESEARCH ASSOCIATES

Name of Individual _____

Item investigated	Problem
Name	
Date of birth	
Place of birth	
Date of marriage	
Place of marriage	
Date of death	
Place of death	
Parents	

Assignment 2: Pedigree Analysis

This assignment also has several parts to it.

1) Use the Pedigree Analysis Forms (Figures 6.2a-c) to outline three case studies. Select two from the stories on the previous pages and one from your own information.

2) Fill in the sources you would search in the appropriate columns.

3) Explain what you hope to obtain by searching that particular source.

4) Place a numbered priority beside the sources (#1 highest priority, #2 second priority, etc.) to indicate the order in which these sources would be searched.

5) Indicate why you would search in this particular order (include proximity, availability, cost to search, etc.).

Figure 6.2a   Pedigree Analysis, Exercise A

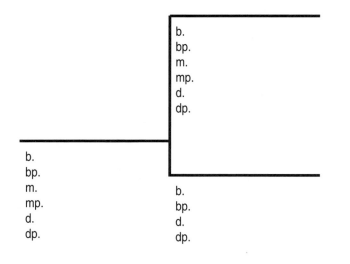

b.
bp.
m.
mp.
d.
dp.

b.
bp.
m.
mp.
d.
dp.

b.
bp.
d.
dp.

Sources to be searched	What you hope to obtain	Priority	Why this step is important

Figure 6.2b   Pedigree Analysis, Exercise B

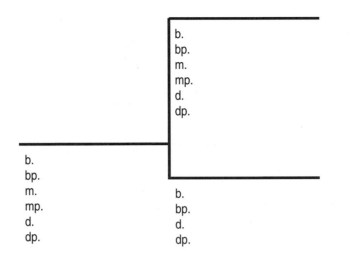

Sources to be searched	What you hope to obtain	Priority	Why this step is important

Figure 6.2c   Pedigree Analysis, Exercise C

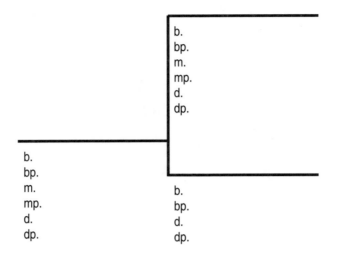

b.
bp.
m.
mp.
d.
dp.

b.
bp.
m.
mp.
d.
dp.

b.
bp.
d.
dp.

Sources to be searched	What you hope to obtain	Priority	Why this step is important

Assignment 3: Using Repositories

Produce three reports describing the genealogical resources of three major repositories in your area which you use on a regular basis. You may use the forms on the following pages. These provide a record of the complete name and address of the repository (for the user's future use), the hours and admittance requirements (in case he or she would like to visit again), a description of their basic collection (such as all federal census indexes, statewide indexes, a strong collection on the New England states if you are a New England researcher, etc.), a listing of any special collections of use to genealogists (in case something is available there that is not available elsewhere), and the costs to use the facilities (loan fees, special services such as interlibrary loan, photocopying, etc.).

Figure 6.3a

GENEALOGY RESEARCH ASSOCIATES

Record Repository Survey

Name of repository ____________________

Address ____________________

Hours ____________________ Cost to use ____________________

Admittance requirements ____________________

Basic Collection

Call number	Item	Comments

Special Collection

Call number	Item	Comments

Figure 6.3b

Record Repository Survey

GENEALOGY
RESEARCH
ASSOCIATES

Name of repository _____

Address _____

Hours _____   Cost to use _____

Admittance requirements _____

Basic Collection

Call number	Item	Comments

Special Collection

Call number	Item	Comments

Figure 6.3c

Record Repository Survey

GENEALOGY
RESEARCH
ASSOCIATES

Name of repository _____

Address _____

Hours _____ Cost to use _____

Admittance requirements _____

Basic Collection

Call number	Item	Comments

Special Collection

Call number	Item	Comments

8/97

Assignment 4: Document Recognition

Identify the documents in figures 6.5 to 6.24 by writing a description of the document on the bottom of the page. For example, document 1 is a township map from Alabama.

Figure 6.4   Document Recognition 1

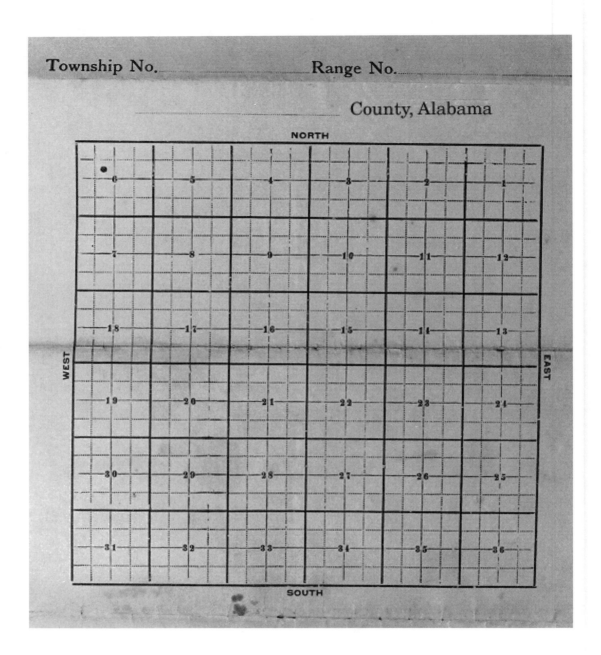

Figure 6.5   Document Recognition 2

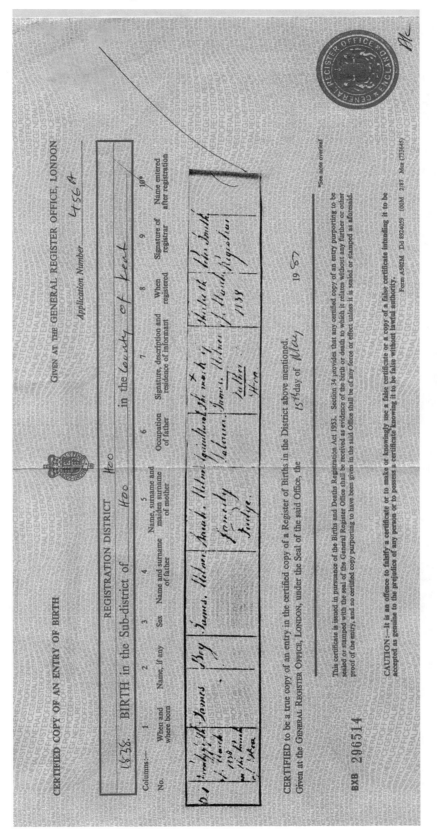

Figure 6.6 Document Recognition 3

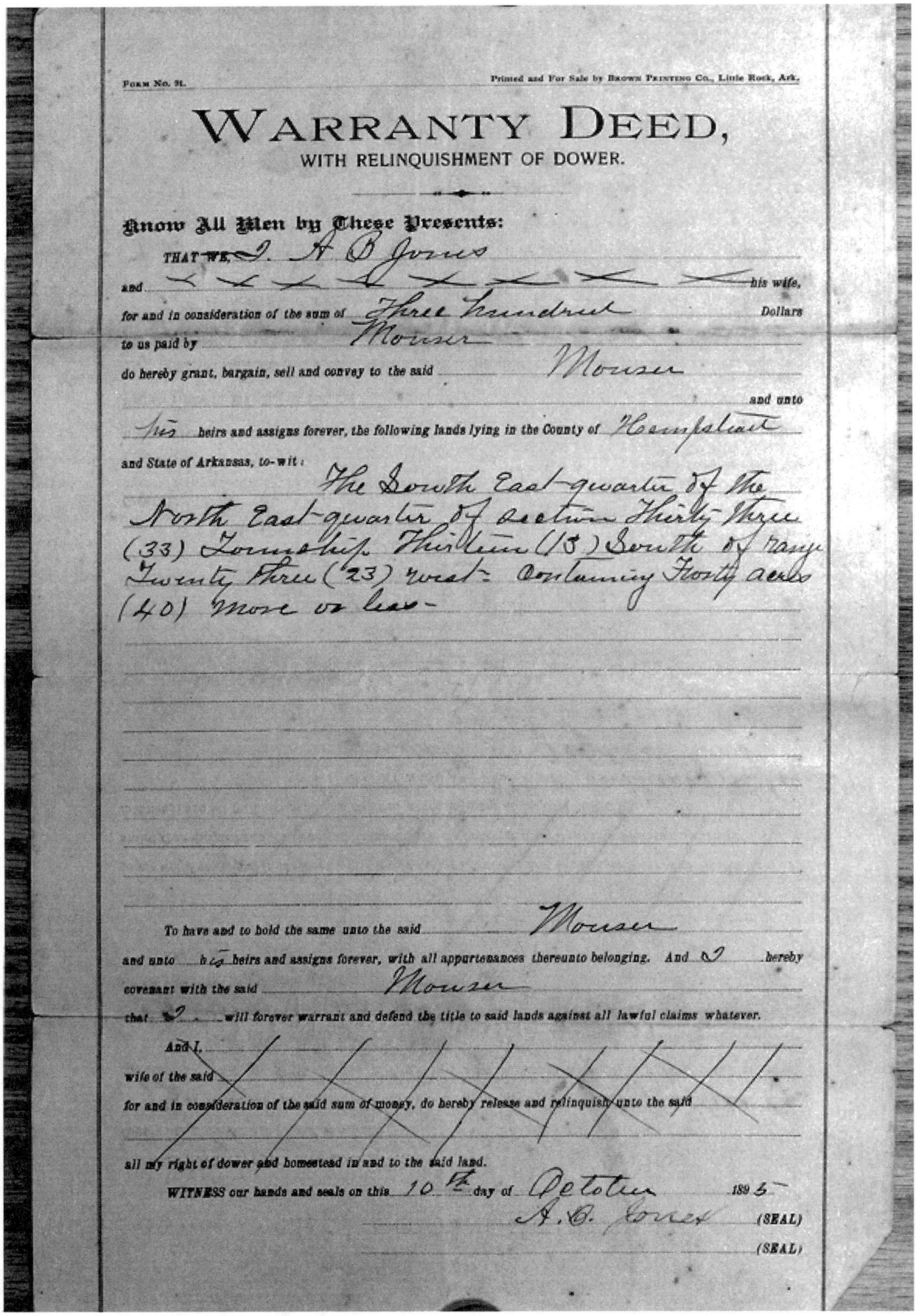

FORM No. 91. Printed and For Sale by BROWN PRINTING CO., Little Rock, Ark.

WARRANTY DEED,
WITH RELINQUISHMENT OF DOWER.

Know All Men by These Presents:

THAT ~~WE~~, I. A. B. Jones
and ~~× × × × × × × ×~~ his wife,
for and in consideration of the sum of Three hundred Dollars
to us paid by Mouser
do hereby grant, bargain, sell and convey to the said Mouser
and unto his heirs and assigns forever, the following lands lying in the County of Hempstead
and State of Arkansas, to-wit: The South East quarter of the North East quarter of Section Thirty Three (33) Township Thirteen (13) South of range Twenty Three (23) west. Containing Forty acres (40) more or less.

To have and to hold the same unto the said Mouser
and unto his heirs and assigns forever, with all appurtenances thereunto belonging. And I hereby covenant with the said Mouser
that I will forever warrant and defend the title to said lands against all lawful claims whatever.

~~And I, wife of the said for and in consideration of the said sum of money, do hereby release and relinquish unto the said~~
all my right of dower and homestead in and to the said land.

WITNESS our hands and seals on this 10th day of October 1895
A. B. Jones (SEAL)
(SEAL)

Figure 6.7   Document Recognition 4

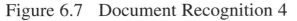

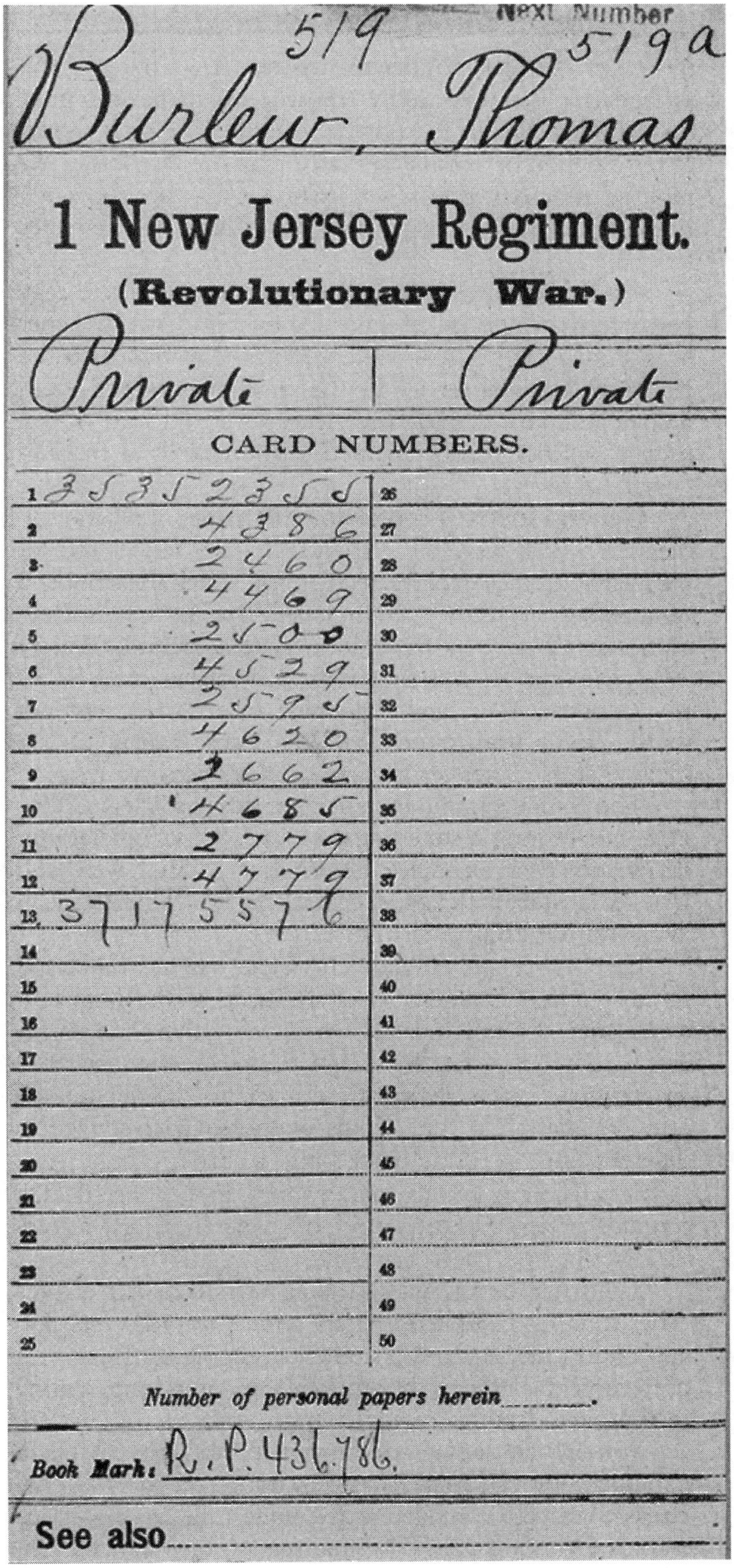

	CARD NUMBERS.	
1	3535 235 5	26
2	4 3 8 6	27
3	2 4 6 0	28
4	4 4 6 9	29
5	2 5 0 0	30
6	4 5 2 9	31
7	2 5 9 5	32
8	4 6 2 0	33
9	2 6 6 2	34
10	4 6 8 5	35
11	2 7 7 9	36
12	4 7 7 9	37
13	3717 5 5 7 6	38
14		39
15		40
16		41
17		42
18		43
19		44
20		45
21		46
22		47
23		48
24		49
25		50

Card header text: 519   Next Number   519 a

Burleur, Thomas

1 New Jersey Regiment.
(Revolutionary War.)

Private | Private

Number of personal papers herein _____.

Book Mark: R. P. 436786.

See also _____

Figure 6.8 Document Recognition 5

DECLARATION FOR WIDOW'S PENSION

ACT OF APRIL 19, 1908—AMENDED BY ACT OF SEPTEMBER 8, 1916, AND ACT OF MAY 1, 1920

State of Minnesota, County of Otter Tail, ss:

On this 3^d day of June, 1922, personally appeared before me, a Notary Public within and for the County and State aforesaid, Luella E. Shaw who, being duly sworn by me according to law, declares that she is 66 years of age and that she was born Sept 10th 1855, at New York State

That she is the widow of Darius N. Shaw, who enlisted Oct 12th 1861, at Lansing, Minn under the name of Darius N. Shaw, as a Privot (Rank) in Company "E" 4th Regiment Minnesota

(Here state company and regiment, if in the Army; or vessels, if in the Navy.)

and was honorably discharged Oct 15th 1862, having served ninety days or more or was discharged for or died in service of a disability incurred in the service and in the line of duty during the Civil War.

That he also served as private in Company "B" 2nd Regiment of Minnesota Calvalry and was honorable discharged on Dec 1865

(Here give a complete statement of all other military, naval, or coast guard service, if any, at whatever time rendered.)

That she was married to said soldier (or sailor) August 4, 1891 under the name of Luella E. Taylor, at Grand Forks N. Dak., by Alex McGregor Pastor M. E. Church that she had been previously married; that he had been previously married, to Milton W. Taylor, + was divorced and Darius N. Shaw had previously married Sylvia Wood and that she died Jan 7 1891

(Here state all prior marriages of either, and give the names and dates and places of death or divorce of all former consorts.)

and that neither she nor said soldier (or sailor) was ever married otherwise than as stated above.

(If any *former* husband rendered military or naval service, here describe same and give number of any pension claim based thereon.)

That said soldier (or sailor) died May 2d, 1922, at Ottertail, Minn; that she was not divorced from him; and that she has not remarried since his death.

That the following are the ONLY children of the soldier (or sailor) under sixteen years of age NOW living, namely:

None, born ______, 1____, at none
______, born ______, 1____, at ______
______, born ______, 1____, at ______
______, born ______, 1____, at ______
______, born ______, 1____, at ______

ATTORNEY FILED
W. L. S.
LAW DIVISION

That the above-named child ______ of the soldier (or sailor) {is / are} ______ now receiving a pension, and that such child ______ {is a / are} member ______ of her family and ______ cared for by her.

That she has Not heretofore applied for pension, the number of her former claim being ______; that said soldier (or sailor) was ______ a pensioner, the number of his pension certificate being 289563.

That she makes this declaration for the purpose of being placed on the pension roll of the United States under the provisions of the ACT OF APRIL 19, 1908, as amended by the ACT OF SEPT. 8, 1916, and ACT OF MAY 1, 1920.

She hereby appoints M. Elliott Waggaman & Co. (De Lapointe Rice and M. Elliott Waggaman), Washington, D. C., her true and lawful attorneys.

(Two attesting and identifying witnesses.)

(1) G. B. Schultz (Signature of first witness.) — Luella E. Shaw (Claimant's signature in full.)
Ottertail Minn (Address of first witness.) — Ottertail Minn. (Claimant's address in full.)
(2) H. G. Schultz (Signature of second witness.)
Ottertail Minn (Address of second witness.)

OFFICE 1922

Subscribed and sworn to before me this 3 day of June, 1922, and I hereby certify that the contents of the above declaration were fully made known and explained to the applicant before swearing, including the words ______ erased, and the words ______ added; and that I have no interest, direct or indirect, in the prosecution of this claim.

H. H. Gruttog (Signature.)
H. GRUTLAG, Notary Public, Ottertail Co. Minn.
My Commission Expires Jan. 24, 1925.
(Official character.)

(SEAL.)

Declaration accepted as a widow's claim under Act of May 1, 1920 ... of attorney ...

Figure 6.9 Document Recognition 6

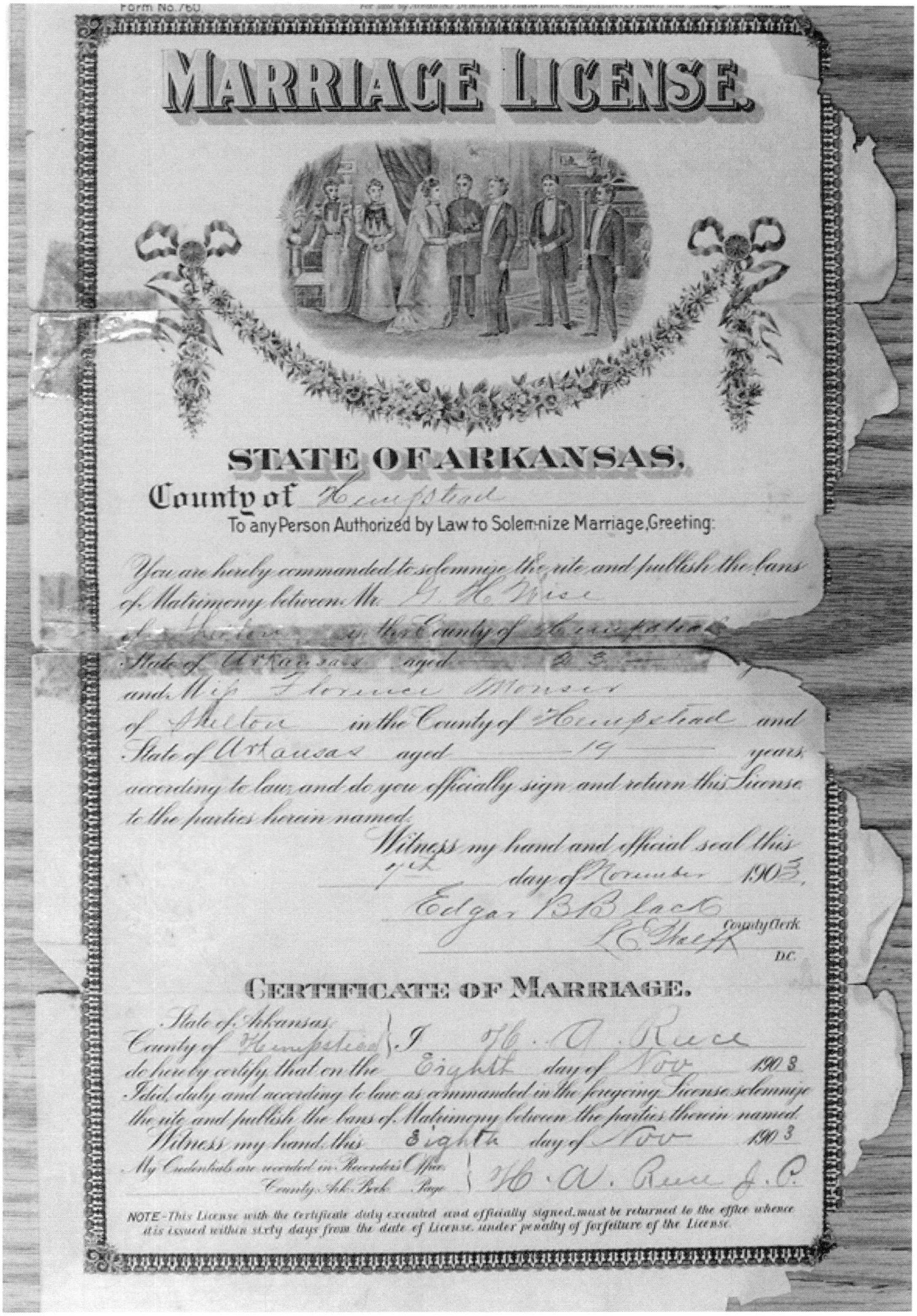

Form No. 760.

MARRIAGE LICENSE.

STATE OF ARKANSAS,

County of Hempstead

To any Person Authorized by Law to Solemnize Marriage, Greeting:

You are hereby commanded to solemnize the rite and publish the bans of Matrimony between Mr. G. H. Wise of [illegible] in the County of Hempstead and State of Arkansas aged 23 and Miss Florence Monser of Shelton in the County of Hempstead and State of Arkansas aged 19 years according to law, and do you officially sign and return this License to the parties herein named.

Witness my hand and official seal this 7th day of November 1903.

Edgar B. Black County Clerk

[illegible] D.C.

CERTIFICATE OF MARRIAGE.

State of Arkansas, County of Hempstead } I H. A. Rice do hereby certify that on the Eighth day of Nov 1903 I did, duly and according to law as commanded in the foregoing License, solemnize the rite and publish the bans of Matrimony between the parties therein named.

Witness my hand this Eighth day of Nov 1903

My Credentials are recorded in Recorder's Office County, Ark. Book Page } H. A. Rice J. P.

NOTE—This License with the Certificate duly executed and officially signed, must be returned to the office whence it is issued within sixty days from the date of License, under penalty of forfeiture of the License.

Figure 6.10   Document Recognition 7

COMPLEMENT TO GENEALOGIES

FAYSSOUX. Fayssoux family. By P. F. Sevens. (Baltimore? 1939?)   (33) 53 p.   FW

FAZAKERLEY.   Pedigree of the late Henry Hawarden-Gillibrand-Fazakerley, and the descent to him
of Fazakerley hall, Gillibrand hall and Lower house in Widnes.   By V. Hussey Walsh.   Exeter, Pollard,
n.d.   21 p.   Reprinted from the Genealogist, vol. 33   FW

FEARNS.   Fearns of Virginia and some allied families.   By E. L. F. C. Ferneyhough.   (Richmond,
Expert Graphics, 1973)   70 p., 8 leaves. illus., maps, coat of arms. 8vo.   FW

FEATHERINGILL.   History of the Featheringill, Bogart, Fruchey, Holmes, and Metcalf families.
By Marjorie F. Waterfield.   (Maumee, O.) 1976.   (64) p.   FW

FEATHERSTONE.   The Featherstones and Halls; gleanings from old family letters and manuscripts.
By Margaret Irwin.   Leominster, Orphans' Print. (1890)   6, 99 p. 16 mo.   FW LI

FECHHEIMER.   Fechheimer family tree.   By Richard Fechheimer.   Highland Park, Ill., author,
n.d.   10 p. 28 cm.   CH

FEDERLE.   Jahrheft des Geschlechts Federle-Feederle.   Heft 1-5.   Bruchsal, 1926-38.   8vo.
illus., plates. ports., tables.   NY

FEE.   A history of the Fee family, with biographical sketches of their descendants from the earliest
available records from 1750 to the present time.   By the granddaughters of the children of Robert and
Rachel Fee.   Chester, S. C., Lantern Print., 1901.   71 p., 2 leaves. 8 plates. 8vo.   NY

FEE.   Fee family in Maryland, Pennsylvania, Kentucky & Ohio, 1703-1944. By Wm. B. McGroarty.
(Alexandria, Va.) 1944.   20 p.   FW

FEE.   A history of the Fee family.   By Ralph E. Pearson.   (Austin, Tex.) 1969-(71?)   4 vols. 28 cm.
Main work, supplements, 1-12, addenda, 1-9 (1601 p. all together including index)   FW KH NY SP

FEE.   Fee family.   By Robert Arthur.   Rev. ed.   New Orleans, La., 1965.   78 leaves.   FW

FEEMAN.   Feeman family, Lebanon County, Pa.   (Schaefferstown, Pa., 1974)   p. 55 - 63. Reprinted
from Historic Schafferstown Record, vol. 8   FW

FEER.   Die Familie Feer in Luzern und im Aargan, 1331-1934.   (By) Eduard Feer.   (Berlin, 1934)
122 p. 25 cm. Also supplement. Berlin, 1936. 31 p. 24 cm.   NY

FEHLIMAN.   Fehliman, Fellman, 1818-1968.   By Jeanne B. F. Seydel.   San Diego, Calif., Neyenesch
Printers, 1968.   76 p.   DP FW OH OL SU

FELDER.   Felder family of South Carolina.   N. p., 1899?   12 p. 8vo.   NY

FELDHAUSEN.   Descendants of Jacob and Theresa Feldhausen.   (By Pearl Anderson)   No imprint.
(54) leaves. ports., coat of arms. 29 cm. Cover title. Mimeo.   KH

FELL.   Fells of Swarthmoor hall and their friends; with an account of their ancestor, Anne Askew,
the martyr ...   By Maria Webb.   London, A. W. Bennett, 1865.   434 p. 2 facsim. front. 16mo.   FW

FELLERS.   Enos Fellers family; background and posterity.   By Forest S. Fellers.   (Toledo, Ohio,
1960?)   68, (4) leaves. port. 30 cm. Bibliography, leaves (69-71)   LA NY

FELLERS.   Enos Fellers family; background and posterity.   (Walhonding, O., 1965)   69, 14 p. 28 cm.   FW

FELLOWS.   Genealogy of the Fellows family in America, from 1635 to 1885.   By Charles S. Fellows.
(Lanesboro, Minn. , M. G. Fellows, printer, 1886?)   7 p. 22 cm. Cover title.   MH

Figure 6.11   Document Recognition 8

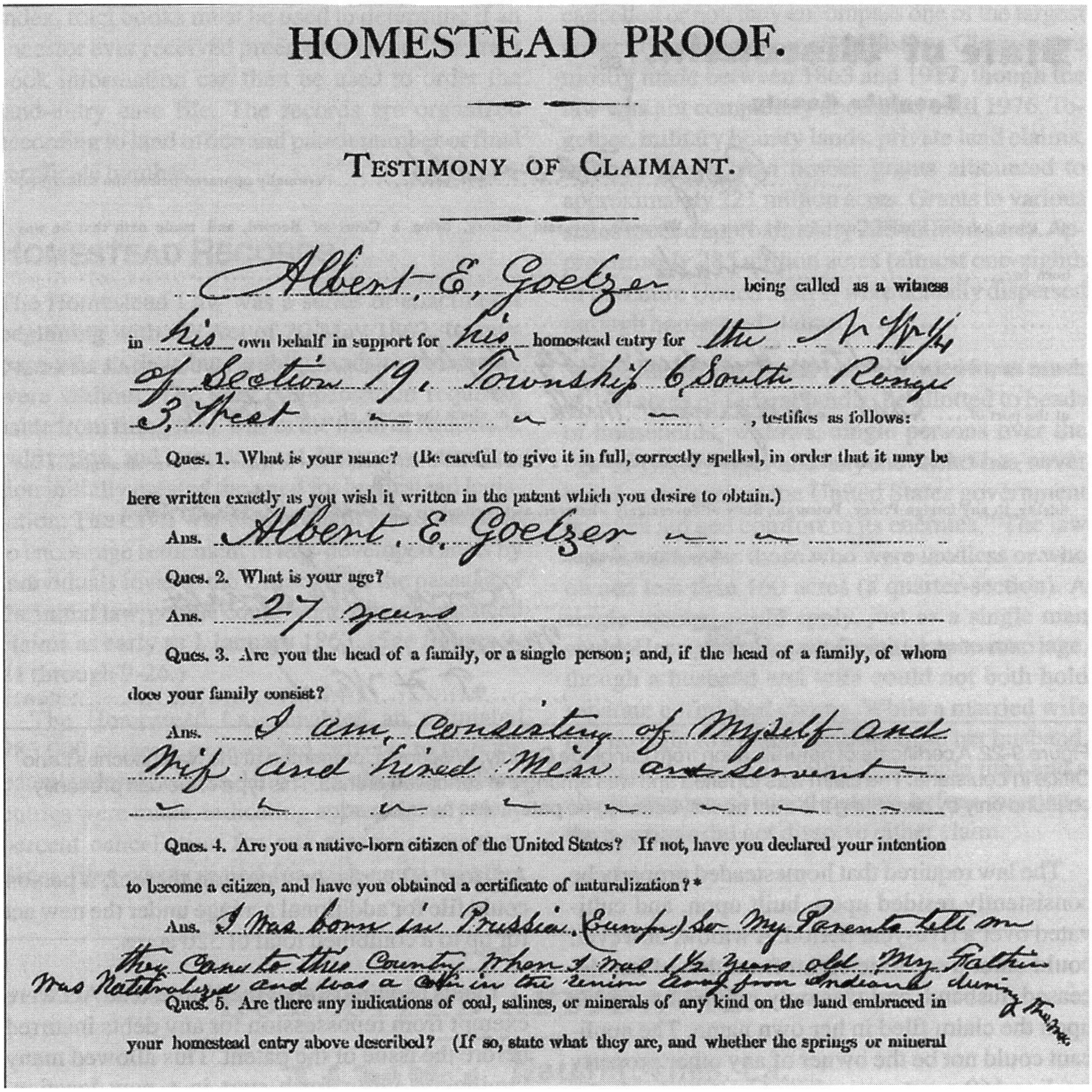

HOMESTEAD PROOF.

TESTIMONY OF CLAIMANT.

Albert E, Goelzer .... being called as a witness

in *his* own behalf in support for *his* homestead entry for *the N W ¼ of Section 19, Township 6 South Range 3 West* .... , testifies as follows:

Ques. 1. What is your name? (Be careful to give it in full, correctly spelled, in order that it may be here written exactly as you wish it written in the patent which you desire to obtain.)

Ans. *Albert, E, Goelzer* ....

Ques. 2. What is your age?

Ans. *27 years* ....

Ques. 3. Are you the head of a family, or a single person; and, if the head of a family, of whom does your family consist?

Ans. *I am, Consisting of Myself and Wife and hired Men and Servant* ....

Ques. 4. Are you a native-born citizen of the United States? If not, have you declared your intention to become a citizen, and have you obtained a certificate of naturalization? *

Ans. *I was born in Prussia (Europe) So My Parents tell me they Came to this Country When I was 1½ years old My Father was Naturalized and was a ___ in the ___ ___ from Indiana during*

Ques. 5. Are there any indications of coal, salines, or minerals of any kind on the land embraced in your homestead entry above described? (If so, state what they are, and whether the springs or mineral

127

Figure 6.12   Document Recognition 9

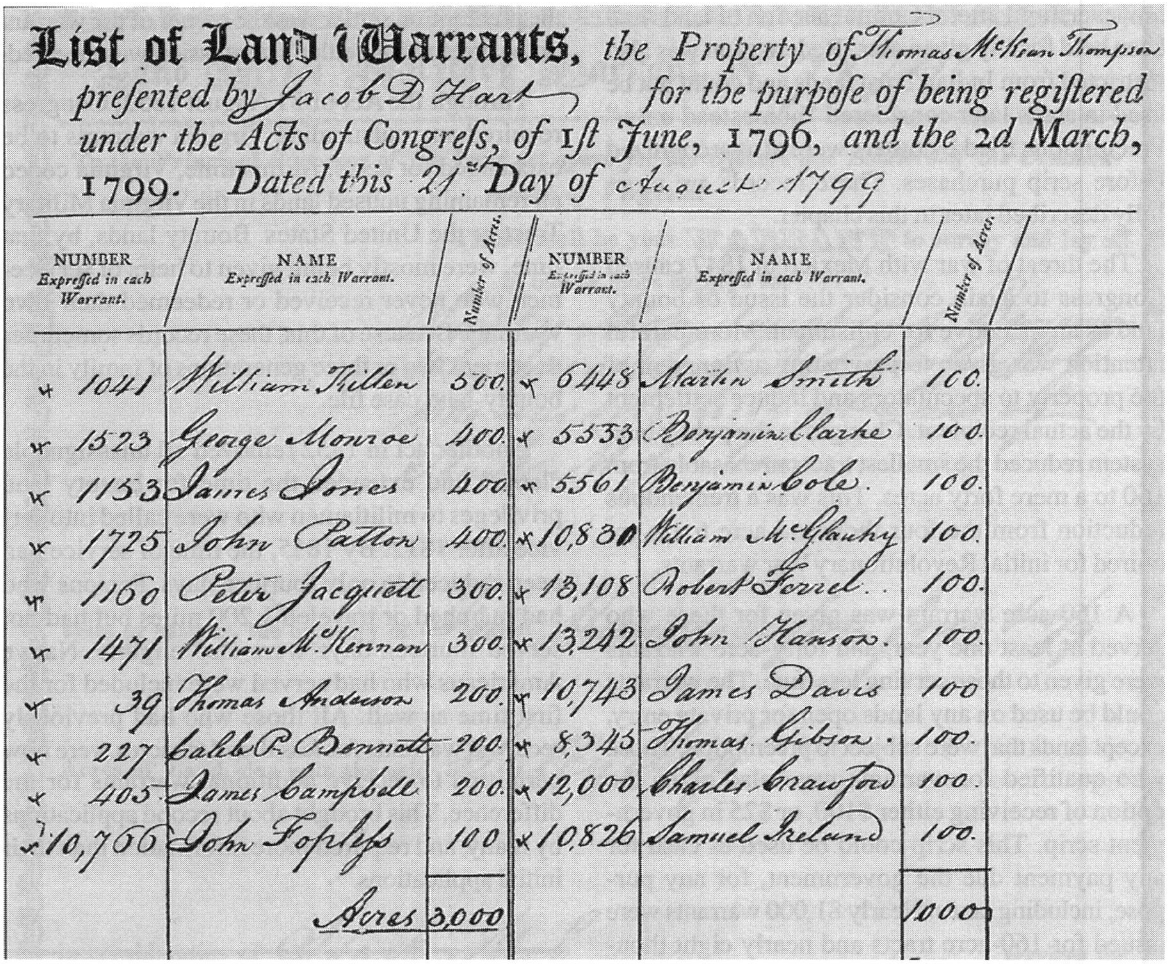

List of Land Warrants, the Property of *Thomas McKean Thompson* presented by *Jacob D Hart* for the purpose of being registered under the Acts of Congress, of 1st June, 1796, and the 2d March, 1799. Dated this 21st Day of *August 1799*

NUMBER Expressed in each Warrant.	NAME Expressed in each Warrant.	Number of Acres.	NUMBER Expressed in each Warrant.	NAME Expressed in each Warrant.	Number of Acres.
1041	William Tilten	500.	6448	Martin Smith	100.
1523	George Monroe	400.	5533	Benjamin Clarke	100.
1153	James Jones	400.	5561	Benjamin Cole	100.
1725	John Patton	400.	10,830	William McGlauhy	100.
1160	Peter Jacquett	300.	13,108	Robert Ferrel	100.
1471	William McKennan	300.	13,242	John Hanson	100.
39	Thomas Anderson	200.	10,743	James Davis	100
227	Caleb P. Bennett	200.	8,345	Thomas Gibson	100.
405	James Campbell	200.	12,000	Charles Crawford	100.
10,766	John Fopless	100	10,826	Samuel Ireland	100.
	Acres	3,000			1000

Figure 6.13   Document Recognition 10

LIST OF ALL THE PASSENGERS

Taken on board the *Brig Henry Clay* — of *New York* ....in any foreign Port or Place.

Names of Passengers.	Ages.	Sex.	Occupation.	Country to which they belong.	Country of which they intend to become inhabitants.	Died on the Voyage.
John Sigot	32 yars	Male	Painter & Glazier	England	State of Indiana	
Hannah Sigot	28 „	Female	none	„	„	
John Alford	25 „	Male	Nail Maker	„	„	
Ann Alford	25 „	Female	none	„	„	
John Elston	25 „	Male	paper Maker	„	„	
Sarah Elston	30 „	Female	none	„	„	
Hannah Jones	48 „	„	„	„	„	
Jacob Jones	22 „	Male	Labourer	„	„	
Elizabeth Jones	16 „	Female	none	„	„	
Mary Jones	12 „	„	„	„	„	
Charlotte Jones	6 „	„	„	„	„	
William Jones	8 „	Male	„	„	„	
Jacob Alford	9 „	„	„	„	„	
Israel Alford	7 months	„	„	„	„	
John Elston Junr	6 „	„	„	„	„	
Jane Rogers	35 yars	Female	„	„	„	
Sarah Rogers	16 „	„	„	„	„	
Elizabeth Rogers	12 „	„	„	„	„	
Stephen Rogers	10 „	Male	„	„	„	
Thomas Rogers	8 „	„	„	„	„	
Wm Rogers	6 „	„	„	„	„	
Mary Rogers	3 „	Female	„	„	„	
John Rogers	6 months	Male	„	„	„	
Richard Seamour	50 yars	„	Mariner	„	„	
Elizabeth Seamour	30 „	Female	none	„	„	
George Seamour	20 „	Male	Mariner	„	„	
Jane Seamour	14 „	Female	none	„	„	
Richard Seamour Jr	9 „	Male	„	„	„	
Hervey Seamour	7 „	„	„	„	„	
Solomon Seamour	2 „	„	„	„	„	
Wm Hardy	30 „	„	Mariner	„	„	
Sarah Hardy	30 „	Female	none	„	„	
John Hardy	7 „	Male	„	„	„	
Sarah Hardy Jr	5 „	Female	„	„	„	
John Lander	34 „	Male	Cabinett Maker	„	„	
Sarah Lander	34 „	Female	none	„	„	
Thomas Lander	9 „	Male	„	„	„	
Mary Lander	4 „	Female	„	„	„	
Louiza Cudliss	35 „	„	„	„	„	
Frederick Cudliss	11 „	Male	„	„	„	
Louiza Cudliss Jr	12 „	Female	„	„	„	
John Cudliss	„	Male	„	„	„	
George Cudliss	„	„	„	„	„	
Eliza Cudliss	17 „	Female	„	„	„	
Elizabeth Lander	25 „	„	„	„	„	
Michael Saberac	35 „	Male	Physician	Paris France	Philada	
Flora Langsley	60 „	Female	none	„	„	
Thomas Medford	45 „	Male	Farmer	England		

Havre De Grace

Signed Wm Beall Jr

Septr 4. 1820.

Figure 6.14   Document Recognition 11

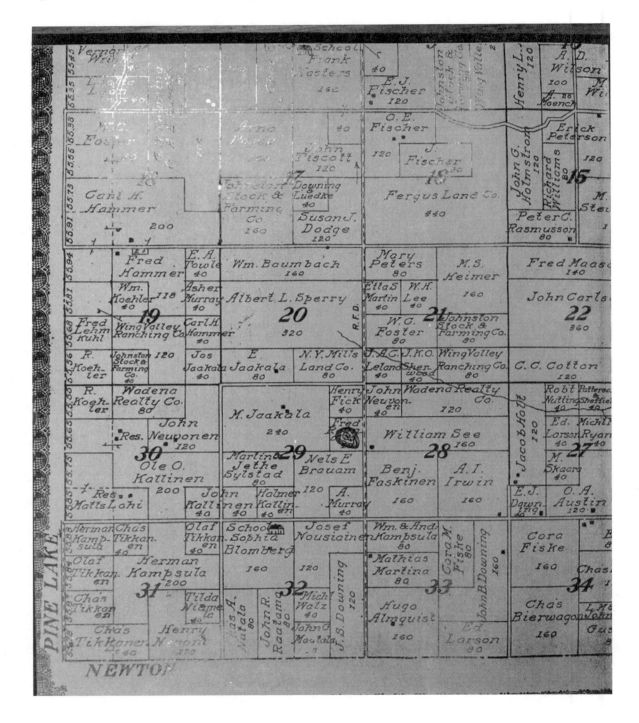

Figure 6.15   Document Recognition 12

Becoming an Accredited Genealogist

Figure 6.16   Document Recognition 13

48. The Hunt Party Reaches Idaho.—Hunt with his party of sixty-five men left St. Louis in the fall of 1810 and passed the winter near St. Joseph, Missouri. In April, 1811, the Astorians began their celebrated journey. During the spring and summer they ascended the Missouri River and passed through portions of the present States of South Dakota, Montana, and Wyoming. On September 16 from the summit of Union Pass, Wyoming, the Hunt party caught their first glimpse of the snowy peaks of the Three Tetons, the most noted landmarks of the Northwest. The sight of the Teton Peaks, once on Idaho soil but now in Wyoming, sent a thrill of joy through the weary travellers. They realized that they were nearing the headwaters of one

WILSON PRICE HUNT.

of the great branches of the Columbia, whose mouth was the cherished goal of their ambitions.

49. They Sail Down the Snake in Canoes.—During late September the Astorians crossed the Teton Pass and entered that beautiful valley of the Teton River known as Pierre's Hole in the present Teton County, Idaho. On October 8 they arrived at Fort Henry in the vicinity of the modern St. Anthony, and occupied for ten days the deserted log cabins built the preceding autumn by Andrew Henry. At this point the party made a sad blunder. They decided to abandon their horses and trust to the river the rest of the way. The Snake was navigable for canoes at this point and the voyagers little realized that, in their rude pirogues, they were attempting to float on one of the world's most treacherous and turbulent streams.

Figure 6.17   Document Recognition 14

meat of ... productive tract of land, bringing to them very substantial returns. In 1910 Mr. Mitchell opened a stock of agricultural implements, hardware, groceries, boots and shoes in Wilder and has since engaged in business as a retail merchant, being now accorded a liberal patronage in recognition of his reliable business methods, his earnest desire to please his patrons and his straightforward dealing. In February, 1918, he was appointed postmaster and is discharging the duties of that office in connection with his business affairs.

In 1905 Mr. Mitchell was united in marriage to Miss Edna Irene Wilson, a native of Iowa, and they have become the parents of three children: Helen and Kenneth, who are attending school; and Lolo, three years of age.

The parents of Mr. Mitchell, J. H. and Sarah (Morse) Mitchell, also become residents of Idaho, removing from Ladora, Iowa, in 1912. The father purchased land near Wilder which he now rents, for he has retired from business, having reached the age of seventy years, while his wife is sixty-eight years of age. They have a daughter, Lilla, who is a trained nurse, having graduated from the State University of Iowa and now making her home in Wilder.

In his fraternal relations Charles E. Mitchell is an Odd Fellow and became a charter member of Wilder Lodge, No. 37. He is also connected with the Modern Woodmen of America. He is keenly interested in everything that pertains to the welfare and upbuilding of the district in which he lives and cooperates heartily in all well defined plans and measures looking to the betterment of the town, the extension of its trade relations and the maintenance of its high civic standards.

FRED H. DAVIS.

The real estate business in Nampa has a prominent and successful representative in Fred H. Davis, who was born in Craftsbury, Orleans county, Vermont, October 28, 1861. His father, Ira Davis, was born in Broom county, Quebec, Canada. He was a veteran of the Civil war and for many years was well known as a tradesman at East Barrington, New Hampshire, where he passed away. His parents were Canadians but were natives of Wales. The mother of our subject was in her maidenhood Sarah Cooey and was also a native of Broom county, Canada, though her parents were born in Belfast, Ireland. She is still living upon the old homestead at East Barrington, New Hampshire, at the venerable age of eighty-seven years. She bore her husband ten children, of whom six grew to manhood and womanhood, five of them remaining in the New England states. One brother of our subject, Samuel Davis, is and has been for many years prominent in the city government of Manchester, New Hampshire.

Fred H. Davis was educated in the old New England schools until the age of twelve, when the family removed to Manchester, New Hampshire, which remained his home until he was eighteen. At that period in his life he came to Idaho, settling in Hailey, where he remained, however, but a short time. He then went to Rocky Bar, engaging in mining in its immediate vicinity for about sixteen years, at the end of which time he went to Silver City. While there residing he was elected to the legislature, serving one term and not only doing effective work in taking care of the interests of his constituents but also ably supporting all measures which he considered of value to the state. He was afterwards appointed by Governor Frank Hunt and the secretary of state to take complete charge of the Idaho mineral exhibit at the Pan American Exposition at Buffalo, New York.

Upon his return to Idaho Mr. Davis chose Nampa as his place of residence and in 1916 he became connected with the United Stores Company of Shoshone county. However, he maintained this relationship for but a short time, for he was returned to the legislature under Governor Alexander, again doing valuable work in the halls of legislation. After the expiration of his term he returned to Nampa, where he engaged in the real estate business, his wife being his able assistant. He has met with more than ordinary success, being a man of rare business tact and ability as well as of experience, and the highest principles have ever guided his business deals. It is therefore but natural that he has won the trust and confidence of all who have had business relations with him. He is thoroughly informed in regard to local conditions and values, and his advice and judgment are often sought in

Figure 6.18 Document Recognition 15

BIOGRAPHICAL SKETCHES.

JAMES H. ALLSTOT, farmer and stock raiser, Section 20, P. O. Bennet; is a brother of George W. Allstot, and came to Lancaster County with the family in 1870, his father is recognized as one of the pioneers and favorably known as an agriculturist. James H. was born in Parke County, Ind., November 3, 1847, came to Dubuque County, Iowa, with his parents when quite young, and there spent his youthful days. For four years was a resident of Marion County, Iowa. He has secured a fair start in life by untiring industry and promises in the near future to be numbered among the stalwart farmers of the State.

S. P. BARRETT, A. M., Principal of Bennet Public schools, favorably known as being closely associated with the educational interests of Lancaster County, is the subject of this sketch. He is a native of Ohio and was born in Kingsville, Ashtabula Co., June 7, 1834, was reared in his native State, receiving superior educational advantages. He attended and graduated from Kingsville Academy, after which he entered the University of Rochester, at Rochester, N. Y., in 1856, and graduated from that institution in 1859. In the fall of the same year he engaged in teaching school at Chattanooga, Tenn., where he taught two years; whence he removed to Buchanan, Mich., where he became Principal of the public schools of the city, which place he filled four years. He then engaged in mercantile business in Nunda, N. Y., for one year, in which place he also taught previous to his entering college at Rochester, N. Y. His whole subsequent life to the present, 1882, has been devoted to teaching as follows: two years at Kingsville Academy, Ohio; three years at Buchanan, Mich.; four years at Dallas City, Ore., and three years at Baker City, Ore. In 1879, becoming desirous of obtaining rest from his continued labors, he located on a farm in Nebraska. It is a short distance west of Bennet, on Section 5, and one of the most desirable homes in the precinct. Since he has been in Nebraska, in connection with conducting his farm, he has taught school, having been the Principal of the Bennet schools for several terms as an educator; and the satisfaction he gives the people may be inferred from the fact that the public is ardent in his praise. Prof. Barrett has a good command of language, does a full share of thinking, is a good judge of human nature, is social and genial, has an aptness to make and retain friends, and is honorable in all his motives, measuring with precision the wants of the future. In 1862, Miss Mary J. Hovey, of Nunda, N. Y., became his wife; by this union they have five children; Hovey P., Jay A., Grace M., Edith A., and Inez D. Mr. and Mrs. Barrett and the three eldest children are members of the Baptist Church. Prof. Barrett has been associated with that denomination since 1851, and his wife since 1852.

P. J. BRATT'S SONS, dealers in hardware, agricultural implements and furniture, prominently identified in eastern Nebraska, and favorably known in commercial circles, is the firm of P. J. Bratt's Sons, although but a short time has elapsed since they were established here. Their present large and increasing trade is evidence of sterling business qualifications. A. Bratt, the senior member of the firm, is a native of Illinois, and was born in Bureau County, Ill., August 26, 1854. When young removed with his parents to Rock Island County, Ill., where his father, Mr. P. J. Bratt, engaged in merchandising at Coal Valley and was widely known as one of the substantial merchants of that country for many years. His death occurred in 1874. His sons conducted the business at Coal Valley until 1880, when they established their business in Bennet. In the summer of 1880 they erected their large and well arranged establishment. In the autumn of that year they opened it. The subject of this sketch during his sojourn in Bennet, has been closely associated with its progress. Upon the organization of the town, he was appointed Treasurer of the Town Board. In 1879 Miss Laura E. Clark, of Illinois, a native of Ohio, became his wife. They have one son, Harry. Mr. Barrett is a Master Mason. John P. Bratt, the junior member of the firm of P. J. Bratt's Sons, is a native of Bureau County, Ill., and was born February 9, 1857, removed with his parents when young to Coal Valley, Rock Island Co., Ill., where he was raised and educated. In company with his brother A., assumed his father's business after his death. In 1878 came to Nebraska and purchased a half section of land in Stockton Precinct, but did not come to the State to reside until 1880, when he resided for a time in Stockton. He is largely interested in buying and selling real estate, in connection with his other business. While in Stockton Precinct he was Justice of the Peace and member of the School Board. In June, 1881, was appointed Justice of the Peace in Bennet, and the same autumn elected to this office, which at the present time (1882), he holds. He is a gentleman of pleasing address, and is eminently popular with all who form his acquaintance. Is a Master Mason and Third Sergeant of Co. I. N. N. G.

E. N. COBB, farmer and stock raiser, Section 23, P. O. Bennet. He is a native of Wayne County, Penn., and was born December 18, 1844; resided in his native State until the breaking out of the war, when he enlisted in the Fifty-sixth Pennsylvania, after serving three months was discharged on account of ill health. He soon re-enlisted in the Seventeenth Pennsylvania, served two months and was transferred to the Eighteenth United States Infantry. He participated in a number of warm engagements, among those were Stone River and Chickamauga, at the latter battle he was severely wounded in the ankle, after which he was on detached service until the close of the memorable battle of Lookout Mountain, when he rejoined his regiment. Was honorably discharged at Louisville, Ky., September 10, 1865. After the war, returned to Pennsylvania, and for seven years was a resident of Susquehanna County, after which he came to Nebraska. He married, April 28, 1869, Miss Raphel Hewit. By the union they have had five children, George F., Calvin D., Minnie B., Zady G.; lost one, Maud, died in 1882. Mr. Cobb is First Lieutenant of Company I, Nebraska National Guards, and a member of G. A. R. and O. D. of Upright Post No. 62. He is thoroughly conversant with military tactics and takes a live interest in military affairs. Is a member of the I. O. O. F., P. G. and School Director for District 78.

FRANK COGGESHALL, farmer and stock raiser, Section 26, P. O. Bennet. Deserving of special mention in the history of Nebraska is the subject of this sketch. He is a native of New Haven, Conn., and was born April 13, 1848. His earlier days were spent and education received principally in his native State. When quite young he manifested a strong desire to visit the Western country, and before the war, then a mere youth, came to Iowa, where some relatives resided, remaining a considerable length of time, when he returned to his home in New Haven. In 1864, tendered his services to the union cause, enlisting as a drummer boy, and served in a Connecticut regiment, until the close of the Rebellion, when he was honorably discharged. For a few years after the war was engaged in freighting, across the plains. In 1869, located his present farm, and from that time has been identified by the developments of Lancaster County, although not constantly a resident. His farm is one of the most desirable in the precinct, on which is situated an attractive and comfortable residence. Mr. Coggeshall is a logical reasoner, thoroughly conversant with the events of the day, and an entertaining conversationalist. He married in 1880, Miss Livey Kelsey, of Illinois, a lady whose graces of mind and heart endear her to a large circle of friends.

W. H. DAVIS, agent for the B. & M. R. R. Mr. Davis is a native of Indiana, and was born in Parke County, July 15, 1855, was reared and educated in the Hoosier State. He commenced and learned telegraphing on the Lake Shore and Michigan Southern Railroad, after which he was connected with the Grand Rapids and Indiana Railroad, also the Michigan Central, with the latter company was operator for two years, at Porter, forty miles east of Chicago. The autumn of 1879, came to Nebraska and entered the employ of the B. & M. Co., as assistant agent at Sutton, on the main line, continuing for a time, when he became agent and operator at Hampton, having charge of that office six months; thence to Bennet. On the 28th of November, 1877, Mr. D. was wedded to Miss Minnie Cheney, of Furnessville, Ind. By this union they have one daughter, Dora, born in 1879.

M. B. DECK, physician and surgeon, is a native of West Virginia, and was born in Martinsburg, October 26, 1852. His father, Abraham, was a native of that State, and his maternal ancesters (Faris) were among the pioneers of Virginia. The subject of the sketch was reared and educated in his native State and took up the study of medicine in the office of Dr. N. D. Baker, after which he attended the university of Maryland, at Baltimore, graduating in March, 1878, commenced practice at Darksville, W. Va.; came to Nemaha County, Neb., in September, 1881, continuing until January, 1882, when he came to Bennet, and formed a partnership with Dr. Piper. He married May 25, 1880, Miss Lottie Benson, of New Jersey. They have one son by this union, Harry.

CAPT. L. P. DERBY, Postmaster of Bennet. There are but few citizens, for a radius of many miles around Bennet, that are more popularly known or highly esteemed than Capt. Derby. He is a native of Hancock County, Ill., and was born February 14, 1844. When quite young he removed with his parents to Williams County, Ohio. His father was a contractor and builder in West Unity, where the subject of this sketch was educated, raised and learned the painter's trade. On the 18th of September, 1861, he displayed that spirit of patriotism which has characterized his career, by enlisting in Company B, Sixty-eighth Ohio Volunteer Infantry, under Capt. Sidney Sprague. At the battle of Fort Donelson his eyes became injured to such an extent that they never fully recovered. Participated at the battle of Pittsburgh Landing, was at Matamoras, on the Central Mississippi campaign, Siege of Vicksburg, first and second battle at Jackson, Miss., Meridian raid, operations against Atlanta, and with Sherman on his famous march to the sea. After which he was at Columbus, Raleigh, Goldsboro and other minor engagements. At the battle of Champion Hills he received a slight flesh wound. On the 22nd of February, 1866, was promoted to Second Lieutenant of the Fourteenth United States Infantry, continuing in the service of the West and South until 1871, when he resigned as First Lieutenant of the Eleventh United States Infantry. After the long and continued years of a soldier's life, repaired to his old home in Ohio. Settled in Bennet in 1878, following different pursuits until 1881, when he was appointed Postmaster. In June, 1880, when Company I, of N. N. G. was organized, he was appointed Captain, which office he still holds. Is a member of the G. A. R. and on the deputy staff. Capt. Derby has had a varied experience, is a brilliant conversationalist, and on the whole is one of the most genial and companionable of men. In 1879, Miss Mary Henderson, of Grand Rapids, Mich., became his wife. By this union they have two children, Winnie and Arthur.

G. W. EGGLESTON, grain and coal dealer, is a native of England and was born in Lincolnshire, February 23, 1850. Came to America with parents when young, living for a time near Akron, Ohio, after which in Peoria County, Ill., where his father William was engaged in agricultural pursuits. The family also for several years resided in Cedar County, Iowa and emigrated from that point to Nebraska, the senior Eggleston locating in Lancaster County. The subject of this sketch took up his permanent abode in the State in 1873, and commenced tilling the soil near Bennet. In 1875 engaged in merchandising, continuing one year, when he established present business which has grown under his careful supervision to be lucrative and substantial. He married in October, 1877, Miss Edith Gouram, of Nebraska. They have two children, George W. and Frank LeRoy. Mr. E. is a member of the I. O. O. F.

W. H. FROST, farmer, Section 24, P. O. Bennet. This enterprising young agriculturist is a native of England and was born in Chesterfield, June 18, 1857. When quite young he came to America with his parents. For a time the family resided in Utah, but eventually, in 1870, they located in Lancaster County, Neb., being among the pioneers of Nemaha Precinct. Mr. Charles Frost, father of W. H., was closely identified with the early development and the progress of the county to the time of his demise, August 27, 1880. Mrs. Jane Frost died in Otoe County, June 24, 1879. She had been over in that county attending church when taken sick. The first house the family had on their new farm was destroyed by fire a few years after their arrival and was a serious drawback as it contained a large amount of grain, as well as the loss sustained by being deprived of the building. W. H. was reared on a farm and devotes his entire attention to agricultural pursuits in which branch he is making a success. In 1879 Miss Annie Bayless, a native of Quincy, Ill., became his wife. They have had two children, Charles is living, Eva died August 7, 1881.

DAVID A. GRAU, contractor, builder and architect. This popular gentleman is a native of St. Lawrence County, N. Y., and was born April 18, 1842. When he was quite young came West with his parents. His father, who was a blacksmith by trade, located in Columbia County, Wis., being among the pioneer vulcans of that country, and was prominently identified among the early settlers. In 1861 the subject of this sketch tendered his services to the country, enlisting October 8, in Company D, Tenth Wisconsin Volunteer Infantry. Participated in many of the notable events of the war. Among those was Perrysville, Ky., Stone River, Kenesaw Mountain, Resaca, and Atlanta. Was with Sherman. Served three years and was discharged in Milwaukee, Wis., November 4, 1864. Returned to Columbia County and resided there for a time, when he went to Iowa where he pursued his vocation of contracting and building, eventually returning to Wisconsin, and in 1880 came to Nebraska, locating in Lincoln, and was interested in the building of many of the basements of the substantial and attractive edifices of that city, among them the *Journal* office, Kelly's block, and the C. C. Burr building. In the autumn of 1881 he came to Bennet. Mr. G. is one of the most thoroughly experienced builders in the country and has attained a wide and well merited reputation. He is a member of the K. of P. and of the Grand Army of the Republic.

A. GRIBLING, harness and saddlery, one of the pioneer substantial business men of Bennet, is the subject of this sketch. He is a native of New York, and was born in Herkimer County, August 28, 1841. When quite young he was deprived of his father by death. His boyhood days were spent in gaining an education in his native county. In the spring of 1862 he commenced to learn the harness and saddlery trade, at Fredonia, N. Y. In August of that year, he tendered his services to the Union cause, enlisting in Company B, One Hundred and Twelfth New York Volunteer Infantry, under Gen. Dix. Soon after being mustered in, he was put on detached service, being placed in the Seventh Massachusetts Battery. His first engagement was at Deserted House, Va., and the next Hanover Junction, near Richmond, thence to New Port and Washington. Was called to New York City during the riot, but on his arrival it had subsided, and he returned to Washington, thence to New Orleans. Was with Gen. Banks on the famous Red River expedition. On returning, camped for several months at Morganzies Bend, after which was at Little Rock, Duvall's Bluffs and Montgomery, where he rejoined his regiment. Was honorably discharged at Buffalo, N. Y., on July 1, 1864. Again located at Fredonia, N. Y., and completed his trade. In 1865, came west, and after a temporary sojourn in Iowa and Illinois, returned to New York, not to remain, however. After a few months' sojourn, he became a resident of Rockford, Ill. For a time worked as a journeyman, after which he embarked in trade, continuing to reside in that city two years. In 1868 came to Nebraska, locating four miles north of Bennet, engaging in agricultural pursuits. Continuing in that capacity until he engaged in trade in Bennet in 1872, with the exception of a short time spent in Lincoln. Mr. G. was the first and only harness and saddlery man in Bennet, and the large and lucrative trade that he has built up is prima facie evidence of his popularity. From 1876 to 1879, he was Bennet's efficient Postmaster. Upon the organizing of the Town Board, he was elected one of that body. Mr. G. is a member of the I. O. O. F., and Recording Secretary of the Nebraska Horsethief Association. In 1873, Miss Ida Graves, an estimable lady, became his wife. She is a native of New York.

THORER HANSON, farmer and stock raiser, P. O. Bennet, Lancaster Co., Neb. This substantial agriculturist and well known gentleman, is a native of Norway, and was born in Christiana, August 26, 1832. Educated and learned the cabinet making trade in his native country, and pursued that vocation until 1866, when he came to America. Located temporarily in Chicago, Ill., in the employ of a lumber company. Moved to Oconto, Wis., and engaged work in his trade. In 1867, his family, which he left in Norway, came to the United States, and took up their abode in Oconto. In 1868, came to Nebraska, locating in Nebraska City, and for one year worked at the furniture trade. Mr. H. being a superior workman, always commanded the highest wages. On the 12th of April, 1869, located on eighty acres of land, where he now resides. Not having enough land to demand his entire time, he engaged in working at his trade in Lincoln, for his Nebraska City employers, who had a branch house there. Continued working in Lincoln until 1873, when he turned his entire attention to farming. Has been adding from time to time to his estates, and at present, 1882, has 320 acres. This year he has erected a residence which is a striking contrast to the one that was first erected in Lancaster County, for his home. Mr. H. is an industrious, progressive citizen. He is closely identified with the Norwegian Lutheran Church, and has done much toward the organization of the church society in Nemaha Precinct. In Norway, on the 29th of December, 1857, Miss Theo Andersen became his wife. They have had twelve children—Helmer, Torval, Maria, Emma, Richard, Walter, Nora, Hubert, Sherman, Adolph, Gerhard and lost one, Matilda, died in Oconto, Wis.

JAMES H. HARPER, farmer and stock raiser, Section 2, P. O. Bennet. Among those that figured at an early day in the State of Nebraska, is the subject of this sketch. Mr. H. is a native of West Virginia, and was born December 7, 1839. His early life was spent in that State, and he was there educated, and learned the harness and saddlery trade. The autumn of 1859 found him in the Territory of Nebraska, and located at Nebraska City, where he worked at the harness trade for upward of four years, when in company with Mr. Enoch Riggels, he succeeded his employer in business. The style of the firm for a considerable length of time, was well known as Harper & Riggels. Mr. H. eventually sold out, and returned to the scenes of his childhood, West Virginia. Sojourning temporarily, came again to Nebraska, and engaged in working at his trade in Nebraska City, continuing two years, when he went to Julesburg and engaged in the photographing business for a time; returned to Nebraska City, residing until the spring of 1869, when he located on his present farm. His estate consists of 120 acres, under a high state of cultivation,

Figure 6.19   Document Recognition 16

142

Parish Record of Burials.

1858			
Dec. 23	Frank Mitchell Hart	6 m.	St. George's Yard
25	Maria Jones	67 y.	" "
26	Robert Henry Woodhead	4 m.	" "
31	Betsey Herbert	42 y.	" "
1859			
Jan. 15	Elizabeth Watkins	2 w.	St. George's Yard
March 22	Josiah C. Hook	82 y.	Greenwood, N. Y.
April 14	Alexander H. Forest	7 y.	Vale Cemetery
" 15	Ann Jane Pritchard	4 y.	St. George's Yard
25	Albert Hough	31 y.	St. Johnsville
May 1	James Cleary	10 m.	Vale Cemetery
30	Ormon Jennings	47 y.	Universalist Ground
June 28	Mary E. Mix	30 y.	Duanesburgh
"	George Horace Adams	1 y.	St. George's Yard
29	Robert McFarlane	6 w.	St. George's Yard
July 20	Hannah Hayes	34 y.	Amsterdam
Aug. 6	William Henry Ouderkirk	15 y.	St. George's Yard
Sep. 28	Harvey Davis	68 y.	St. George's Yard
Oct. 14	Joseph Miller	1 y.	St. George's Yard
Nov. 2	Mary Jane Martin	7 m.	Vale Cemetery
4	Robert William Bryen	4 m.	St. George's Yard
6	Stephen S. Riggs	51 y.	Vale Cemetery
Dec. 26	Ellen Cecile Page		St. George's Yard
1860			
Jan. 29	John Webber	3 m.	" " "
30	Frederick V. Skinner	16 m.	" " "
Feb. 10	William Jones	4 m.	" " "
"	Mary Ella Gilbert	4 y.	" " "
17	Jay Cady Freeman	6 m.	Vale Cemetery
22	Henry Stevens	2 y.	" "
April 4	Mary Hearsey	83 y.	St. George's Yard
8	Mary Frances Brignall	8 y.	
April 9	William C. Rogers	29 y.	Vale Cemetery
May 8	Robert Fuller	22 y.	St. George's Yard
10	Margaret Mechlin	52 y.	Canajoharie
June 4	Annie Sacia	16 y.	Canajoharie
21	Melissa Seymour	53 y.	Presbyterian Yard
Sep. 14	Charles Winkler	3 y.	St. George's Yard
25	Sophia Winkler	6 m.	" " "
26	Irving Stevens		Vale Cemetery

Figure 6.20   Document Recognition 17

years, 4 montns anu
ceased was born in
March 29, 1831. A
its removed to Lewis-
ed there and in Au-
20 years of age; was
burn common schools
ademy. He came to
1, and entered into
Salmon Falls Mfg.Co.,
f the weaving for 24
1881. In 1882 he be-
ith the Rollinsford
Salmon Falls Bank, as
asurer and cashier, of

he has been trustee
he past 25 years; was
house of representa-
64; selectman in 1883-
r at the annual town
y years. The follow-
isters survive him. –
., Augusta, Me.; Wm.
ill; E. G. Wood, Bos-
Wood, Boston, and
Wood of this place.
occur Friday, the Rev.
fficiating, after which
be taken to Auburn for
deceased was a man
and respected by all

l board, selectman, representative and
member of the last constitutional
ntion held at Concord. He was a
er of Granite Lodge, A. F. and A. M.,
as also a prominent member of the
regational society. He was for many
connected with the Salmon Falls Mfg.
ing been overseer of the weaving
on leaving the mill, he went into the
sford Savings Bank. His health has
gradually falling for three or four
and for the last two years he has
unable to engage in active business.
s a much respected citizen, and his
will be deeply regretted by a large
of relatives and friends.

Obituary.   1890

MRS. C. F. WOOD.—Died, March 25, Mrs. Charles F. Wood of Salmon Falls. By the death of Mrs. Wood the community in which she lived, and all to whom she was known, have sustained a severe loss. She combined in herself an harmonious proportion of qualities which made her influence exceedingly valuable. Her Christian character led to a consecration of purpose, a singleness of aim, which were felt in all she said and did. Her interest in the Church of Christ, and in the spiritual welfare of those around her, led her to be active, prompt, vigilant in religious service of any kind, in the regular attendance on all appointed gatherings for worship, in the Sunday-school, in all those means by which a small parish finds it necessary to add to the resources of the society, and, above all, to the cultivation of fraternal, social intercourse and good feeling. Mrs. Wood was never intrusive or aggressive in her methods; but when it was best for her to lead on any desired occasion she did it simply, kindly, gracefully, being still more willing to yield to others if the object could be equally served, and interested in every good suggestion which came from other sources. There was an innate refinement of feeling and sense of propriety which pervaded, like an atmosphere, her Christian activity, making it acceptable and welcome. To the church to which her constant aid and unfaltering loyalty have been so long essential, and in which her efficient, discreet and kindly influence has been so much enjoyed, her loss is very sad. But her memory is gratefully cherished, making her Christian faith and life still an

Figure 6.21   Document Recognition 18

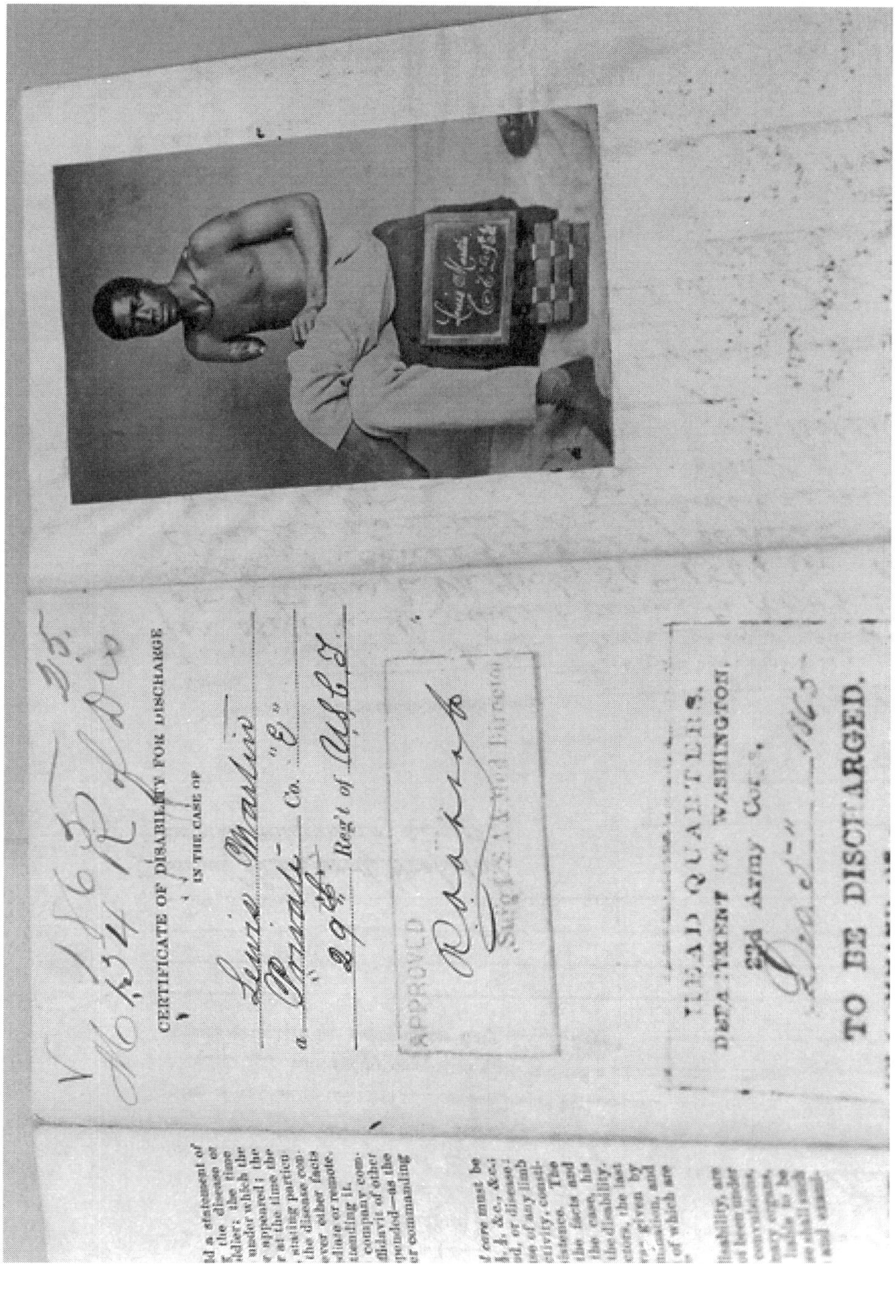

Figure 6.22   Document Recognition 19

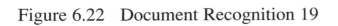

Figure 6.23   Document Recognition 20

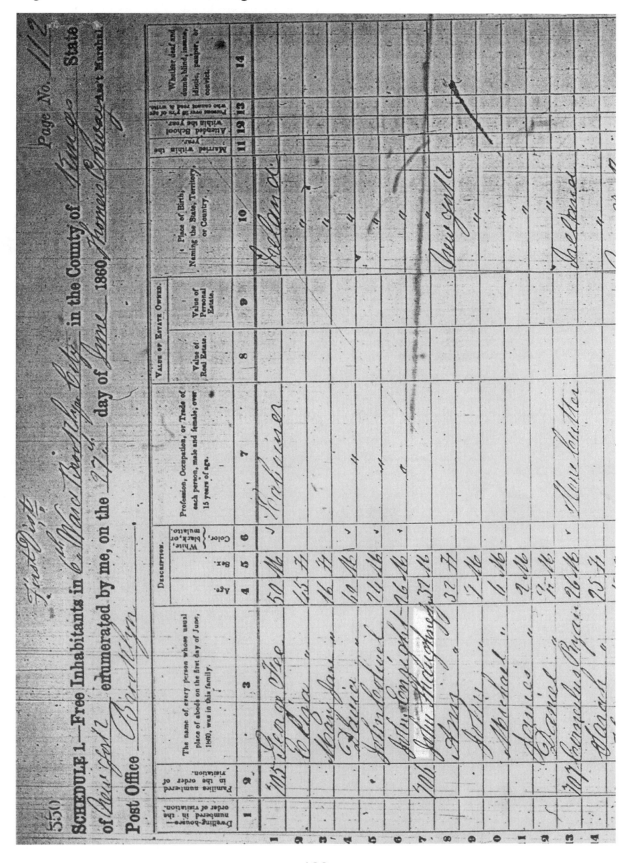

Assignment 5: Document Transcription

Transcribe one of the following documents (Figures 6.24-6.27b)

Figure 6.24   Document Transcription 1

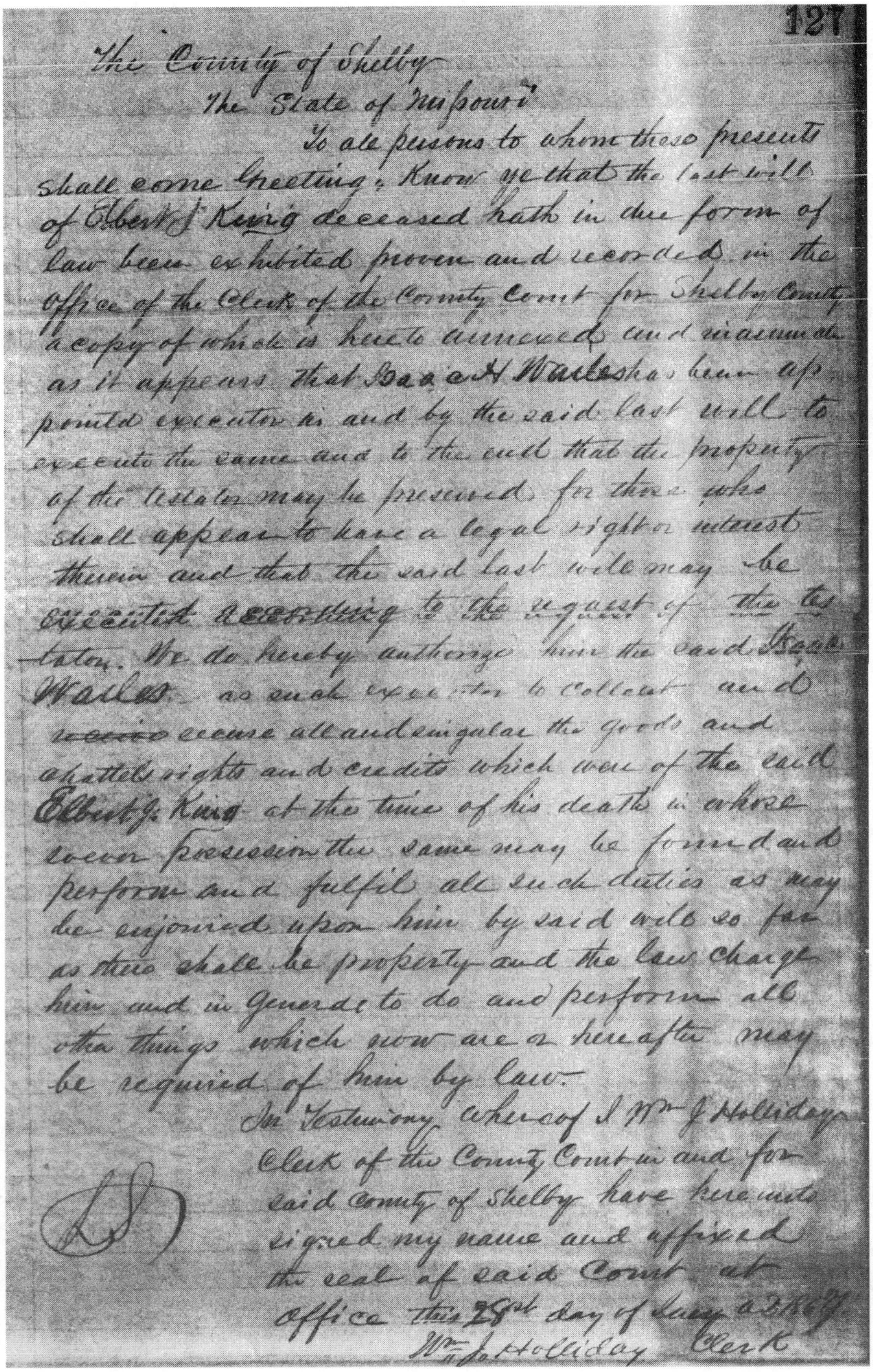

127

The County of Shelby
The State of Missouri
To all persons to whom these presents
shall come Greeting, Know ye that the last will
of Elbert J King deceased hath in due form of
law been exhibited proven and recorded in the
Office of the Clerk of the County Court for Shelby County
a copy of which is hereto annexed and inasmuch
as it appears that Isaac H Wailes has been ap
pointed executor in and by the said last will to
execute the same and to the end that the property
of the testator may be preserved for those who
shall appear to have a legal right or interest
therein and that the said last will may be
executed according to the request of the tes
tator. We do hereby authorize him the said Isaac
Wailes as such executor to collect and
secure all and singular the goods and
chattels rights and credits which were of the said
Elbert J. King at the time of his death in whose
soever possession the same may be found and
perform and fulfil all such duties as may
be enjoined upon him by said will so far
as there shall be property and the law charge
him and in general to do and perform all
other things which now are or hereafter may
be required of him by law.
In Testimony whereof I Wm J Holliday
Clerk of the County Court in and for
said County of Shelby have hereunto
signed my name and affixed
the seal of said Court at
office this 28th day of Jany AD 1867
(LS)
Wm J Holliday Clerk

Figure 6.25   Document Transcription 2

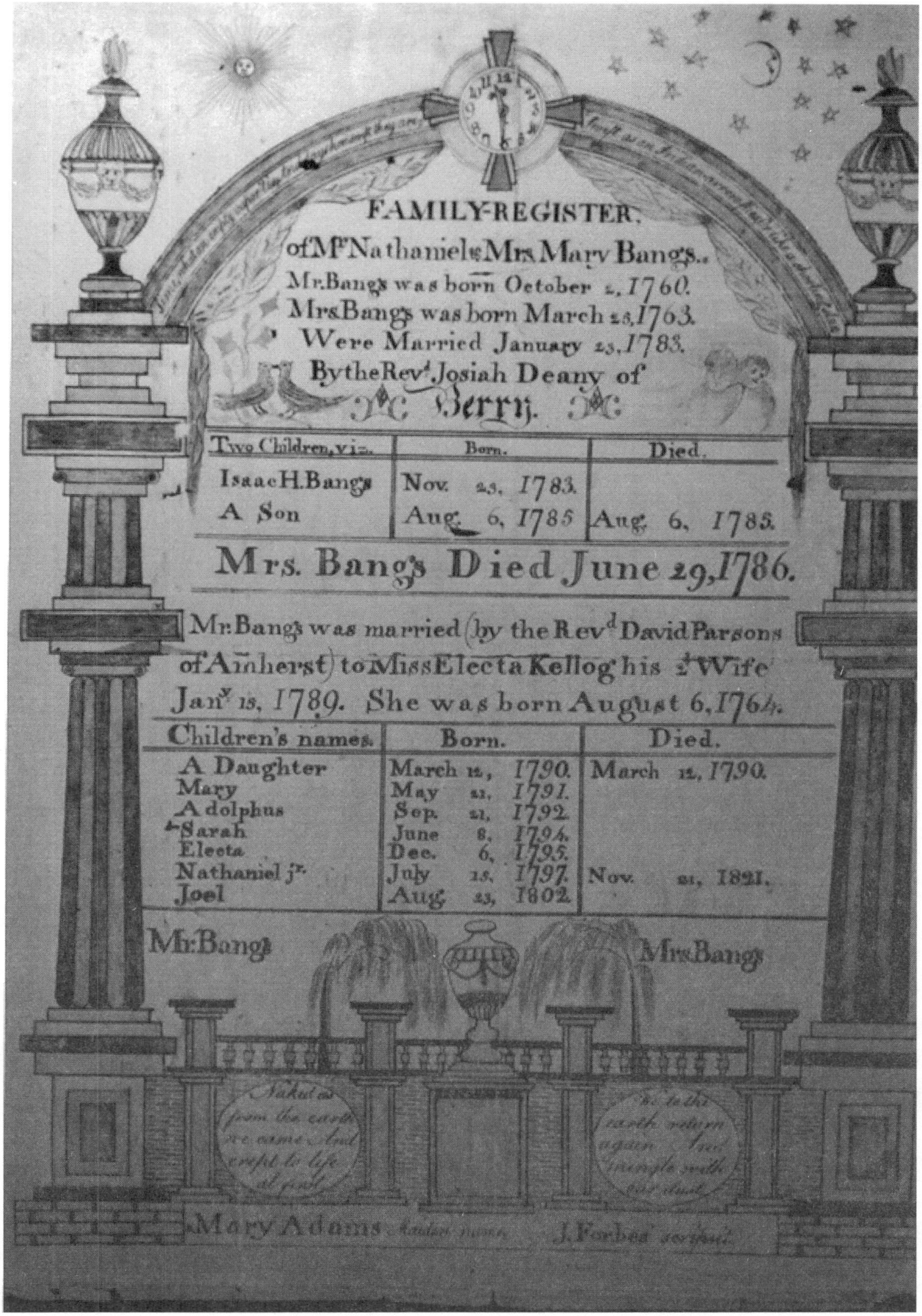

Figure 6.26   Document Transcription 3

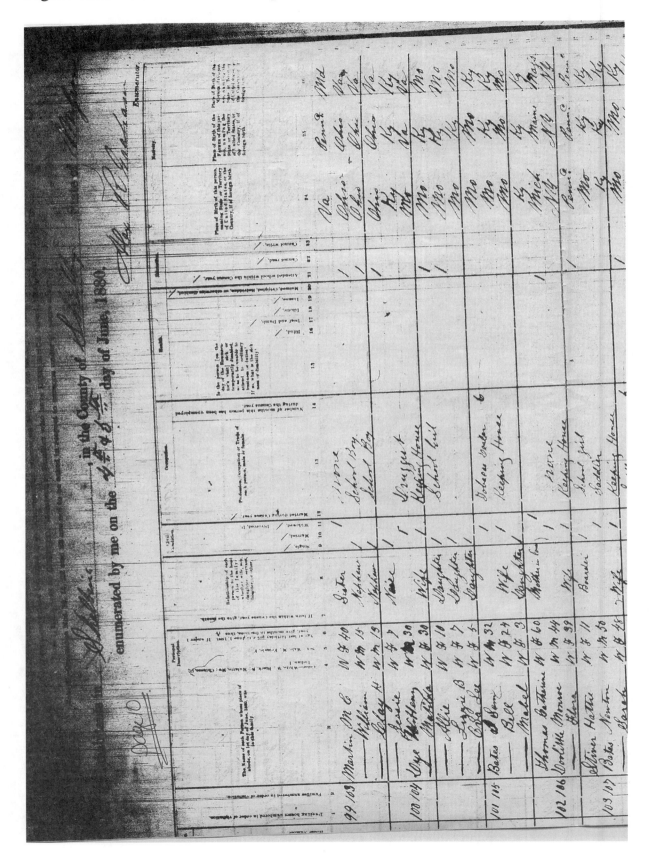

Figure 6.27a   Document Transcription 4

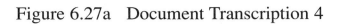

Figure 6.27b   Document Transcription 4 (second page)

Figure 6.28   Research Log of a Student Under Pressure Using Eastern States Sources in a Test Situation

[This is a sample of sources selected by a student doing one of the story problems in this chapter. She has done an excellent job searching the major genealogical collections, military indexes, and compiled genealogies.]

Figure 6.28   Research Log (second page)

[This same student has now finished her analysis of previous research on this family and has moved to original records on the family itself.]

Research Log

Ancestor's name

Lewis Humphreys

Objective(s)

Locality: *NJ*

Date of search	Location/ call number	Description of source (Author, title, year, pages)	Comments (Purpose of search, results, years and names searched)	Doc. number
	848735	grantor deed index 1785–1901 Cumberland cos NJ corres list of flms	determine possible land ownership "order system difficult	
	0854577 it. 4	Cumberland Co. 1804–1818 Surrogate ct. Admins + guardianships Index of wills, inventories etc in the office of the Secy of State prior to 1901	Administration Book A Not avail SF FHL V. 1 p. 271–327	nil
	973 DZhe 1969	Hinshaw, William Wade Encyclopedia of American Quaker Genealogy	V. 2 (NJ)	
	974.9 K28L	(Hinshaw) NJ Quaker Mtg Records	not searched	
	2194 – 2197	(NJ) Hinshaw Index to Quaker Mtg Records Swarthmore College	" "	
		OH Warren Co. Washington twp	no records	
	977.1763 H2h index searched	OH Warren Co. Hist. index	copy p. 692, 701, 859	
	974.994 X2j 1800	NJ 1800 NJ 1800 Cumberland county census index	no Humphries— any spelling	
	974.9 B2qe index	Nissen, Mrs. Carl Index to NJ Genesis, 1953–1971	nil Lewis, James Humphreys etc.	
	974.9 B2g	Stryker-Rodda, Kenn Index to the Genealogical Magazine of New Jersey (1st 30 volumes) Vol. 1 – index to first 30 volumes Vol. 3 " Vol 4 "	Humphries etc. James 24:84 – not relevant nil Lewis nil Vols. 31–40 " Vols 41–50 " indexes	
	974.9 M2n	Norton, James New Jersey in 1793 aged 18 and 45 between	males nil	
	896945	p. 903 Comly, George N. Comly Family from England's will	Analysis of the Walter Humphries family of Burlington NJ who was a Quaker America. Phil. J.B. Lippincott Co. Phil 1939 dated 26 Nov 1698. He left son Joshua	

the lineis is not carried down further

146

Figure 6.29 Report of a Student Using Eastern States Sources in a Test Situation

[This is a sample of sources selected by a student doing one of the story problems in this chapter. She has done an excellent job searching the major genealogical collections, military indexes, and compiled genealogies.]

REPORT ON LEWIS HUMPHREYS FAMILY

The goal of this research is to confirm family details on Lewis Humphreys, born about 1750, possibly in NH or MD who married in 1782 Elizabeth, born about 1751. Lewis died 4 Mar 1805 at Greenwich, Cumberland in New Jersey. Lewis and Elizabeth had a son Jones Humphreys, born on May 26th 1792, in Cumberland Co. New Jersey who married on the 29th of March 1813 at Bridgeton, Cumberland Co., and who died February 9th 1879 in WA Twp., Warren Co., Ohio. The birthplace of Lewis Humphreys is particularly sought.

No birth or christening for Lewis or James Humphreys appeared in New Jersey in a search of the International Genealogical Index (IGI), a date base containing millions of individuals found in primary and secondary sources. In fact, the Humphreys name did not show up in the 161 in any context in Cumberland County, New Jersey in this time period. It should be noted that the surname is variously spelled Humphreys, Humphrys, and Humphries and that occurrences of the name without the terminal s might refer to the same family. We checked all spellings.

We next searched various printed sources which index NJ genealogical records with a statewide scope. These included: *The New Jersey Family Index* which covers compiled genealogies, books and periodicals. One possible source in vol. 51:5-10 of the *"Genealogical Magazine of NJ"* was not on the shelf. In a *New Jersey Biographical Index: Covering some 100,000 Biographies,* there was no James or Lewis although some 19th century Humphreys appear. *The Index to Military Men of NJ 1775-1815* included six men who served in the Revolutionary war time period, two from the War of 1812, and one from 1791 had no Lewis. *The New Jersey Marriage Records 1689-1890* confirmed the inventory of Lewis Humphries, Cumberland Co. 1805 and NJ Tax Lists 1772-1822 showed that Lewis was taxed on the June-August list in 1803.

Following through with the above information, we checked the Cumberland county deeds index, grantors, 1785-1901 and the Surrogate Court index to administrations and guardianships but found no Lewis Humphreys in either of them. If Lewis did not own land, his name would not be among deeds.   Likewise if he had no real property, he might not appear be in guardianship records even though his son James Humphreys was a minor in 1805.

Returning to military records, Lewis was purportedly of an age, appropriate for service in the Revolutionary War. However, a search of the *Index to Revolutionary War Service Records* found no record of him. A Lewis Humphreys served in the 5th South Carolina Regiment, and we will return to him later. *New Jersey in 1793*, used as a substitute for the missing 1790 census, includes the names of men between the ages of 18 and 45 who appeared on Military lists. Lewis Humphreys is not included, but since he is believed to have been born about 1750, he may have been over 45 years of age.

Since Lewis Humphreys apparently was not involved in military service it seemed possible that the family might be Quakers. William Wade Hershaw's *Encyclopedia of American Quaker Genealogy* provides a fairly comprehensive index to people of the Quaker persuasion Humphries are well represented in volume in which covers several southeastern PA and NJ meetings. The only mention of the given name Lewis is to a James Lewis Humphreys in the Philadelphia Monthly Meeting records of 1790. This does not seem to be the Lewis in question, but the family might have had Quaker background.

There are several genealogical collections which cover NJ people and which have been indexed. Charles Garner was a well known genealogist whose work focused on Northwestern NJ. Although several Humphreys families of the late seventeenth and early eighteenth centuries appear in his records, none involved later families.

Two additional collections, those of John Dornan and Gilbert Cope, pertain to Quaker families. Mr. Copes work focused on PA and included some Philadelphia and Humphreys but none form South Jersey, Although Mr. Dornan's records center on New Jersey, the Lewis Humphreys family is not mentioned. In fact, the only Humphreys is one Cornelius with CT, NY and PA connections.

As mentioned on page 2, a Lewis Humphreys served from South Carolina in the Revolutionary War. We searched the AIS census indexes for 1790, 1800, and 1810 and found a Lewis Humphries in Spartansburg District of SC (p 185) in 1810. This would indicate that he remained in South Carolina and is not related to your Lewis. Lewis Humphreys appearance on the 1803 Cumberland Co. New Jersey tax list is included.

It is important to note that 1790, 1800, 1810, and 1820 federal census records for New Jersey do not exist. The one exception is the 1800 census for Cumberland Co. New Jersey, but Humphreys is not there. Census records have enormous value as a finding and locating aid and are extremely important in research. The absence of those critical records for the time period in which we should find Lewis is most regrettable. However, since he appears in no other states index for 1790 or 1800, it may indicate that he was living in some county in New Jersey other than Cumberland.

Several New Jersey genealogical societies publish journals which encompass a wide variety of genealogical records and materials. Kenn Strykker Rodda has indexed volumes 1-50 of the Genealogical Magazine of New Jersey, published by the Genealogical Society of New Jersey, Lewis Humphreys' name does not appear here nor in the index to New Jersey Genesis, another publication.

Turning finally to the *History of Warren County Ohio*, there are two sketches concerning James Humphreys and his son William. Although county history sketches are sometimes inaccurate, they often provide valuable clues for further research. In this case (p. 692) the author states that James Humphreys was <u>born on the Delaware River</u> 26 May 1792 and migrated to Ohio in 1815. He was both a farmer and a boatman. His occupation as a boatman may be significant because he came from an area of New Jersey which lies on the mouth of the Delaware River. Virtually the Atlantic Ocean. His ancestors may have been maritime people.

The discussion is somewhat confusing as it is not clear which man married "thrice". If James had a first wife, Phebe Rose, her family could provide additional clues. It is interesting to note that James apparently had a son Lewis, probably named for his grandfather. A further brief check of the IGI presented other connections among the families in OH.

In summary, we checked a vast number of sources covering all aspects of NJ records from the county through the state and national levels. Lewis Humphrey's name appears only on an 1803 tax record and a record of the inventory taken at the time of his death. The lack of 1790 and 1800 NJ census records is a significant hindrance to locating him further as it appears that he was Cumberland county only briefly. Since he did not serve in the Revolutionary war, he may have been a Quaker but the lack of service is by no means conclusive evidence. Records of his descendants in OH seemed to be plentiful.

We would make the following suggestions for further research.

1. Obtain a copy of the 1805 inventory of Lewis Humphreys

2. Seek a death record for James in OH to confirm the maiden name of his mother.

3. Ascertain the religious affiliation of the family and search denomination records.

4. Pursue compiled genealogies. Although a search of the holdings of the family history library indicates no book on the Humphreys in NJ, there are some 30 books covering various Humphreys in other states.

5. Engage a researcher who is knowledgeable in Southwest Jersey records to pursue the family there. For example, there may be a Cumberland county repository which holds special indexes to local records.

Instructor's Analysis

This was a good report. The goal was clearly stated up front. Reasoning for searching the various record groups was stated including an explanation of the spelling variations. Major state-wide collections were searched and the results were reported. When the individual did not appear in a particular record group, the student explained why, and what other records should be searched next.

A wide variety of record types were searched including the IGI, land and property, compiled genealogies, military records, church records, biographical indexes, federal census records, county histories, etc. Good suggestions were given for further research possibilities.

This student completed this project in four hours. If the researcher had had more time, a study of the historical background of the area could have led to other states and their records.

Student Project

On the next five pages, another student took on a project assigned for a two-hour period. This student was given the pedigree chart in figure 6.31 with the instructions to select a goal and to proceed. The student was given this clue: there were family traditions that Henrietta's father was from Canada, which was verified on the 1880 census.

The student first searched the 1880 census to determine exactly what clues were given (see figure 6.32). This was another good report. The student's report was concise and showed a knowledge of basic record types. The student spent much of her time typing the information neatly onto research logs and abstracts so she was not able to do as much research as she would have liked, but her reports looked very professional. One can clearly see what was done and not done in her work. This points out an important aspect in our research. We must allow enough time to compose a good report with supporting abstracted materials for our client.

Figure 6.30 Student Four-Generation Pedigree Chart Indicating Research Goal

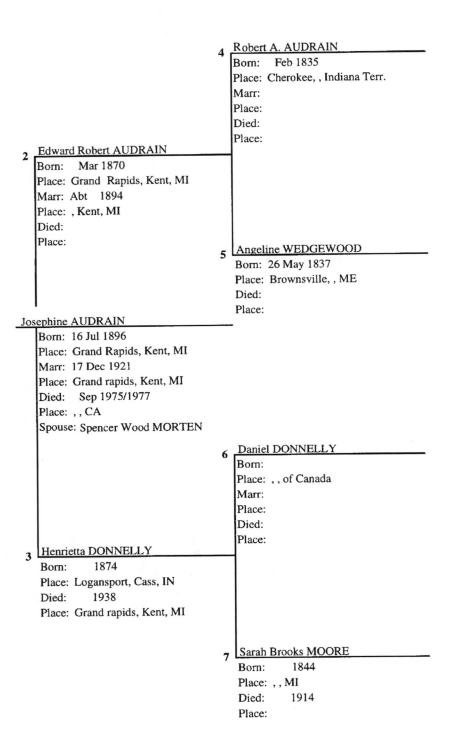

4 Robert A. AUDRAIN
Born: Feb 1835
Place: Cherokee, , Indiana Terr.
Marr:
Place:
Died:
Place:

2 Edward Robert AUDRAIN
Born: Mar 1870
Place: Grand Rapids, Kent, MI
Marr: Abt   1894
Place: , Kent, MI
Died:
Place:

5 Angeline WEDGEWOOD
Born: 26 May 1837
Place: Brownsville, , ME
Died:
Place:

Josephine AUDRAIN
Born: 16 Jul 1896
Place: Grand Rapids, Kent, MI
Marr: 17 Dec 1921
Place: Grand rapids, Kent, MI
Died: Sep 1975/1977
Place: , , CA
Spouse: Spencer Wood MORTEN

6 Daniel DONNELLY
Born:
Place: , , of Canada
Marr:
Place:
Died:
Place:

3 Henrietta DONNELLY
Born: 1874
Place: Logansport, Cass, IN
Died: 1938
Place: Grand rapids, Kent, MI

7 Sarah Brooks MOORE
Born: 1844
Place: , , MI
Died: 1914
Place:

Figure 6.31 Student 1880 U.S. Census Transcription

1880 Census—United States

Family History Department

State	Michigan
County	Kent
Date	9 June 1880
Enumeration district number	135
Town/Township	City of Grand Rapids
Sheet number	257 B
Page number	28
Microfilm roll number	1,254,588

Page	Dwelling number	Family number	Names	Color	Sex	Age prior to June 1	Month of birth in census year	Relationship to head of house	Single	Married	Widowed	Divorced	Married in census year	Occupation	Other information	Can't read or write	Place of birth	Place of birth of father	Place of birth of mother	Enumeration date
28		222 277	Dunn, Susan	W	F	56			1		1			Washer Woman			Ire	Ire	Ire	
			Joseph	W	M	16		Son	1					Laborer			Mich	Ire	Ire	
	222	278	Irwin, William H.	W	M	39				1			1	Farmer			Mich	NY	Canada	
	222	279	Sarah	W	F	36		Wife		1			1	Keeping House			Mich	NY	Canada	
			Emma	W	F	2		Dau	1								NY	M	NY	
			Donnelly, Nettie	W	F	5		Step Dau	1								Ind	Can	Mich	
	[?]	[?]	Brown, Henry	W	M	32				1				House Painter			Mich	Ire	Ire	
			Lyda A.	W	F	88		Wife		1				Keeps House			New York	Mass	Mass	

Figure 6.32 Student Research Report on Ancestry of Henrietta Donnelly

---

Research Report
Ancestry of Henrietta Donnelly

16 July 1997

The focus of this research session was to learn more about the family of Henrietta Donnelly. The 1880 Census had been searched previously for this family, but since the extract was not available to provide needed information, the citation was looked up. The enumeration district number had been given as 185, but the actual entry was located in enumeration district 135. At this time, Henrietta was living with her mother and step father, William M. Irwin. Indication was given that Sarah and William had been married within the census year. An attempt was made to locate this family in the 1900 census to gather more information about the family structure, but no entry was found for William or Sarah Irwin.

The Indiana Biographical Index was searched to see if a biography of Daniel Donnelly had been written and included in a county history of the area. An entry was located for Daniel P. Doney, but the reference clearly referred to a different individual. No other entries were found.

The Kent County, Michigan marriage indexes were searched next to locate the marriage record of Sarah Donnelly and William Irwin. The only entry for Sarah Donnelly showed a marriage to Henry Langley. Since it was possible that this could have been another marriage of Sarah, the indexes were searched for a Sarah Langley or Donnelly to William Irwin. No entry was found for this marriage.

More information is needed about Henrietta's father and mother. It is recommended that the death certificate for Henrietta be requested from the state of Michigan. Also, more time is needed to search for the family of Daniel and Sarah Donnelly in the 1870 census of Cass County, Indiana. This census is not indexed and will require more time to locate this family. There was also a state census taken in Indiana in 1877 that might be helpful in locating this family. Another recommended search would be to look through the county histories of Cass county to see if the Donnellys are mentioned in the history or biographies of the area. There are also several more statewide indexes that might be helpful in locating this family. The marriage records of Cass County, Indiana could also be searched for the marriage of Daniel and Sarah.

Figure 6.33 Student Research Log on Donnelly Family

```
                        Donnelly Family Research Log

Date          Call Number     Description of Source                      Results
7/16/97       FHL             1880 Census of Kent County, Michigan
              #1,254,588      searched for Henrietta Donnelly's family      1

7/16/97       FHL             1900 Michigan Soundex (I-650)
              #1,245,029      searched for William M. Irwin
                                [searced W. M., Willy, William, William M.]  Nil
                              searched for Sarah Irwin                       Nil

7/16/97       FHL             Indiana Biographical Index
              #6331353        searched for Daniel Donnelly                   2
                                [searched Donely, Donley, Donly, Donnelly]

7/16/97       FHL             History of Northeast Indiana, vol. 2, ed. by Ira
              US/CAN            Ford, Chicago, IL:1920.
              977.27          searched for Daniel P. Doney                   Nil
              H2f               [not Daniel Donnelly, husband of Sarah Brooks
              v. 2              Moore]

7/16/97       FHL             Kent County, Michigan Marriage Index, A-D
              #1,377,934        1842-1926
              item 1          searched for Sarah Donnelly                    3
                              searched for Nettie Donnelly                   3
              item 2          E-J
                              searched for William Irwin                     4
              item 2          K-Mc
                              searched for Henry Langley                     5
                              searched for Sarah Langley                     Nil
```

Figure 6.34 Student Listing of Indexed Information

Indiana Biographical Index
FHL #6331353

Doney, Daniel P.   IN0003   Vol. 2   p. 219

IN003   Ford, Ira, ed. <u>History of Northeast Indiana</u>, Chicago, IL:1920

Marriage Index A-D
Kent County, Michigan
1842-1926
(FHL #1,377,934 item 1)

<u>page 181</u>

Donely, Sarah - Henry Langley   Book 6   Page or No. 182

Donnelly, Nettie - E. R. Audrain   Book 11   Page or No. 58

Marriage Index E-J
Kent County, Michigan
1842-1926
(FHL #1,377,934 item 2)

<u>page 166</u>

Irwin, William F. - Sarah J. Thomas   Book 6   Page or No. 173
Irwin, William - Carrie W. Worden   Book 11   Page or No. 20
Irwin, Will - Ethel De Man   Book 15   Page or No. 243
Irwin, Wm. - Catherine Henry   Book 17   Page or No. 51
Irwin, William H. Jr. - I. Kuemerle   Book 19   Page or No. 22

Document Recognition Answers

1. County land plat from Alabama.

2. Civil registration certificate from Hoo, Kent, England, for 1838

3. Warranty deed with relinquishment of Dower for Hempstead County, Arkansas, in 1895

4. New Jersey Revolutionary War Service Record

5. Civil War Widows Pension

6. Marriage license for Hempstead, Arkansas, for 1903

7. Bibliography of genealogies from the Library of Congress

8. Testimony of Claimant, Homestead Application Packet

9. Land Warrant

10. New York Ship Passenger List

11. Land plat for Minnesota, Otter-Tail County, of Finnish settlers

12. German baptismal record in 1894

13. A state history of Idaho

14. Surname histories as part of a county history

15. Biographical histories of Lancaster County, Pennsylvania

16. Death and burial records

17. An 1890 newspaper obituary

18. A Civil War Union army military disability discharge paper

19. A letter to President Lincoln and his response in 1865

20. An 1860 census page from Brooklyn, Kings County, New York

Suggested Readings

Amundson, Margaret. "Rebutting Direct Evidence with Indirect Evidence: The Identity of Sarah (Taliaferro) Lewis of Virginia." *National Genealogical Society Quarterly 87*, no. 3 (1999): 217-240.

Clifford, Karen. "Documentation and Evaluation of Evidence." Breaking Through Brick Walls; UGA Conference, 16-17 April 1999; Salt Lake City, Utah, S-98. (May be ordered from Repeat Performance, 2911 Crabapple Lane, Hobart, IN 46342, session S-98.)

Humphrey, John T. "Reconstructing Families on the Colonial Frontier." *Meet Me In St. Louis; Federation of Genealogical Societies and St. Louis Genealogical Society, 11-14 August 1999*; St. Louis, Missouri, T-75. (May be ordered from Repeat

Performance, 2911 Crabapple Lane, Hobart, IN 46342, session T-75.)

Jones, Thomas W. "Going Beyond the Bare Bones: Reconstructing Your Ancestors' Lives." *Meet Me In St. Louis; Federation of Genealogical Societies and St. Louis Genealogical Society, 11-14 August 1999*; St. Louis, Missouri, T-74. (May be ordered from Repeat Performance, 2911 Crabapple Lane, Hobart, IN 46342, session T-74.)

Leary, Helen F. M. "Resolving Conflicts in Direct Evidence: Identity and Vital Dates of Mary Kittrell." *National Genealogical Society Quarterly 87*, no. 3 (1999): 199-205.

Leary, Helen F. M. "Using the Analytical Method to Define the Problem and Direct Our Search." *Meet Me In St. Louis; Federation of Genealogical Societies and St. Louis Genealogical Society, 11-14 August 1999*; St. Louis, Missouri, T-49. (May be ordered from Repeat Performance, 2911 Crabapple Lane, Hobart, IN 46342, session T-49.)

Myers, Marya. "Discovering Identity through Indirect Evidence: Elizabeth James of Bristol, Rhode Island." *National Genealogical Society Quarterly 87*, no. 3 (1999): 206-216.

Rose, Christine. "What Is 'the Preponderance of the Evidence'"? *National Genealogical Society Quarterly* 83 (March 1995): 5.

Sherrill, Charles A. "Analysis of a Court Case File." *Meet Me In St. Louis; Federation of Genealogical Societies and St. Louis Genealogical Society, 11-14 August 1999*; St. Louis, Missouri, T-60. (May be ordered from Repeat Performance, 2911 Crabapple Lane, Hobart, IN 46342, session T 60.)

Preparing Research Guides

Personal Research Guides

In addition to teaching, I incorporated by sole proprietorship into a corporation a few years ago. I discovered the value of putting together my own study guides for each state where I do research to help me save time. Since the examinations you take, either through the FHL or BCG, are, in essence, open-book examinations, these guides can be very helpful in your exam, but more importantly in your personal research and your own business.

I have continually added to these guides throughout the years and it is amazing how large they have become. I use these book-size compilations for each state constantly as ready references. Even if you are not the enthusiast that I am on genealogy, you should at least put together a notebook of the various research guides provided by the different national organizations.

I have found the following information summaries essential for my own notebooks:

1. Topography, geography, and riverways of the area

2. Historical background of the area

3. Prevailing customs in a particular area and during a specific time period

4. Languages used and key genealogical terms in those languages

5. Paleography tips

6. Sources available for the area

7. Repositories or large data bases available

8. Periodicals dealing with the area

9. Methods of using the sources of the area

Other Useful Topics

Other items that I've found helpful in my research are included below. You may wish to add these to your reference notebooks.

Call Numbers. The state call numbers listed in figure 7.1 for finding printed sources can be very useful when working in the Family History Library or any other library that uses the Dewey Decimal Classification System. When you are there, in a hurry, and already aware of the major published collections, look quickly at this list and then locate the aisle for the state you are interested in. It is helpful to include these numbers with each state guide.

Maps. Historical maps are helpful aids to keep in your state research guide. Check book vendors, used bookstores, publishing companies, etc. for maps pertinent to your area. I have many large binders of early state maps collected over several decades. (Whenever I produced a map for a client, I made a copy for myself.)

Timelines. By placing an individual's life into an historical timeline, related historical events will surface that can lead you to other sources. Therefore, state historical timelines, as well as general timelines, are important to have in your research guide.

Figure 7.1 Sample Dewey Decimal Subject Classifications for North America

970 North America			976.3	Louisiana
971	Canada		976.4	Texas
971.1	British Columbia		976.6	Oklahoma
971.2	Canadian Northwest		976.7	Arkansas
971.3	Ontario		976.8	Tennessee
971.4	Quebec		976.9	Kentucky
971.5	New Brunswick			
971.6	Nova Scotia	**977**	**North Central States**	
		977.1	Ohio	
972	**Mexico**	977.2	Indiana	
		977.3	Illinois	
973	**United States**	977.4	Michigan	
		977.5	Wisconsin	
974	**Northeastern States**	977.6	Minnesota	
974.1	Maine	977.7	Iowa	
974.2	New Hampshire	977.8	Missouri	
974.3	Vermont			
974.4	Massachusetts			
974.5	Rhode Island	**978**	**Western States**	
974.6	Connecticut	978.1	Kansas	
974.7	New York	978.2	Nebraska	
974.8	Pennsylvania	978.3	South Dakota	
974.9	New Jersey	978.4	North Dakota	
		978.6	Montana	
975	**Southeastern States**	978.7	Wyoming	
975.1	Delaware	978.8	Colorado	
975.2	Maryland	978.9	New Mexico	
975.3	District of Columbia			
975.4	West Virginia	**979**	**Far Western States**	
975.5	Virginia	979.1	Arizona	
975.6	North Carolina	979.2	Utah	
975.7	South Carolina	979.3	Nevada	
975.8	Georgia	979.4	California	
975.9	Florida	979.5	Oregon	
		979.6	Idaho	
976	**South Central States**	979.7	Washington	
976.1	Alabama			
976.2	Mississippi			

Preparing a Personal State Guide

An example of the types of materials I gather for my individual research guides, "The State of Delaware—An Abbreviated Personal State Guide," begins on page 179.

In this example, I purposely selected a state where I am neither accredited nor certified. Thus, it should reflect a newcomer's perspective. As I found new sources and entered them in my guide, different impressions would come to me as to how those sources would be used in research. I've made tips for you in the margins so you will see what I was thinking about.

Later these insights will help me to locate new sources and provide faster techniques for accomplishing the necessary work. Following this pattern, you'll be able to put together the basic sources and methods of research for the states you are interested in studying.

Library Guides

Libraries and other repositories produce guides to their collections. The Family History Library produces the *SourceGuide* with research outlines as mentioned previously in this book. The National Genealogical Society also produces manuals. I place those I have found most helpful in my personal state research guides.

Guides produced by libraries and repositories throughout the United States usually provide information concerning hours of operation, phone numbers, location, and the extent of their collection. Samples can be found in figures 7.2, 7.3, 7.4, and 7.5. These guides lead you to relevant sources.

Figure 7.2 University of North Carolina at Chapel Hill Library Guide for the Louis Round Wilson Library Reprinted by permission from the University of North Carolina at Chapel Hill, Louis Round Wilson Library.

THE UNIVERSITY OF NORTH CAROLINA AT CHAPEL HILL

LIBRARY GUIDE

Louis Round Wilson Library

Louis Round Wilson Library opened in 1929 and served as the main campus library for over fifty years. After three years of extensive renovation, Wilson Library reopened on August 17, 1987. Now it houses four special collections: the Manuscripts Department (including the Southern Historical Collection and the University Archives), the Maps Collection, the North Carolina Collection (including the North Carolina Collection Gallery), and the Rare Book Collection. Also in Wilson Library are the Photographic Services Section and the office of the Associate University Librarian for the Special Collections (962-0114). The collections contain over 300,000 books, 12,000,000 manuscripts, 500,000 photographs, and 200,000 maps.

WILSON LIBRARY HOURS

Monday-Friday   8:00 AM to 5:00 PM

Saturday   9:00 AM to 1:00 PM
Manuscripts Department
North Carolina Collection
Rare Book Collection

Sunday   1:00 PM to 5:00 PM
North Carolina Collection

North Carolina Collection Gallery
Monday-Friday   9:00 AM to 1:00 PM

CLOSED UNIVERSITY HOLIDAYS

MANUSCRIPTS DEPARTMENT
Fourth Floor   962-1345

The Manuscripts Department acquires, preserves, and services the majority of the manuscripts in the campus library system, organizing them in four major components. The **Southern Historical Collection**, the largest component, is a center for research in Southern history. It contains letters, business papers, legal documents, diaries, plantation journals, photographs, oral history tapes and transcripts, and other documents accumulated by individuals, families, and institutions in North Carolina and other southern states. The **University Archives** preserves the unpublished records of the University from its founding and contains manuscript minutes of the Board of Trustees and Faculty, student records, correspondence, and other non-current records of University officials. **General and Literary Manuscripts** includes a variety of materials from states outside the South, several groups of English literary manuscripts, and one large collection of family papers from Popayan, Colombia. The **Southern Folklife Collection** was established as a component of the department in 1986 through the combination of Folk Music Collection created by faculty members of the Curriculum in Folklore and the John Edwards Memorial Collection, acquired by the University in 1983. It holds approximately 42,000 sound recordings of traditional southern music and other source materials for the study of Southern folklore.

Figure 7.2 University of North Carolina at Chapel Hill Library Guide for the Louis Round Wilson Library (continued). Reprinted by permission from the University of North Carolina at Chapel Hill, Louis Round Wilson Library.

MAPS COLLECTION
First Floor   962-3028

The Maps Collection offers the principal map reference service for the campus library system. It also provides research assistance for map materials and instruction in the use and reading of maps. The Maps Collection files serve as a guide to the collection, to maps and atlases found in Davis and the departmental libraries, and to map materials in general. The Collection contains sheet maps for all world areas, covering a range of topics that includes topography, demography, administrative divisions, and history. There is a good collection of U.S. historical maps, especially of the Southern states. The atlas collection contains general, national, regional, city, and historical and other topical atlases. Other volumes in the Maps Collection include gazetteers and geographical dictionaries, bibliographies, cartographical reference volumes, catalogs of map collections and map publishers, and map depository publications.

NORTH CAROLINA COLLECTION
Second Floor   962-1172

The North Carolina Collection preserves an incomparable collection of materials about North Carolina and by North Carolinians. Here are housed not only books and pamphlets but also publications and reports of governmental agencies, businesses, religious bodies, and professional organizations. Other items include newspapers and periodicals, scrapbooks, textbooks, broadsides, maps, pictures, recordings, microforms, and both subject and biographical newspaper clippings. The North Carolina Collection also serves as a repository for printed materials issued by the University, and collects and maintains files of departmental publications and reports of various organizations on campus. The archival copies of theses and dissertations are kept in the collection. Among the special collections within the North Carolina Collection are the Thomas Wolfe Collection, consisting of manuscripts and published works by and about Wolfe, and the Sir Walter Raleigh Collection of materials relating to English efforts to colonize North America. The **North Carolina Collection Gallery** (East Wing) features both permanent and changing exhibits of textual materials as well as the Collection's historic furnishings, art works, artifacts, and keepsakes.

RARE BOOK COLLECTION
Third Floor   962-1143

The Rare Book Collection has over 90,000 printed volumes, 16,000 prints and broadsides, and 1,170 manuscripts, dating from 2,500 B.C. to the present and covering the full range of human knowledge. Materials are selected for the Collection based upon date (before 1800 for European imprints, 1820 for American), fragility, value, and/or subject. The Collection has particularly strong holdings of incunabula, sixteenth-century imprints (most notably the Estienne family of scholar-printers), English literature, French history, and the history of the book. Special subject strengths include Samuel Johnson, Charles Dickens, George Cruikshank, George Bernard Shaw, crime and detection fiction, Sherlock Holmes, Spanish *Cronistas*, Southern history (after 1821), Confederate imprints, nineteenth-century British and American publishing history, World Wars I and II, and Spanish plays.

PHOTOGRAPHIC SERVICES
First Floor   962-1334

The Photographic Services Section provides specialized copying for library patrons. Services include quick copying of book pages, microfilming, copyflo (paper) prints from microfilm, and still photography (negatives, prints, and slides). The photographic archives of the North Carolina Collection are located here and are a useful resource for researchers seeking illustrations.

Figure 7.3   Floor Plan of the Family History Library Obtained Before a Visit

Reprinted by permission. Copyright © 1992 by The Church of Jesus Christ of Latter-day Saints.

Family History Library - Floor Layouts

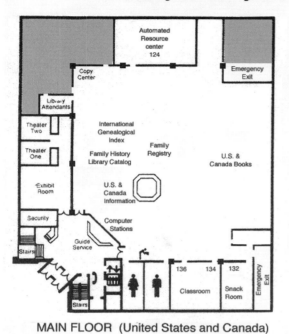

MAIN FLOOR (United States and Canada)

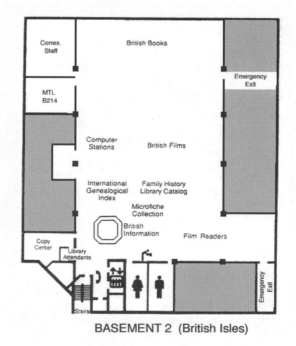

SECOND FLOOR (United States and Canada)

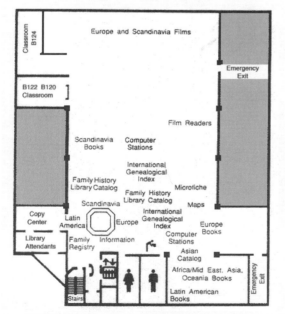

BASEMENT 1 (Europe, Scandinavian, Latin America, and International)

BASEMENT 2 (British Isles)

Figure 7.4 Informational Pamphlet: Genealogical Research at The Library of Virginia. Reprinted by permission from the Library of Virginia, Richmond, Virginia.

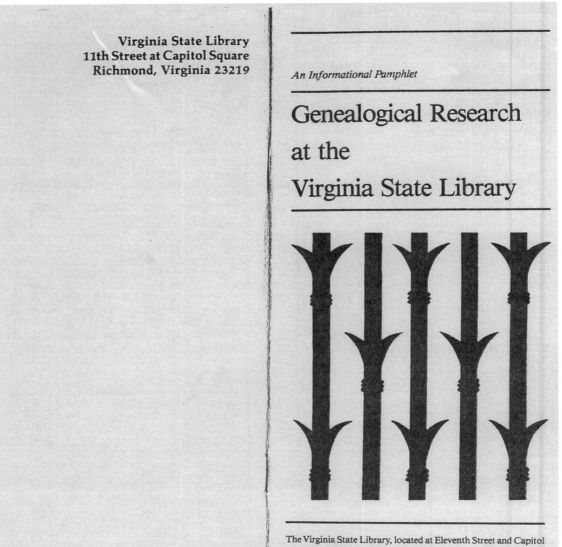

Virginia State Library
11th Street at Capitol Square
Richmond, Virginia 23219

The Virginia State Library's logogram depicts the stylized papyrus design of the brass gates at the main entrance.

An Informational Pamphlet

Genealogical Research at the Virginia State Library

The Virginia State Library, located at Eleventh Street and Capitol Square in Richmond, Virginia, is open to the public between the hours of 8:15 A.M. and 5:00 P.M. from Monday through Saturday, except on legal holidays.

The State of Delaware—An Abbreviated Personal State Guide

STATE	CALL NUMBERS		NATIVE RACES
Delaware	FHL State Call No.	975.1	Lenni Lenape or Delawares
	Kent County	975.14	Algonkian
	New Castle County	975.11	Nanticoke
	Sussex County	975.17	

[In the timeline below, various sources are given in brackets suggesting the genealogical consequences of these historical events.]

Timeline

1609   Henry Hudson, working for the Dutch West India Company of Britain, locates the Delaware River. [**Could lead to a search of the Dutch West India Company records if the ancestor sought after was thought to have lived in this time period.**]

1610   Another English explorer, Samuel Argall, names the area after the governor of Virginia, Lord De La Warr.

1631   Dutch found Zwaanendael colony as part of the Dutch West India Company (near Lewes today). Indians massacre settlers.

1638   Wilmington (then called Fort Christiana) settled by Swedish colonists, first permanent settlement in Delaware; fort is built; area named New Sweden. [Could lead to a search of the early Swedish colonists.]

1651   Peter Stuyvesant, Governor of Dutch New Amsterdam (now New York), builds Fort Casimir on site of New Castle. [Search of Dutch military records.]

1654   Swedes capture Fort Casimir and name it Fort Trinity.

1655   Stuyvesant recaptures Fort Casimir, Swedes surrender to Dutch.

1664   England conquers Dutch American colonies. Delaware part of Duke of York's Province.

1672   War between Dutch & English.

1673   Dutch capture New York and recover colonies.

1674   By the Treaty of Westminster, English regain control.

1682   Delaware granted to William Penn as part of Pennsylvania Province by Duke of York. Called the "Three Lower Counties." Lord Baltimore of Maryland disputes grant. [Early Delaware records, especially court and land, may be in Pennsylvania.]

1701   Delaware is formally separated from Pennsylvania.

1704   Pennsylvania governs but Lower Counties form own assembly.

1763   For next 5 years Mason and Dixon survey Delaware boundaries.

1777   Capital moved from New Castle to Dover. British occupy Wilmington.

1787   Delaware first state to ratify U.S. Constitution.

1802   E. I. du Pont builds first powder mill near Wilmington. [Search Revolutionary War records also in close surrounding states.]

1812   British blockade Delaware River. [Search War of 1812 records.]

1829   Chesapeake and Delaware Canal opened. [Immigrants could have found employment on these canals. Could account for movement throughout the state.]

1861   Delaware refuses to secede from Union but has many Confederate sympathizers. [May need to search Confederate as well as Union records.]

1937   Nylon invented at Wilmington. [Could have resulted in greater job opportunities in Wilmington. If I can't find a person where he's supposed to be, maybe he found work in Wilmington.]

Overview

Tip 82: This information tells me I may want to search the records of Maryland and Virginia if I cannot find someone in Delaware.

Geography and Topography. Delaware, the second smallest state in the United States, lies along the Atlantic seacoast sharing the Delaware Peninsula with parts of Maryland and Virginia. It is a low, flat plain with rolling hills and valleys covering its northern tip. There are two main land regions: the coastal plain and the piedmont.

Tip 83: I'll need an early map of these waterways as land records will most likely mention them. See Map 8.1 which follows.

Waterways. The Delaware River is the largest and most important river linking the Atlantic Ocean with northern Delaware, parts of New York, Pennsylvania, and New Jersey. Appoquinimink Creek and the Smyrna River flow into it. The Christiana River forms Wilmington Harbor. Brandywine Creek is the Christiana's chief tributary. The many streams including the Broadkill, Indian, Mispillion, Murder Kill, and the St. Jones rivers that emptied into the Delaware Bay and the Atlantic Ocean attracted early settlers.

In the southwest, the Nanticoke River flows across Maryland and into the Chesapeake Bay. Ocean ships cross the Delaware Bay to reach the Delaware River and the Rehoboth River. The Indian River bays in southeastern Delaware had great sand reefs. During the War of 1812 a network of canals, highways, and the Delaware River transported Delaware's products to Baltimore, New York, Philadelphia, and Washington, D.C.

Major Industry and Economic Factors. Farm land was very important in the state. It was affected by the weather and the topography. The weather is humid with hot summers and generally mild winters.

Unique Features. Delaware was the only state with counties divided into areas called "hundreds." It was also the only state in which the legislature could amend the state constitution without the approval of the voters.

Historical Background

Early Settlements and Migration Trails

Tip 84: It is not necessary to reiterate every historical event as you begin this activity. The information will grow as your knowledge of the area expands. If you feel weak in a particular area, attend conferences, seminars and classes that focus on those areas of weakness.

The Dutch established the first settlement at Zwaanendael (Lewes today) in 1631, but by 1632 the Indians had massacred the settlers and burned their fort. The two Indian tribes in the area at the arrival of white explorers were the Algonkian and the Nanticoke.

Swedish settlers came in 1638 and founded the colony of New Sweden. They built Fort Christiana at present day Wilmington. New settlers from Sweden and Finland expanded the colony northward. These early Finnish settlers came aboard Swedish ships. Between 1638 and 1655 the Swedes controlled the area.

Between 1655 and 1664 the Dutch took over control of the area, but

Table 7.1 Railroad Distances—1880 Railroad Distances from Baltimore to Wilmington and Other Major Cities

Annapolis MD	.35	Detroit MI	.697
Louisville KY	.716	Philadelphia PA	.98
Boston MA	.421	Fredrick MD	.62
Lynchburg VA	.216	Richmond VA	.170
Charleston SC	.606	Fredericksburg VA	.108
Manassas VA	.72	Sandusky OH	.595
Charlottesville VA	.155	Gettysburg PA	.46
Martinsburg VA	.100	Savannah GA	.716
Chicago IL	.801	Gordonsville VA	.134
Milwaukie WI	.886	St. Louis MO	.920
Cincinnati OH	.580	Hanover PA	.46
Montreal Canada	.586	Washington D.C.	.38
Cleveland OH	.517	Harper's Ferry VA	.81
Nashville TN	.900	Westminster MD	.20
Columbus OH	.512	Harrisburg PA	.85
New Orleans LA	1384	Wilmington DE	.70
Culpeper VA	.107	Indianapolis IN	.700
New York NY	.185	Wilmington NC	.406
Cumberland MD	.178	Lancaster PA	.80
Petersburg VA	.191	York PA	.57

Tip 85: I thought you might enjoy this 1880 Railroad Distances chart. It really brought home to me how close Pennsylvania, Maryland, New Jersey, and Virginia are to Delaware.

in 1664 England captured all of New Netherland including the Delaware region, and ruled it as part of the colony of New York. During this time period, many English people came from the surrounding states of Virginia, Maryland, New Jersey, New York, and from England itself.

William Penn founded Pennsylvania in 1681 and wanted Delaware in order to establish a connection between his colony and the Atlantic Ocean. A year later the Duke of York gave the Delaware region to Penn as a territory of the Pennsylvania colony. Penn established representative government for both the colony and the territory.

In the 1680s the Delaware region became known as the Three Lower Counties because it was located down the Delaware River from Pennsylvania. Pennsylvania continued to grow in the late 1600s and added new counties. Colonists in the Three Lower Counties were fearful that they would soon have a minority voice in the government. Delegates from the Three Lower Counties refused to meet with those from Pennsylvania in 1701. Penn gave them a separate legislature which met in 1704, but Pennsylvania governed those counties until the Revolutionary War.

In the 1700s there were several established roads leading through southern Delaware and Maryland. In 1762, in the Wyoming District of northern Pennsylvania, far up the Susquehanna, a speculating company from Connecticut (known as the Susquehanna Company) claimed the area and sent out parties to the outrage of the Delaware Indians' chief and the Iroquois. One night the chief of the Delaware Indians was killed and his village burned. The Delaware waited for an opportunity to take revenge.

Late in 1761 the Crown began requiring proof of sale from the Indians before colonists could set foot on the land. This halted the western movement, but not before Indian resentment boiled up in Pontiac's Rebellion in 1763. This was a fierce and bloody war that raged on the western frontier during much of 1763.

In addition to Pennsylvania's hold on Delaware between 1684 and 1732, Lord Baltimore of Maryland laid claim to southern and western Delaware. In 1698 the Scotch-Irish also came to this area looking forward to worshipping under the Presbyterian faith. Some Roman Catholics arrived as early as 1730.

During and after the Revolutionary War the Wilmington area became the center of the nation's flour mill industry. More Catholics came into the area around 1790 when several French families escaped from uprisings in the West Indies. During this time period a flourishing slave trade brought black people into the area and they constituted nearly one-fourth of the population.

In 1802 Eleuthere Irenee du Pont, a French immigrant, established a powder mill on the Brandywine Creek near Wilmington. This mill was the center of Delaware's great chemical industry known even today as DuPont Chemical.

Tip 86: This network of canals and riverways indicates that there are potentially more records available in neighboring cities and states.

During the War of 1812, the lack of British goods encouraged industries in Delaware. A network of canals, highways, and the Delaware River transported Delaware's products to Baltimore, New York, Philadelphia, and Washington, D.C.

Although many of the native races, particularly the Lenni Lenape, lived quite peacefully among the European settlers, the introduction of white settlements on Indian lands forced most of them to move to Pennsylvania, Ohio, and West of the Mississippi River. Several Delaware Indian tribes live on reservations today in Oklahoma and Ontario, Canada.

Early settlers migrated from Delaware to New Jersey, Maryland, and Pennsylvania, and by 1749 there was an established route of migration from the northeastern states going through Pennsylvania to Wilmington, Delaware and on to Baltimore, Maryland where it turned south to Virginia.

Delaware, a slave state, during the Civil War had strong ties with both the Union and the Confederate states. Delaware fought on the Union side during the Civil War, but many Delawareans felt that the Confederate states should have been allowed to secede peacefully from the Union. Farms and industry prospered during and after the Civil War, and the growth of railroads in the 1850s helped the farmers move their crops to market. Because of improved transportation, farm values in southern Delaware increased. See distances to markets in table 7.1.

An excellent source is Edward Noble Vallandigham's *Delaware and the Eastern Shore: Some Aspects of a Peninsula Pleasant and Well Beloved* published in 1922 in Philadelphia: J. B. Lippincott Company. Also "The Quaker Colonies: A Chronicle of the Proprietors of the Delaware," by Sydney G. Fisher provides a lovely illustrated explanation of the area as part of the series produced by the New Haven: Yale University Press, 1920, *The Chronicles of America* series, vol. 8. Both are available in the Family History Library.

Prevailing Customs, Language, and Paleography

Since there was a tug-of-war between the Dutch, the Swedes, and the English in the pre-Penn period of the Delaware Valley, if there is reason to believe the sought-after individual lived among the early Swedes or Dutch, it would be important to understand the language and living customs that would be reflected in the records. Dr. J. Thomas Scharf's *History of Delaware*, originally published in 1888, provides excellent background materials involving the customs of the people involved. Back when lengthy titles were in vogue, Benjamin Ferris wrote *A History of the Original Settlements on the Delaware, From Its Discovery by Hudson to the Colonization Under William Penn: To Which is Added an Account of the Ecclesiastical Affairs of the Swedish Settlers, and a History of Wilmington, from Its First Settlement to the Present Time* (Wilmington: Wilson and Heald, 1846). This area covers what was Delaware and parts of Maryland, New Jersey, Pennsylvania, and New York and the book is available at the FHL in both book and film format (film 1036276). The Swedish settlements are covered in several good sources. The Genealogical Publishing Company reprinted Amandus Johnson's *The Swedish Settlements* on the Delaware in 1969. "A brief history of the Colony of New Sweden," by Carolus David Arfwedson was covered in the *Proceedings and Addresses: Pennsylvania German Society*, vol. 18, 1909, which discussed both the Swedish and the Pennsylvania German influence in the settlement and development along the Delaware River. It is found on FHL films 0982161 and 1432969.

New Sweden on the Delaware, 1638-1655 by C. A. Weslager is found in the Swedish area of the Family History Library. This book published in Wilmington, Delaware by Middle Atlantic Press, in 1988, focuses on the zenith of New Sweden's history when it was an elongated colony that encompassed both sides of the Delaware river and its tributary streams from the capes as far north as Trenton (except for the territory in the vicinity of Fort Nassau) without having any stated width. As his introduction states, "No state lines existed when New Sweden attained its full size, and Delaware, Maryland, New Jersey, and Pennsylvania became separate colonies."

There were several minorities in Delaware. Being full-blooded Finn myself, I was thrilled to see so many sources for this early minority group in Delaware. *Delaware 350: Amerikansiirtolaisuuden Alku = Amerikaemigrationens början = the Beginning of Finnish Migration to the New World: Exhibition Catalogue* by Olavi Koivukangas was published in my family's ancestral home of Turku, Finland: Migrationsinstitutet, (1988). Don't let the title frighten you because the text is in Swedish, Finnish, and English. A copy is at the FHL. *The Delaware Finns, or, The First Permanent Settlements in Pennsylvania, Delaware, West New Jersey and Eastern Part of Maryland* by Evert Alexander Louhi was published in New York by Humanity Press in 1925 and is located in the FHL. *The Finns on the Delaware, 1638-1655: An Essay in American Colonial History* by John Henry Wuorinen (New York: Columbia University Press, 1938) is also at the FHL.

Other minority groups include the early Native American tribes of the area, the Amish, and the Loyalists. FHL film 1009062 covers *Delaware's Forgotten Folk: the Story of the Moors & Nanticokes* by Clinton Alfred Weslager (Philadelphia: University of Pennsylvania Press, 1943). Available as well in the Library of Congress, on film as well. He also wrote *The Nanticoke Indians: Past and Present* (Newark, Del.: University of Delaware Press, 1983). This includes a discussion of descendants of the Nanticoke Indians living in Delaware and New Jersey. Allen B. Clark in *This Is Good Country: A History of the Amish of Delaware, 1915-1988* (Gordonville, Penn.: Gordonville Print Shop, 1989) produced a revised edition of the original *History of the Amish of Delaware*, 1963. This book includes information on the Amish in Kent County and Dover. Finally, *The Delaware Loyalists by Howard Bell Hancock* (Wilmington, Del.: Historical Society of Delaware, 1940), is available on FHL film 1000154. I hesitate to include the Black residents of Delaware as a minority since they constituted one-fourth of the population in the late 1700s. They were not freed until 1865. Several indexed slave schedules and recent publications covering early burial records are being introduced.

The fact is, Delaware has an abundance of published source materials. However, to standardize their formats, most publications delete many details and descriptions included in the original documents. Some of this deleted information could be crucial to distinguishing two same-named families in an area. For example, in *Genealogy Research: Methods and Sources,* volume 1, by the American Society of Genealogists, 1980, Milton Rubincam indicated:

> The most famous church in Delaware is Holy Trinity (Old Swedes') in Wilmington. . . . In 1890 The Historical Society of Delaware published *The Records of Holy Trinity (Old Swedes') Church, Wilmington, Delaware, from 1697-1773, with Abstracts of English Records from 1773-1810,* translated and edited by Horace Burr . . . the reader is cautioned that Mr. Burr and his assistants made many errors in translation and transcription, and no doubt printers contributed additional errors.

Maps and Gazetteers

A Gazetteer of Maryland and Delaware, by Henry Gannett, originally published in 1904 and reprinted by the Genealogical Publishing Company in 1976, and on microfilm 982220 item 3 through the FHL, will help locate small town names. Town names and rivers may also be located in L. W. Heck's *Delaware Place Names,* produced by the Government Printing Office in Washington, D. C., 1966.

Research Strategies

Maryland lies on the south and west, Pennsylvania on the north, and across the Delaware Bay is New Jersey and New York. Each of these states may have records on Delaware families. For example, Maryland land patents (1684–1732) often formed the basis for land titles in the south and western parts of Delaware. Look for records in both states.

Delaware citizens resented heavy English taxes and were very supportive of the Revolutionary War. Only one small battle took place on its soil, but the British often marched across the state. Many families moved back and forth between Delaware and the surrounding states of Pennsylvania, Maryland, and New Jersey.

Below are samples of sources to search in Delaware for an ancestor born in the various time periods indicated, with notes on their use.

Conducting research in the 1600s

1. For information on the period between 1638 and 1655, see Amandus Johnson's *The Swedish Settlements on the Delaware*

Tip 87: It became evident that this area needed to be studied as a region, so I looked for other sources such as this one.

1638-1664. 2 vols. 1911 Baltimore: Genealogical Publishing Co., 1969 reprint.

Tip 88: Look for records under subject headings of Swedish, German, or Dutch genealogy.

2. For information on the period from 1648 to 1664, see Dr. Charles T. Gehring's *New York Historical Manuscripts: Dutch,* vols 18-19. Delaware Papers (Dutch period). Baltimore: Genealogical Publishing Co., 1981.

3. For the period 1664-1682, when the English ruled Delaware, consult *New York Historical Manuscripts: Dutch*, vols 20-21. Delaware Papers (English Period). Baltimore: Genealogical Publishing Co., 1977.

4. *Delaware's Fugitive Records,* which are cataloged as Archives Inventory #2 at the Bureau of Archives and Records Management, Hall of Records, in Dover, Delaware, list the records in New York and Pennsylvania, between 1682-1776. They are available on microfilm in the Family History Library as well.

5. A source to help find a denomination of an ancestor is: Weis, Frederick Lewis. *The Colonial Clergy of Maryland, Delaware and Georgia.* Reprint. Baltimore: Genealogical Publishing Co., 1978.

Conducting research in the 1700s

1. The available birth records from about 1680 to 1913 are on FHL films 006424 to 006430. Some christenings from 1759 to 1890 are indexed on FHL film 006423. The Bureau of Vital Statistics in Delaware has prepared an index to Delaware marriages, baptisms, births, and deaths from 1680 to 1913 which have been microfilmed on 18 reels by the Family History Library on FHL films 006416 to 006433. See the complete list below. These are arranged alphabetically by surname starting with marriages on films:

Marriages	(A-B 1680-1850)	0006416
Marriages	(C-D 1680-1850)	0006417
Marriages	(E-G 1680-1850)	0006418
Marriages	(H-K 1680-1850)	0006419
Marriages	(L-O 1680-1850)	0006420
Marriages	(P-S 1680-1850)	0006421
Marriages	(T-Z 1680-1850)	0006422
Baptisms	(A-Z 1759-1890)	0006423
Births	(A-B 1861-1913)	0006424
Births	(C-E 1861-1913)	0006425
Births	(F-I 1861-1913)	0006426
Births	(J-L 1861-1913)	0006427
Births	(M-R 1861-1913)	0006428

Births	(S-V 1861-1913)	0006429
Births	(W-Z 1861-1913)	0006430
Deaths	(A-G to 1888)	0006431
Deaths	(H-Q to 1888)	0006432
Deaths	(R-Z to 1888)	0006433

2. The Hall of Records, in Dover, Delaware, accomplished a great centralizing system of records with many indexes for the state, especially involving court records. First search existing indexed records such as the *Joseph Brown Turner Collection,* various biographies, bibliographies, the indexes of the Bureau of Archives and Record Management listed throughout this report, the indexes of the Historical Society of Delaware, the *IGI*, the *Ancestral File,* and other *FamilySearch* programs, and the *Charles Henry Black Collection*. All of these are located in the FHL.

Tip 89: Be sure to look at originals whenever possible and obtain qualified help to translate foreign words, if necessary. Remember that both the paleography and the language may be difficult to read.

3. If the individual being sought after was from Sussex or Kent county, a search of early records in the 1790s, the 1782 tax records, and early land or probate records, might lead you to an area or locality. Once the locality has been discovered, court records should be searched. William Penn decreed that public expenses should be paid for by taxing the people, so tax assessment records covered most people and they should be searched. These records give more than the names of the persons paying taxes. They might also give previous residences, occupations, death dates, land transfers, and taxes on estates. The FHL has microfilmed county tax records for many years between about 1726 and 1850. Rent rolls similar to quit rents were maintained in the Proprietary Colony of Delaware and the surrounding counties of Maryland and Pennsylvania. These required payments, and were similar to today's property taxes.

4. If the individual cannot be located in Delaware but was on the seacoast, the records of New Jersey or the coastal counties of Maryland or Virginia should be searched.

5. The wills to the three counties of Delaware have been fully indexed to 1800 (Kent County 1680-1948 FHL microfilm 006492-006493; New Castle County 1682-1885 FHL microfilm 006545; and Sussex County 1682-1948 microfilm 006618).

6. Delaware's servicemen are recorded on microfilm and available through the Family History Library for the colonial wars and the Revolutionary War. One excellent source it the *List of Officers of the Colonies on the Delaware and the Province of Pennsylvania, 1614-1776* edited by John B. Linn & William Henry Egle and indexed by Robert Barnes. Baltimore, Md.:

*Tip 90: Search
Revolutionary War
records.*

Clearfield Co., 1992 (reprinted by Genealogical Publishing Company, Inc. for Clearfield Co.). This reprint of: *Pennsylvania Archives.* Second Series, v. 9, p. 621-818, includes a new index and covers the officers of the colonies on the Delaware, 1614-1681; Officers of the Province of Pennsylvania, 1681-1776; Provincial officers of the three lower counties, New Castle, Kent, and Sussex; Provincial officers for the three original counties, Chester, Philadelphia, 3nd Bucks, 1682-1776; and Provincial officers for the additional counties, 1729-1776.

Conducting research in the 1800s

1. Use technology to find the ancestor in a specific county. Search the CD-ROM indexes region-wide to locate your ancestor in a particular county and state (see Table 8.3). Also search the original records indicated by the above indexes according to the locality in which your ancestor was located.

2. Because birth and death records were not complete until 1913, use substitute vital records such as church records, cemetery records, probate records, etc., whenever a vital record cannot be located. Cemetery records are especially fruitful. Those vital records that were preserved were kept by the Bureau of Vital Statistics in Delaware and filmed by the Family History Library on eighty-seven reels covering births 1861-1913 and deaths 1855-1910 with a partial index. See FHL microfilms 006323 to 006409.

3. The wills of the three counties of Delaware have been fully indexed to 1885 (Kent County 1680-1948 on FHL microfilms 006492 to 006493, New Castle County 1682 to 1885 on FHL microfilm 006545, and Sussex County 1682 to 1948 on microfilm 006618).

4. The FHL has also microfilmed Gilbert Cope's manuscript collection entitled A List of Marriage License Bonds, So Far as They Have Been Preserved in New Castle County, Delaware 1744-1836. This list of marriage license bonds, so far as they have been preserved in New Castle County, Delaware, 1744-1836 was filmed from the original handwritten manuscript at the Historical Society of Pennsylvania in Philadelphia.

5. Marriages may also be found in records produced by the Clerk of the Peace in Delaware (and filmed in 1949) entitled Marriage Bonds, 1855-1861 and Marriage Licenses 1889-1894 on eighteen reels of films (FHL microfilm 006416 to 006433).

6. After the Civil War a major change in population occurred as many of the early settlers moved west and were replaced by Irish Roman Catholic and German settlers. Delaware's military

servicemen for the War of 1812 and the Civil War are recorded on microfilm at the FHL.

Conducting research in the 1900s

1. World War I draft records on microfilm are available through the FHL. They could provide birth dates, birth places, and names of parents for men born between the 1870s and 1900.

2. World War II records are recorded in William H. Conner's *Delaware's Role in World War II, 1940-1946*, and these records could lead to military service records, birth and death dates for those born prior to 1913, etc.

3. By the 1920s, industry had brought more immigrants to the area, mainly from Italy, Poland, and Russia (Jews). Therefore, passenger lists, naturalization records, passport indexes, ethnic newspapers, ethnic religions, etc., should be searched, because they often provide the home town in the old country, the actual birth date, and parentage. Remember that these naturalization, passport, citizenship, and other twentieth century records will not normally be found at the state level but at the federal level. After World War II a migration of blacks to the urban areas of Delaware occurred, so families should be found on census records to determine previous states of residency.

4. The Social Security Death Benefits Index, available at the FHL and other genealogical libraries, will also provide death dates and clues for further research. By requesting form SS-5 from the Social Security Administration (instructions are available on the CDs), you could receive a copy of an individual's original application for a Social Security Number. It would contain his/her name, birth date and place, and often the parents' names. Ordering a copy of the death certificate could also prove very rewarding.

Major Libraries and Vital Records Repositories

Bureau of Archives and Records Management
Hall of Records
Dover, DE 19901

Tip 91: Search genealogical sources in surrounding states.

National Archives - Mid-Atlantic Region
9th and Market Streets
Philadelphia, PA 19107

The Historical Society of Delaware/
The Delaware Genealogical Society
505 Market Street Mall
Wilmington, DE 19801

The Historical Society of Pennsylvania/
The Genealogical Society of Pennsylvania
1300 Locust Street
Philadelphia, PA 19107

Bureau of Vital Statistics
Jesse S. Cooper Memorial Building
William Penn Street
Dover, DE 19901 (birth and death records from 1861 to present)

Tip 92: I like to make aids which help me find information more quickly. For example, table 7.2, Selected Index and Reference Works Available on CD-ROM, is a handy table I put together from any CDs which covered the state of Delaware and the surround region. If the person I am looking for has disappeared, using this table I can search an entire area in a matter of minutes. Of course they are all indexes and references, but they can lead me to excellent Delaware sources. I've included information on how to obtain this information.

Most of the following CDs are produced by and available from the Banner Blue Division of Brøderbund Software, Inc. Banner Blue purchased the CDs originally produced by Automated Archives. The majority of those originally produced were census CDs. Therefore, if you are using the older version of the CDs they will have an Automated Archives label. Many errors, omissions, and labeling problems were discovered by users over the years. Corrections were made on the new CDs currently offered as compatible with the *Family Tree Maker*™ (FTM) computer software program. The CDs are also operable by using the *Family Archive Viewer* which is a separate software program if you do not wish to use the FTM software. [Since FTM quickly and easily accesses the files of the *Personal Ancestral File* family records data so that I can do immediate searches, I find it a wonderful program to own.] Some of the CD numbers have changed because FTM has combined CDs as better compression techniques have become available. Currently the Banner Blue Division is doing the majority of business with these products. A current list of genealogy CDs produced by all companies given by topic and locality is available by sending a self-addressed, stamped over-sized envelop to Genealogy Research Associates, Inc., 2600 Garden Road, Suite 224, Monterey, CA 93940. Requesting a current catalog would be most advantageous.

Recently the Genealogical Publishing Company formed an alliance with Brøderbund Software's Banner Blue Division to produce valuable CDs for all genealogists. *The Genealogist's All-in-One Address Book* contains thousands of names, addresses, phone numbers, and other information vital to researchers. This includes information on agencies, societies, libraries, archives, courthouses, professional bodies, periodicals, and services that are basic to family history research. It is listed as FTM 115 in Table 7.2.

Table 7.2 Selected Indexes and Reference Works Available on CD-ROM

Year	CD #	Description of Resource
1784-1811	FTM 146	Military Volunteer Records: Induction and Separation Rolls
Pre 1790	FTM 310	Census Index: Includes DE, MD, NJ, NY, PA, VA
1790	FTM 311	Census Index: Includes DE, MD, NJ, NY, PA, VA (some reconstructed from tax lists)
1800	FTM 312	Census Index: Includes DE, MD, NJ, NY, PA, VA
1810	FTM 313	Census Index: Includes DE, MD, NJ, NY, PA, VA
1820	FTM 314	Census Index: Includes DE, MD, NJ, NY, PA, VA
1830	FTM 315	Census Index: Includes DE, MD, NJ, NY, PA, VA
1840	FTM 316	Census Index: Includes DE, MD, NJ, NY, PA, VA
1850	FTM 317	Census Index: Includes DE, MD, NJ, NY, PA, VA
1860	FTM 318	Census Index: Includes DE, MD, NJ, NY, PA, VA
Mortality	FTM 164	Census Mortality Index: DE 1850-1880; PA 1870 & 1880; VA
1830/1853	GenRef	Early American Gazetteers
1870	FTM 319	Census Index: U.S. Selected States/Counties; DE & VA
1870	CD 288	Baltimore, MD
1870	FTM 286	Census Index: PA East
1870	FTM 290	Census Index: VA & WV
Marriages	FTM 4	Marriage Index: Selected Counties of MD, VA & NC
History	CD A-1	U.S. History Source Book of American History
Native American	OC	Indian Records
History	FTM 113	Histories Series
Genealogies	FTM 114	Early American Families, by Frederick Virkus, (also on FTM 113)
Reference	FTM 115	Genealogist's All-in-One Address Book: Genealogist's Tool Address Book; County Courthouse Book; Directory of Family Associations
Reference	CD A-2	Ancestry Reference Library Five Resource Books: *The Tool Source: A Guidebook of American Genealogy; Ancestry's Red Book: American's State, County and Town Sources; The Library: A Guide to the LDS Family History Library; The Library of Congress: A Guide to Genealogical and Historical Research; The Archives: A Guide to the National Archives Field Branches*

Also, the *Roll of Honor: Civil War Union Soldiers* is an excellent finding aid. If you feel you are searching for someone who died in the Civil War in Delaware, the *Roll of Honor* is the only official memorial to the Union dead ever published. All 27 volumes are on this CD.

Each month more *World Family Tree* CDs are being produced by FTM. These are genealogies sent in by customers and friends. Also check the *Pedigree Resource Files* CDs, www.myfamily.com and www.kindredkonnections.com for other large pedigree data bases. Although they are secondary sources, since they are so quick to search and provide names and addresses of suppliers, they should not be overlooked as a source for any area in the world.

Although all genealogists might not be desirous of a CD on early emigrants, if you are looking for someone who came to these shores between 1607 and 1776, the Genealogical Publishing Company has also announced *The Complete Book of Emigrants, 1607-1776* with approximately 140,000 names. These are Peter

Wilson Coldham's four-volume *Complete Book of Emigrants* and *The Complete Book of Emigrants in Bondage and its Supplement*. This CD contains virtually every reference to English emigrants that can be found in contemporary English records such as port books, shipping registers, apprenticeship lists, plantation records, Treasury and Chancery records, and records of forced transportation and exile. With the built-in search engine you are allowed to do a free-text search for names, dates, places, ships, occupations, neighbors, etc. This can be a real time saver.

Ancestry provides several excellent reference tools on CD regarding genealogical research. *The Ancestry Reference Library*, listed as CD A-2 in table 7-2, includes *The Source: A Guidebook of American Genealogy; Ancestry's Red Book: American State, County & Town Sources; The Library: A Guide to the LDS Family History Library; The Library of Congress: A Guide to Genealogical and Historical Research;* and *The Archives: A Guide to the National Archives Field Branches*. When you purchase this CD you also receive a bonus resource of an 1854 gazetteer. Products may be ordered from Ancestry by calling 1-800-ANCES-TRY (262-3787). They also have an excellent resource on the Internet at http//www.ancestry.com. Here the *Social Security Death Master File* as well as various collections of other information including marriages and immigration records are available.

GenRef, Inc., at 874 West 1400 North, Orem, UT 84057 produces several CDs of a general nature to genealogists. *The Vital Records Assistant* produces computer-generated letters to request birth, marriage or death certificates from vital records offices in the United States. It is a fill-in-the-blank program customized for each user. *The Early American Gazetteer* contains two pre-1860 gazetteers which can be used as a locator for towns which no longer exist. It is also good for finding rivers, post offices on the 1850 census and other statistical information during this time period. GenRef has also produced a *Social Security Death Benefits* CD with a different search engine. Items may be ordered by calling 1-801-225-3256, writing to the above address, or searching the Internet at www.genref.com.

The Indian Question produced by Objective Computing, P.O. Box 51246, Indianapolis, IN 46251 is the most comprehensive encyclopedic resource on the history of native North American Indians. It covers over 300 texts including the original 1850 encyclopedia on American Indians by Henry Schoolcraft. This CD can be ordered by calling 317-475-9904 or writing to the address above.

Census records, tax lists, and other large data bases

This category of records is most helpful as a finding aid to pinpoint the individual you are looking for in a particular locality. Once the individual is located in a specific place, county and town records may be searched for more clues. The information below can serve as a caution in using CD-ROM technology. The label, or title, doesn't always indicate everything that is included. For example:

1. CD310 includes a 1677 Upland District tax list when Delaware was considered part of Pennsylvania. It also includes an index to New Jersey, New York, and Pennsylvania's pre-1790 census and tax lists.

2. CD311 includes not only the Delaware reconstructed 1790 census index, but also Pennsylvania, Maryland, New York, and New Jersey for the same year.

3. CD312 includes not only the Delaware 1800 census index, but also the same year for Pennsylvania, Maryland, New York, and New Jersey.

4. CD313 includes the 1810 census index for Delaware, New Jersey, and Pennsylvania, and CD149 covers New York. New Jersey's index includes tax lists for several counties from 1810-1818.

5. CD314 covers both the 1820 census and an 1828 tax list for Delaware. However, the three surrounding states are found on CD139, which also includes a New Jersey listing between 1824 and 1829.

6. CD315 covers all four states for 1830 as well as all counties in 1837.

7. CD316 on the 1840 census covers Delaware (including a tax list for 1842), New Jersey, and Pennsylvania. The New York 1840 census is found on CD141.

8. CD317 covers the 1850 census for Delaware, New Jersey, and Pennsylvania. Check the New York 1850 census on CD42 for migration from Delaware   into that area.

9. CD318 covers the 1860 census for Delaware, New Jersey, and Pennsylvania. The New York 1860 census index is found on CD21.

10. CD164, Mortality Records for Delaware 1850-1880, appears to be a good source for African-American references. Pennsylvania is also on this CD.

11. Check CD146, *Military Volunteers Induction and Separation Rolls 1784-1811*, for military personnel.

Once again, the CD numbers are changing as, for example, all the 1860 census records are being placed on one CD.

Genealogical Collections, Histories, and Indexes

1. The Bureau of Archives and Records Management (at the Hall of Records, Dover, DE 19901) has a Genealogical Surname File that indexes surnames mentioned in genealogical and local histories. They will search the file for you if you include a large SASE with your request.

2. The Rev. Joseph Brown Turner Collection, which has about three thousand alphabetically arranged genealogies and pedigrees, is also in the Archives and Records Management Building and is available on microfilms 006272 through 006300 at the Family History Library.

3. To search for a published biography, see *A Bibliography of Delaware through 1960 and Bibliography of Delaware, 1960-1974*, by Henry Clay and Marion B. Reed (Newark, Del.: University of Delaware Press, 1966, 1976).

4. The Historical Society of Delaware at Wilmington has a surname file of about five hundred thousand cards indexing church records, newspaper obituaries, family histories, and the Catherine Harkness and Jeanette Eckmann Research Files. The file also includes cards submitted by genealogists researching Delaware families. The society will search the index for you for a fee. Please send a SASE. See also the Joseph Brown Turner Collection, and the Charles Henry Black Collection of deeds, wills, and original documents for Sussex and Kent counties in Delaware and Somerset and Worcester counties in Maryland, found on Family History Library films 441425 through 441431.

5. The major genealogical societies in Pennsylvania, New Jersey, and Maryland will undoubtedly have records of Delaware families in their surname indexes.

6. Search the *IGI* for Delaware, Pennsylvania, Maryland, and New Jersey.

7. The Walter G. Tatnall Tombstone Records Collection of nearly 800 small cemeteries in all three counties is available only at the Bureau of Archives and Records Management. 006303.

8. Millard F. Hudson's collection of *Cemetery Records of Sussex County, Delaware* includes transcriptions from 630 cemeteries and is on Family History Library film 006690.

Churches Prior to 1900 and Their Repositories

Before 1900 the major religious denominations in the area were Baptist, Episcopal, Methodist, Presbyterian, and Society of Friends, or Quakers. Church records are another very good source for the genealogist in Delaware, because the Delaware Historical Records Survey (WPA) copied about one hundred volumes of records of individual congregations verbatim. Many of these volumes are indexed. When doing research in the Friend's (Quaker) records, the original record should always be researched. Do not rely upon Hinshaw's compilation alone, even though it is a wonderful search tool.

The Bureau of Archives and Records Management has an inventory of available church records, 1680-1930. A card index to church baptisms, 1759-1890, is on Family History Library film 006423.

The Delaware Historical Records Survey transcribed the registers and minutes of nearly 100 churches of various denominations representing half of the available pre-1900 church records. They are at the Bureau of Archives and Records Management and on microfilm at the Family History Library, films 006304 through 006320. A guide to Delaware's church records is found on Family History Library film #1036702, item 3; and microfiche 6019975, the *Directory of Churches and Religious Organizations in Delaware* (Dover, Del.: Historical Records Survey, 1942).

Once a particular denomination has been selected, search for historical information about that particular church. For example, *An Address, Embracing the Early History of Delaware, and the Settlement of Its Boundaries and of the Drawyers Congregation, With All the Churches Since Organized on Its Original Territory: Delivered in Drawyers Church, Del., May 10, 1842, Being One Hundred and Thirty-one Years Since the Site of the Present House of Worship was Purchased* by George Foot (Philadelphia: Christian Observer, 1842), is the history of the Old Drawyers Presbyterian Church located in St. George's Hundred, New Castle County (1895). Also known as Drawyers Creek Presbyterian Church and First Presbyterian Church in St. Georges Hundred, this is available at the FHL on film 0908689. [With titles like this, we don't need card catalog descriptions.]

A minority church of the time period was that of the Swedish Lutheran Church. From the introduction to *The 1693 Census of the Swedes on the Delaware: Family Histories of the Swedish Lutheran Church Members Residing in Pennsylvania, Delaware, West New Jersey and Cecil County, Maryland, 1638-1693* by Peter Stebbins Craig (Winter Park, Fla.: SAG Publications, 1993) we are told that the book ". . .is based upon the 1693 census of the Swedes on the

Delaware, a census taken to document the colonists' argument to Swedish authorities that there remained a sizable group of Swedes in America who were worthy of help in the form of new pastors for their churches and new religious books in the Swedish language." However, further on we are warned that "The list did not include all persons of Swedish origin then living in the vicinity of the Delaware river. Many who had migrated to Maryland no longer associated with the Swedish churches on the Delaware. Others, whose names appear in the church records of Wicaco and Crane Hook, 1697-1699, apparently were not active church-goers in 1693 when both churches were without a minister." This early Swedish influence covered a great distance. The Swedish log church at Wicaco (now Gloria Dei in Philadelphia) served Swedes living in the Philadelphia area from Chester County to Marcus Hook and from Pennsauken Creek in Burlington County to the southern boundary of Gloucester County in New Jersey. The Swedish log church at Crane Hook (now in Wilmington, Delaware) served Swedes living in New Castle County, Delaware; Cecil County, Maryland; and Salem County, New Jersey.

Addresses for contacting these churches include:

BAPTIST
American Baptist Historical Society
1106 South Goodman Street
Rochester, NY 14620

METHODIST
United Methodist Archives Center
Drew University
Madison, NJ 07940

PRESBYTERIAN
Presbyterian Historical Society
425 Lombard Street
Philadelphia, PA 19147

ROMAN CATHOLIC
Diocese of Wilmington Archives
P. O. Box 2247
Greenville, DE 19807

SOCIETY OF FRIENDS
Friends Historical Library
Swarthmore College Library
Swarthmore, PA 19081
(Newcastle County Hicksite records)

Baltimore Yearly Meeting
Stony Run Meetinghouse
5114 North Charles St.
Baltimore, MD 21210
(for Kent and Sussex counties)

Quaker Collection
Magill Library
Haverford College
Haverford, PA 19041
(New Castle County Orthodox records)

Genealogical Periodicals

1. The *Delaware Genealogical Society Journal* is published by the Delaware Genealogical Society.

2. The *Maryland and Delaware Genealogist* was published until his recent death by Raymond Clark, Jr. Both periodicals are available at the Family History Library in Salt Lake City and at other genealogical libraries.

Guides to Further Sources

1. *Delaware Family Histories and Genealogies,* by Donald O. Virdin (St. Michaels, Md.: Raymond B. Clark, 1984) is a bibliography and surname index to 215 published Delaware genealogies. It is available at the Family History Library, book US/CAN 975.1 A1 No. 11.

2. *Preliminary Inventory of the Older Records in the Delaware Archives.* Dover: Division of Historical and Cultural Affairs, Bureau of Archives and Records, 1978. (Also available on FHL fiche 6331225.)

3. Reed, Henry Clay and Marion B. Reed. *A Bibliography of Delaware through 1960.* Newark, Del.: University of Delaware Press, 1966. (Available in the FHL US/CAN 975.1 A3r.)

4. Reed, Henry Clay and Marion B. Reed. *Bibliography of Delaware, 1960-1974.* Newark, Del.: University of Delaware Press, 1976.

5. *Research Outline: Delaware*, Series US-STATES, No. 8, Salt Lake City: Family History Department, 50 E. North Temple Street, Salt Lake City, UT 84150.

6. Rubincam, Milton. *"Delaware," Genealogical Research: Methods and Sources.* Revised Edition. Washington, D.C.: American Society of Genealogists, 1980, pp. 261-71.

7. *Delaware's Fugitive Records: An Inventory of the Official Land Grant Records Relating to the Present State of Delaware.* Dover: Department of State, Division of Historical and Cultural Affairs, 1980. (Inventory No. 2.) Also available on FHL film 1,0333,995. Describes Delaware land records found in New York and Pennsylvania archives.

A Selected List of Published Sources on Delaware

deValinger, Leon, Jr. *Calendar of Kent County, Delaware, Probate Records, 1680-1850*. Dover: Public Archives Commission, 1944.

_____. *Calendar of Sussex County, Delaware, Probate Records, 1680-1800*. Dover: Public Archives Commission, 1964.

Historical Research Committee. Delaware Society of the Colonial Dames of America. *A Calendar of Wills, New Castle County, 1682-1800*. 1911. Reprint. Baltimore: Genealogical Publishing Co., 1969.

Original Land Titles in the Delaware, Commonly Known as the Duke of York Records... 1646 to 1679. Wilmington: Sunday Star Print [1899].

Weinberg, Allen and Thomas E. Slattery. *Warrants and Surveys of the Province of Pennsylvania Including the Three Lower Counties, 1759. 1965*. Reprint. Knightstown, Ind.: Bookmark, 1975.

SUMMARY

Now that I have put together a summary of techniques and sources on this state, I add the research outline or manual I have collected from others such as that which follows from the Family History Library; I also add maps, guides, and other research tools as I come across them.

Some people wonder why I go through this exercise instead of just photocopying pages out of books and highlighting the important parts. I found that as I make up my notebooks, type in the materials, and organize information which is new to me, I remember it better. It is like entering information into a genealogy computer program. As you enter the information, you come to recognize things you had not noticed before.

On the following pages you will see an actual Research Outline for Delaware. You will see that I have added several sources to that provided in this outline including some electronic items. But there is still much more not covered in my own pages. Sources are constantly being added and should be added to your own notebooks.

The assignment which follows will guide you through the process of making your own research notebooks.

Figure 7.5 Now Outdated Research Outline for Delaware.

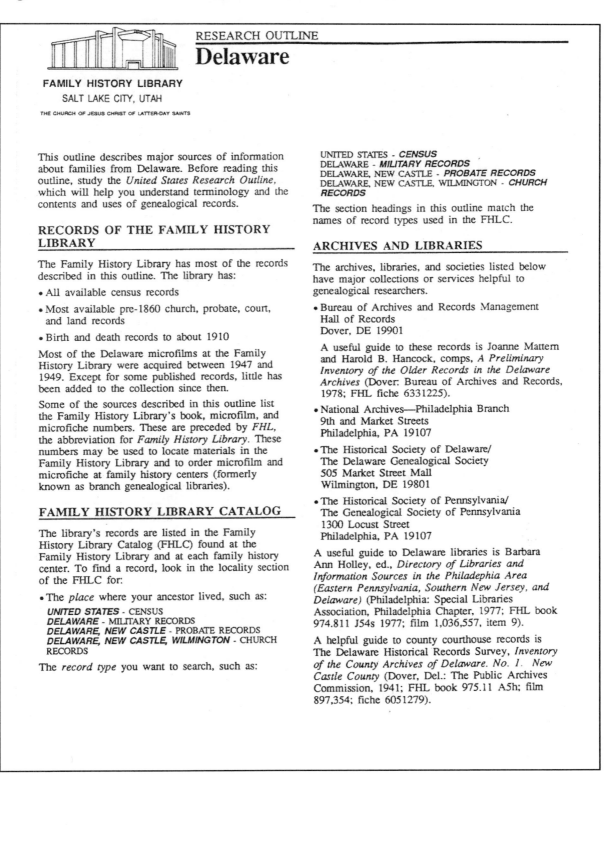

RESEARCH OUTLINE
Delaware

FAMILY HISTORY LIBRARY
SALT LAKE CITY, UTAH

THE CHURCH OF JESUS CHRIST OF LATTER-DAY SAINTS

This outline describes major sources of information about families from Delaware. Before reading this outline, study the *United States Research Outline*, which will help you understand terminology and the contents and uses of genealogical records.

RECORDS OF THE FAMILY HISTORY LIBRARY

The Family History Library has most of the records described in this outline. The library has:

• All available census records

• Most available pre-1860 church, probate, court, and land records

• Birth and death records to about 1910

Most of the Delaware microfilms at the Family History Library were acquired between 1947 and 1949. Except for some published records, little has been added to the collection since then.

Some of the sources described in this outline list the Family History Library's book, microfilm, and microfiche numbers. These are preceded by *FHL*, the abbreviation for *Family History Library*. These numbers may be used to locate materials in the Family History Library and to order microfilm and microfiche at family history centers (formerly known as branch genealogical libraries).

FAMILY HISTORY LIBRARY CATALOG

The library's records are listed in the Family History Library Catalog (FHLC) found at the Family History Library and at each family history center. To find a record, look in the locality section of the FHLC for:

• The *place* where your ancestor lived, such as:

UNITED STATES - CENSUS
DELAWARE - MILITARY RECORDS
DELAWARE, NEW CASTLE - PROBATE RECORDS
DELAWARE, NEW CASTLE, WILMINGTON - CHURCH RECORDS

The *record type* you want to search, such as:

UNITED STATES - **CENSUS**
DELAWARE - **MILITARY RECORDS**
DELAWARE, NEW CASTLE - **PROBATE RECORDS**
DELAWARE, NEW CASTLE, WILMINGTON - **CHURCH RECORDS**

The section headings in this outline match the names of record types used in the FHLC.

ARCHIVES AND LIBRARIES

The archives, libraries, and societies listed below have major collections or services helpful to genealogical researchers.

• Bureau of Archives and Records Management
Hall of Records
Dover, DE 19901

A useful guide to these records is Joanne Mattern and Harold B. Hancock, comps, *A Preliminary Inventory of the Older Records in the Delaware Archives* (Dover: Bureau of Archives and Records, 1978; FHL fiche 6331225).

• National Archives—Philadelphia Branch
9th and Market Streets
Philadelphia, PA 19107

• The Historical Society of Delaware/
The Delaware Genealogical Society
505 Market Street Mall
Wilmington, DE 19801

• The Historical Society of Pennsylvania/
The Genealogical Society of Pennsylvania
1300 Locust Street
Philadelphia, PA 19107

A useful guide to Delaware libraries is Barbara Ann Holley, ed., *Directory of Libraries and Information Sources in the Philadephia Area (Eastern Pennsylvania, Southern New Jersey, and Delaware)* (Philadelphia: Special Libraries Association, Philadelphia Chapter, 1977; FHL book 974.811 J54s 1977; film 1,036,557, item 9).

A helpful guide to county courthouse records is The Delaware Historical Records Survey, *Inventory of the County Archives of Delaware. No. 1. New Castle County* (Dover, Del.: The Public Archives Commission, 1941; FHL book 975.11 A5h; film 897,354; fiche 6051279).

Figure 7.5 Research Outline for Delaware (continued)

BIBLE RECORDS

The *Daughters of the American Revolution (DAR) Collection* at the DAR Library in Washington, D.C. includes many Bible records of Delaware. These are indexed in Daughters of the American Revolution, Delaware, *Old Bible Records with Charts and Genealogical Sketches*, 13 vols. (Newark, Del.: N.p., 1944-73). The Family History Library has the following:

```
Vols. 3-8, 13 . . . . . FHL book 975.1 V29d
Vols. 1-2 . . . . . . . FHL film 845-762
Vols. 3-5 . . . . . . . FHL film 834,763
Vols. 6-9 . . . . . . . FHL film 845,764
Vols. 10-12 . . . . . FHL film 845,765
Vol. 13 . . . . . . . FHL film 1,321,078, item 5
```

Another partial index to the DAR collection of Bible records is E. Kay Kirkham, *An Index to Some of the Bibles and Family Records of the United States*, vol. II (Logan, Utah: Everton Publishers, 1984; FHL book Ref 973 D22kk v.2).

The Bureau of Archives and Records Management is actively collecting and indexing Bible records. You can write to the bureau for more information about the current status of this collection.

BIOGRAPHY

The Bureau of Archives and Records Management has a *Genealogical Surname File* that indexes surnames mentioned in genealogies and local histories. The archives will search it for you, if you include a large, self-addressed, stamped envelope with your request.

A representative biographical encyclopedia is *Biographical and Genealogical History of the State of Delaware...*, 2 vols. (Chambersburg, Pa.: J.M. Runk & Co., 1899; FHL film 1,000,155).

CEMETERIES

The Walter G. Tatnall Tombstone Records collection has inscriptions from nearly 800 small cemeteries in all three counties. It is available at the Bureau of Archives and Records Management and at the Family History Library (FHL film 006,303). A card index to it is only at the Bureau of Archives and Records Management.

Millard F. Hudson's collection of *Cemetery Records of Sussex County, Delaware* includes transcriptions from 630 cemeteries. It is at the Bureau of Archives and Records Management and at the Family History Library (FHL film 006,690).

CENSUS

Federal

Many federal census records are at the Family History Library, the National Archives, and other federal and state archives. The *United States Research Outline* provides detailed information about these records.

The Family History Library has the U.S. federal censuses of Delaware from 1800 to 1910. The 1790 census is missing, and the 1890 census was destroyed. A substitute for the 1790 census created from tax lists is Leon Devalinger, Jr., *Reconstructed 1790 Census of Delaware* (Washington, D.C.: National Genealogical Society, 1962; FHL 975.1 X2d 1790; film 1,000,156; fiche 6019928).

Statewide indexes are available for the 1800, 1810, 1820, 1830, 1840, 1850, 1860, and 1870 censuses. Indexes for these censuses are available in both book and microfiche format. Soundex (phonetic) indexes are on microfilm for part of the 1880 1880 census and all of the 1900 census completely.

Mortality schedules for 1850, 1860, 1870, and 1880 are at the Bureau of Archives and Records Management. The 1850, 1870, and 1880 schedules are indexed.

State

A 1782 state census exists for six "hundreds" (townships). It has been reconstructed from tax lists for the remainder of the state in Harold B. Hancock, *The Reconstructed Delaware Census of 1782* (Wilmington: Delaware Genealogical Society, 1973; FHL book 975.1 X2r).

CHURCH RECORDS

Many religious groups have kept records of Delaware families. Before 1900 the largest denominations were the Baptist, Episcopal, Methodist, Presbyterian, and Society of Friends.

The Bureau of Archives and Records Management has an inventory of available church records from the 1680s to the 1930s. A card index to church baptisms, 1759 to 1890, is on FHL film 006,423 (listed in the FHLC under DELAWARE - VITAL RECORDS - INDEXES).

The Delaware Historical Records Survey transcribed the registers and minutes of nearly 100 churches of various denominations. This collection represents almost half of the available pre-1900 church records. These are at the Bureau of Archives and Records Management and on microfilm at the Family History Library (FHL films 006,304-20).

Figure 7.5 Research Outline for Delaware (continued)

The Bureau of Archives and Records Management and the Historical Society of Delaware house excellent collections. The Family History Library has copies of records for groups such as the Presbyterians and Society of Friends.

The Family History Library has histories for the Baptist, Presbyterian, Episcopal, and Methodist churches, as well as biographies and genealogies of colonial clergymen.

A useful aid to locating Delaware churches is *Directory of Churches and Religious Organizations in Delaware* (Dover, Del.: Historical Records Survey, 1942; FHL book 975.1 E4h; film 1,036,702, item 3; fiche 6019975).

Many denominations have collected their records into central repositories. The following are addresses of regional archives:

Baptist

American Baptist Historical Society
1106 South Goodman Street
Rochester, NY 14620

Methodist

United Methodist Archives Center
Drew University
Madison, NJ 07940

Presbyterian

Presbyterian Historical Society
425 Lombard Street
Philadelphia, PA 19147

Roman Catholic

Diocese of Wilmington Archives
P.O. Box 2247
Greenville, DE 19807

Society of Friends

Friends Historical Library
Swarthmore College Library
Swarthmore, PA 19081
(Newcastle County Hicksite records)

Baltimore Yearly Meeting
Stony Run Meetinghouse
5114 North Charles St.
Baltimore, MD 21210
(for Kent and Sussex counties)

Quaker Collection
Magill Library
Haverford College
Haverford, PA 19041
(New Castle County Orthodox records)

COURT RECORDS

Delaware courts that kept records of genealogical value were established as follows:

1684- *Chancery courts* are countywide courts with
pres. jurisdiction over equity matters.

1701- *Courts of common pleas* are established in
pres. each county and hear minor civil suits, minor criminal cases, appeals from lesser courts, adoptions, and terminations of parental rights.

1792- *Orphans courts* have countywide jurisdiction
pres. over property rights, estates of minors, guardianships, and adoptions.

1831- *Superior courts* are county courts with
pres. jurisdiction over major criminal and civil cases.

The office of clerk of the peace, or prothonotary, dates from 1642. The clerk of the peace was clerk of the levy court, court of general quarter session, court of oyer and terminer, and court of common pleas.

Most of the county court records for the period 1676 to 1699 have been published and are available at the Family History Library. The library has microfilms of chancery court dockets from 1749 to about 1860, and orphans court dockets from 1728 to about 1860. These are listed in the FHLC under DELAWARE, [COUNTY] - COURT RECORDS.

The Bureau of Archives and Records Management has the original court records, including the court of general quarter sessions, oyer and terminer, justice of the peace, and common pleas, as well as superior court and supreme court records.

DIRECTORIES

The Family History Library has Wilmington city directories for:

- 1814, 1845, 1853, . . FHL fiche 6044647-50 1857
- 1862-1901 . . . . . . FHL films 1,377,595-05
- 1934 . . . . FHL film 1,307,613

The most extensive collection of city and business directories is at the University of Delaware Library, Newark, DE 19717-5267.

EMIGRATION AND IMMIGRATION

People

Delaware was first settled by the Swedes in 1638. The area was conquered by the Dutch in 1655 and then by the English in 1664. From 1682 to 1776 the "three lower counties on the Delaware" River (New Castle, Kent, and Sussex), were part of the province of Pennsylvania.

Figure 7.5 Research Outline for Delaware (continued)

The Delaware River brought the original European settlers to Delaware. For more than three centuries it served as a waterway connecting many Delaware towns to each other and to Philadelphia.

A frequently used land migration route was from Philadelphia to Wilmington and then on to Baltimore. There was very little migration from New York and New Jersey to Delaware, but many people migrated back and forth among Delaware, Pennsylvania, and Maryland.

The earliest colonists, the Swedes, the Finns, and the Dutch, soon became anglicized. A rather large group of Quakers came to Delaware from Pennsylvania in the late 1600s and early 1700s. English, Welsh, and particularly Ulster Scots migrated after 1717 to Philadelphia and northern Delaware. They settled in New Castle County in such numbers that by 1776, more than half the county was Presbyterian.

During the nineteenth century, the heaviest migration continued to flow into the Wilmington area of New Castle County. During most of the century, Roman Catholic Germans and Irish were most numerous, but in the last decade Italian, Polish, and Jewish immigrants arrived in great numbers. In the early twentieth century, many Ukrainian and Greek immigrants moved to Delaware.

Records

Records of major ethnic groups are listed in the FHLC under DELAWARE - MINORITIES. The following books may be helpful if you are searching for an early Swedish or Dutch ancestor:

Johnson, Amandus. *The Swedish Settlements on the Delaware, 1638-1661.* 2 vols., 1911. Reprint. Baltimore: Genealogical Publishing Co., 1969. (FHL book 975.1 H2j.)

Gehring, Charles T. *New York Historical Manuscripts. Dutch.* 2 vols. *Vols. 17-19. Delaware Papers (Dutch Period)* and *Vols. 20-22. Delaware Papers (English Period).* Baltimore: Genealogical Publishing Co., 1977, 1981. (FHL book 974.7 N2d.)

Few passenger lists of Delaware ports exist. The Family History Library and the National Archives have passenger lists on microfilm for the port of Wilmington for the years 1820, 1830-31, 1833, and 1840-49 (FHL film 830,246). These lists are included in *Copies of Lists of Passengers Arriving at Miscellaneous Ports...Atlantic and Gulf Coasts...*listed in the FHLC under UNITED STATES - EMIGRATION AND IMMIGRATION. For indexes to these lists, see *Supplemental Index to Passenger Lists...Atlantic and Gulf Coast*

*Ports....*listed in the FHLC under UNITED STATES - EMIGRATION AND IMMIGRATION - INDEXES.

You may also need to search the passenger lists of Philadelphia, New York, and Baltimore. About 8,000 early arrivals are listed in Carl Boyer, 3rd, *Ship Passenger Lists: Pennsylvania and Delaware, 1641-1825* (Newhall, Calif.: Carl Boyer, 1980; FHL book 973 W3sb). More detailed information on immigration sources is in the *United States Research Outline.*

Names of colonial immigrants listed in published sources are indexed in P. William Filby, *Passenger and Immigration Lists Index*, 9 vols. (Detroit: Gale Research, 1981, 1985, 1986, 1987; FHL book Ref 973 W33p). The first three volumes are a combined alphabetical index published in 1981. The next four volumes are a cumulated 1982 to 1985 supplement. The last two volumes are 1986 and 1987 supplements.

GAZETTEERS

Guides to historical place names in Delaware include:

U.S. Geological Survey. *National Gazetteer of the United States: Delaware 1983.* Washington, D.C.: Government Printing Office, 1984. (FHL book 975.1 E5n.) This book has a map of Delaware hundreds (county subdivisions, similar to townships) and an alphabetical list of geographical sites, such as cemeteries and churches, that are named on topographical survey maps.

Heck, L. W. *Delaware Place Names.* Washington, D.C.: U.S. Government Printing Office, 1966. (FHL book 975.1 E2h.)

GENEALOGY

Most archives, historical societies, and genealogical societies have special collections and indexes of genealogical value. These must usually be searched in person. Major Delaware manuscript collections of compiled genealogies include the following:

Name File. The Historical Society of Delaware has a surname file of about 500,000 cards. It indexes church records, newspaper obituaries, the Catherine Harkness and Jeanette Eckmann research files, and the family history files at the historical society. Also included are cards submitted by genealogists researching Delaware families. The society will search it for you for a fee.

Genealogical Surname File. This file is at the Bureau of Archives and Records Management. It indexes surnames mentioned in genealogies and

Figure 7.5 Research Outline for Delaware (continued)

local histories. The archives will search it for you, if you include a large, self-addressed, stamped envelope with your request.

Joseph Brown Turner Collection. This excellent collection has correspondence, newspaper clippings, and about 3,000 alphabetically arranged genealogies and pedigrees. It is available at the Bureau of Archives and Records Management and at the Family History Library (FHL films 006,272-300).

Charles Henry Black Collection. This collection has deeds. wills, and other original documents for Sussex and Kent counties in Delaware and Somerset and Worcester counties in Maryland. It was filmed at the Historical Society of Pennsylvania and is available at the Family History Library (FHL films 441,425-31). The collection is listed in the FHLC under DELAWARE, KENT - GENEALOGY.

Genealogical Collection. This is an alphabetically-arranged collection of published family history pamphlets and articles. It was microfilmed in 1949 at the Bureau of Archives and Records Management and is available at the Family History Library (FHL films 006,410-11).

A bibliography and surname index to 215 published Delaware genealogies is Donald Odell Virdin, *Delaware Family Histories and Genealogies* (St. Michaels, Md.: Raymond B. Clark, 1984; FHL book 975.1 A1 No. 11).

HISTORY

The following important events in the history of Delaware affected political jurisdictions, family movements, and record keeping.

1638	Swedes began settling in the Delaware area.
1655	The area was conquered by the Dutch.
1664	Delaware became a British colony.
1682-1776	Pennsylvania's governor controlled much of Delaware, although Delaware had its own provincial assembly after 1703.
1684-1736	The colonial government of Maryland laid claim to southern and western Delaware.
1776	Delaware declared its independence from Britain and established a government separate from that of Pennsylvania.
1787	Delaware became the first state.
1861-65	During the Civil War, Delaware was a Union state.

One of the best sources for studying the history of Delaware is John Thomas Scharf, *History of Delaware, 1609-1888*, 2 vols. (Philadelphia: L. J. Richards & Co., 1888; FHL film 1,000,154). This work is indexed in Gladys M. Coghlan and Dale Fields, *Index to History of Delaware, 1609-1888, by J. Thomas Scharf*, 3 vols. (Wilmington: Historical Society of Delaware, 1976; FHL book 975.1 H2s Index).

LAND AND PROPERTY

The earliest land grants were given by the Swedes and Dutch. When the English acquired the area, land grants were issued by the proprietary of James, Duke of York, in New York. Jurisdiction fell to William Penn in 1682. Land was granted by this proprietary until the Revolutionary War. Records of the Penn proprietary are located in the Bureau of Archives and Records Management.

County land records were filed in the county courts. The county recorders have deeds, mortgages, and leases from the late 1600s to the present. The Family History Library has copies of deeds and deed indexes, warrants, surveys, patents, and bonds for all three counties. Deeds available on microfilm at the library include:

Kent 1680-1850, index 1680-1873
New Castle 1673-1850, index 1640-1873
Sussex 1693-1850, index 1682-1844

The following publications may be helpful to you:

Original Land Titles in the Delaware, Commonly Known as the Duke of York Records..., 1646 to 1679. Wilmington: Sunday Star Print, [1899]. (FHL book 975.1 R2o; 1903 edition on film 006,616, item 2.)

Delaware's Fugitive Records: An Inventory of the Official Land Grant Records Relating to the Present State of Delaware. Dover: Department of State, Division of Historical and Cultural Affairs, 1980. (FHL book 975.1 A1 no. 7; film 1,033,995, item 4.) This guide refers to Delaware land records found in New York and Pennsylvania archives.

Weinberg, Allen, and Thomas E. Slattery. *Warrants and Surveys of the Province of Pennsylvania Including the Three Lower Counties, 1759*. 1965. Reprint. Knightstown, Ind.: Bookmark, 1975. (FHL book 974.8 A1 No. 130; film 1,036,747, item 2.)

MAPS

The most extensive collections of Delaware maps are at the University of Delaware Library and at the Wilmington Institute Free Library. The Historical Society of Delaware collects land survey maps and atlases of landowners.

Figure 7.5 Research Outline for Delaware (continued)

A valuable atlas that shows names of landowners is Daniel G. Beers, *Atlas of the State of Delaware....* Philadelphia: Pomeroy and Beers, 1868. (FHL fiche 6332689.)

Delaware maps for the years 1790, 1810, 1823, 1838, 1862, 1878, 1884, and 1917 are at the Family History Library (FHL film 002,083). The best atlas for showing changes in county formation and boundary disputes is The Newberry Library, John H. Long, ed., *Historical Atlas and Chronology of County Boundaries, 1788-1980,* vol. 1 (Boston: G.K. Hall & Co., 1984; FHL Ref book 973 E7hl v. 1).

Full color county and state road maps are available for a fee from:

Department of Highways and Transportation
Division of Highways
Mapping Section
Dover, DE 19901

MILITARY RECORDS

Many military records are at the Family History Library, the National Archives, and other federal and state archives. The *United States Research Outline* provides more information on the federal records.

The Bureau of Archives and Records Management has original colonial records, Revolutionary War records, War of 1812 files, militia records for 1765 to 1841, some adjutant general Civil War files, and Spanish-American War records.

You may also want to use the following sources:

Early Wars

Public Archives Commission of Delaware. *Delaware Archives.* 5 vols. Wilmington: [N.p.], 1911-16. (FHL book 975.1 M2d; vol. 1 is on film 928,150; vol. 1 is on film 1,033,612, item 4; vol. 5 is on film 599,318, item 2; vols. 3-5 are on fiche 6051215.) This set contains colonial, revolutionary, and some postrevolutionary military records.

Whiteley, William G. *The Revolutionary Soldiers of Delaware.* Wilmington: Historical Society of Delaware, 1896. (FHL book 975.1 M25w; film 1,036,210.)

Civil War

An index to compiled military service records is available at the Family History Library, but the service records have not been microfilmed and are available only at the National Archives. Pension records also have not been filmed and are available only at the National Archives. A roster of Delaware

volunteers is given in J. Thomas Scharf, *History of Delaware, 1609-1888,* 2 vols. (Philadelphia: L.J. Richards Co., 1888; FHL film 1,000,154).

World War II

A helpful source is William H. Conner and Leon deValinger, *Delaware's Role in World War II,* 2 vols. (Dover: Public Archives Commission, 1955; FHL book 975.1 M25d).

NATURALIZATION AND CITIZENSHIP

Naturalization papers in Delaware were generally filed in the superior courts. The Bureau of Archives and Records Management has naturalization records for:

Kent County 1798-1929
New Castle County . 1811-1906
Sussex County 1795-1852

The Family History Library has naturalization records from the three counties, 1834 to 1870 (FHL film 006,529). New Castle County naturalizations before 1811 were recorded in the deed books. New Castle declarations from 1826 to 1850 are at the Historical Society of Delaware.

Many Delaware residents also filed naturalization applications in the local courts in Philadelphia. An important index is P. William Filby, *Philadelphia Naturalization Records* (Detroit: Gale Research Co., 1982; FHL book 974.811 P4p).

For most naturalization records after 1906, contact the National Archives—Philadelphia Branch. It has Delaware district court naturalizations for 1843 to 1959.

NEWSPAPERS

Delaware's first regular newspaper, the *Delaware Gazette,* began publication in 1785 at Wilmington. Major collections of Delaware newspapers are found at the Historical Society of Delaware, American Antiquarian Society, Library of Congress, and Historical Society of Pennsylvania. The "Delaware Index," an index to the *News Journal* and miscellaneous books and pamphlets from 1871 to the present, is available at:

The Wilmington Institute Library
10th and Market Streets
Wilmington, DE 19801

A surname file that includes obituaries indexed from newspapers is at the Historical Society of Delaware.

Figure 7.5 Research Outline for Delaware (continued)

PERIODICALS

The major genealogical periodicals helpful for research in Delaware are:

Delaware Genealogical Society Journal. 1980-. Published by the Delaware Genealogical Society, 505 Market St. Mall, Wilmington, DE 19801. (FHL book 975.1 D25d.)

Maryland and Delaware Genealogist. 1959-. Published by Raymond B. Clark, Jr., P.O. Box 352, St. Michaels, MD 21663. (FHL book 975 B2m.)

PROBATE RECORDS

Probate records have been kept by the register of wills in each county from 1682 to the present. The Family History Library has probate indexes for Kent and Sussex counties from the 1680s to 1948 and an index for New Castle from 1682 to 1885. Wills, administrations, and guardian accounts to about 1850 are also available at the Family History Library and the Bureau of Archives and Records Management.

More recent probate records, such as settlements, inventories, and guardian bonds, are found at the Bureau of Archives and Records Management.

The following calendars (chronological lists) may be helpful:

deValinger, Leon, Jr. *Calendar of Kent County, Delaware, Probate Records, 1680-1850.* Dover: Public Archives Commission, 1944. (FHL book 975.13 P23c; film 1,035,860, item 4; fiche 6051248.)

deValinger, Leon Jr. *Calendar of Sussex County, Delaware, Probate Records, 1680-1800.* Dover: Public Archives Commission, 1964. (FHL book 975.17 P23c; film 1,035,860, item 5.)

Historical Research Committee. Delaware Society of the Colonial Dames of America. *A Calendar of Delaware Wills, New Castle County, 1682-1800.* New York, 1911. Reprint. Baltimore: Genealogical Publishing Co., 1969. (FHL book 975.11 S2n; fiche 6051273.)

TAXATION

Tax assessments were first taken in 1693 (FHL film 441,413). They were taken sporadically until 1726, and annually thereafter. Many early tax lists have been indexed in Ronald Vern Jackson and Gary Ronald Teeples, *Early Delaware Census Records, 1665-1697* (Bountiful, Utah: Accelerated Indexing Systems, 1977; FHL book 975.1 X2p).

Tax lists to about 1850 are on microfilm at the Family History Library. The original lists to about 1915 are preserved at the Bureau of Archives and Records Management.

VITAL RECORDS

Birth and Death Records

Statewide registration of births began in 1861 but was discontinued in 1863. Registration was resumed in 1881 and was generally complied with by 1921. The Family History Library has microfilms of the birth records from 1861 to 1913 (FHL films 006,323-59).

Although some deaths were recorded as early as 1855, state registration of deaths officially began in 1881 and was generally complied with by 1890. The Family History Library has microfilms of the death records from 1855 to 1910 (FHL films 006,360-409).

The Family History Library also has a card index on microfilm of Delaware birth records, 1861 to 1913 (FHL films 006,424-30) and death records, 1790s to 1888 (FHL films 006,431-33). The information in the indexes is from newspapers, death certificates, and cemetery burial records.

The Delaware Bureau of Vital Statistics has birth and death records from 1861 to the present. You can obtain copies by writing:

Bureau of Vital Statistics
Jesse S. Cooper Memorial Building
William Penn Street
Dover, DE 19901

The current fees for obtaining copies of the state's records are listed in *Where to Write for Vital Records: Births, Deaths, Marriages, and Divorces* (Hyattsville, Md.: U.S. Department of Health and Human Services, August 1987). Copies of this booklet are at the Family History Library and local family history centers. Or you can write to the Bureau of Vital Statistics for current information.

Marriage Records

State registration of marriages began in 1847 and was generally complied with by 1913. These records are not available at the Family History Library. You can obtain marriage records by writing to the Bureau of Vital Statistics (see address given above).

Delaware counties began keeping marriage records as early as 1832. These records have been transferred from the counties to the Bureau of Archives and Records Management. These early county marriage records are not available at the

Figure 7.5 Research Outline for Delaware (continued)

Family History Library; however, the library has acquired some pre-1847 marriage bonds. An index of pre-1850 marriage information found in bonds, probate records, and church records is at the Bureau of Archives and Records Management and at the Family History Library (FHL films 006,416-22).

An example of an early marriage license bond collection is Gilbert Cope, *A List of Marriage License Bonds...in New Castle County, Delaware, 1744-1836* (FHL film 441,415.) Marriages of Delaware residents may also be recorded in adjoining states, such as Pennsylvania and Maryland.

Divorce Records

Divorce proceedings from 1975 to the present are kept by the family court office in the county where the divorce was recorded. For records before 1975 and dating back to the early 1900s, contact the county prothonotary's office (clerk of the court of common pleas). For pre-1900 records, write to the Delaware Legislative Council, Legislative Hall, P.O. Box 1401, Dover DE 19901.

FOR FURTHER READING

These books will give you further information about the records of Delaware:

Mattern, Joanne, and Harold B. Hancock. *A Preliminary Inventory of the Older Records in the*

Delaware Archives. Dover: Division of Historical and Cultural Affairs, Bureau of Archives and Records, 1978. (FHL fiche 6331225.)

Reed, Henry Clay, and Marion B. Reed. *A Bibliography of Delaware through 1960*. Newark, Del.: University of Delaware Press, 1966. (FHL book 975.1 A3r.) This guide discusses libraries, geography, history, courts, biographies, and other subjects.

COMMENTS AND SUGGESTIONS

The Family History Library welcomes additions and corrections that will improve future editions of this outline. Please send your suggestions to:

Publications Coordination
Family History Library
35 N. West Temple
Salt Lake City, Utah 84150

We appreciate the archivists, librarians, and others who have reviewed this outline and shared helpful information.

The *State Research Outline* for Delaware has been used by permission of the Family History Department of The Church of Jesus Christ of Latter-day Saints.
At press time, a new edition of the *State Research Outline* for Delaware was in progress.

Assignment 1: Preparation for Your Own Business

Gather Materials

Gather materials from history books, encyclopedias, conference workshops, class outlines, library handouts, state guides, etc., for the states in which you are specializing.

Prepare State Guides for Each Specialty State

Organize the information for each state in which you wish to specialize. Make a concise, abridged summary of sources such as that shown for Delaware in sample 8 of this chapter. Do not forget to include topographical features and riverways as they affected migration. Read several state histories and make a time line of events. Include with this state summary a copy of the U.S. State Research Outlines from the Family History Library (if you will be using the resources of the Family History Library), outlines from the National Genealogical Society, any booklets or handouts from major repositories within the state which would lead you to sources, and any maps, charts, and guides for the state.

Break your summary down into categories such as:

√ Overview
√ Early settlements
√ Migration trails
√ Sources (include books, genealogical collections, histories, and indexes, both printed and electronic)
√ Churches prior to 1900 and their repositories
√ Major libraries and vital records repositories
√ Genealogical periodicals
√ Guides to further sources
√ Research strategies

If you are preparing a guide for a foreign country also include:

√ Word lists
√ Sample letters in the foreign language
√ Countrywide sources
√ Country libraries

Write a brief description of the methods and sources you would use to locate an ancestor in the 1700s versus the 1800s, etc., for your area of specialization.

One way to do this is to review your research calendar and record the steps you took to arrive at a conclusion. Now determine if you could speed up this process if you had known something you discovered after you made the initial search. Did you discover a new index, a manuscript collection, or published sources?

If you are a research librarian or volunteer, write down the steps you used to help someone. Ask others how they trace someone in a particular record group. People love to share their stories.

Ancestry's Fact Sheets. Orem, Utah: Ancestry, 1998.

Bentley, Elizabeth Petty. *County Courthouse Book*. 2d ed. Baltimore: Genealogical Publishing Co., 1996.

Church of Jesus Christ of Latter-day Saints. *Family History SourceGuide*. CD-ROM. Salt Lake City: Church of Jesus Christ of Latter-day Saints, 1998.

Eichholz, Alice. *Ancestry's Red Book: American State, County & Town Sources*. Orem, Utah: Ancestry, 1992, rev. ed.

Meyerink, Kory. *Printed Sources: A Guide to Published Genealogical Records*. Orem, Utah: Ancestry, 1998.

Mokotoff, Gary. "A Businessman Looks at Professional Genealogy." *A Place to Explore; The National Genealogical Society and the San Diego Genealogical Society,* 3-6 May 1995; San Diego, Calif., 354-356. (May be ordered from Repeat Performance, 2911 Crabapple Lane, Hobart, IN 46342, session F-102.)

Szucs, Loretto Dennis and Sandra Hargreaves Luebking. *The Source: A Guidebook of American Genealogy*, Revised Edition. Orem, Utah: Ancestry, 1997.

The Handybook for Genealogists: United States of America, 9th ed. Logan, Utah: The Everton Publishers, 1999.

Warren, James W. "Getting the Most Mileage from Genealogical Research Trips." *A Place to Explore; The National Genealogical Society and the San Diego Genealogical Society,* 3-6 May 1995; San Diego, Calif., 491-494. (May be ordered from Repeat Performance, 2911 Crabapple Lane, Hobart, IN 46342, session F-137.)

Bibliography of State Guides

As you prepare your personal state guides, you should learn what books have already been published about research in your states. The following list identifies most such books. Do not forget to use the various state research insights found on the *SourceGuide, Ancestry's Red Book, The HandyBook for Genealogists,* and *Printed Sources.*

NEW ENGLAND

Crandall, Ralph J., ed. *Genealogical Research in New England.* Baltimore: Genealogical Publishing Co., 1984.

Lindberg, Marcia Wiswall, ed. *Genealogist's Handbook for New England Research*. 3d ed. Boston: New England Historic Genealogical Society, 1993. [Covers each of the six New England states.]

Sperry, Kip. *New England Genealogical Research: A Guide to Sources.* Bowie, Md.: Heritage Books, 1988.

ALABAMA

Barefield, Marilyn Davis. *Researching in Alabama : A Genealogical Guide.* Easley, S.C.: Southern Historical Press, 1987.

ARIZONA

Spiros, Joyce V. Hawley. *Genealogical Guide to Arizona and Nevada.* Gallup, N.M.: Verlene Publishing, 1983.

ARKANSAS

Norris, Rhonda S. *A Genealogist's Guide to Arkansas Research.* Russellville, Ark.: Arkansas Genealogical Research, 1994.

Ruple, Jack Damon. *Genealogist's Guide to Arkansas Courthouse Research.* N.p., 1989. [Includes directory of circuit, county and chancery clerks.]

CALIFORNIA

Local History and Genealogy Resources of the California State Library. rev. ed. Sacramento: California State Library Foundation, 1991. [Contains a summary of the California State Library's local history and genealogical collections, at Sacramento, and in the Sutro Branch, San Francisco.]

CONNECTICUT

Kemp, Thomas J. *Connecticut Researcher's Handbook.* Detroit: Gale Research, 1981.

Morrison, Betty Jean. *Connecting to Connecticut.* Glastonbury, Conn.: Connecticut Society of Genealogists, 1995.

Sperry, Kip. *Connecticut Sources for Family Historians and Genealogists.* Logan, Utah: The Everton Publishers, 1980.

DELAWARE

Delaware Genealogical Research Guide. N.p.: Delaware Genealogical Society, 1989.

Giles, Barbara S. comp. *Selected Delaware Bibliography and Resources.* N.p.: by the author, 1990.

DISTRICT OF COLUMBIA

Angevine, Erma Miller. *Research in the District of Columbia.* Arlington, Va.: National Genealogical Society, 1992.

Schaefer, Christina K. *The Center: A Guide to Genealogical Research in the National Capital Area.* Baltimore: Genealogical Publishing Co., 1996.

FLORIDA

Bodziony, Gill Todd. *Genealogy and Local History : A Bibliography.* New rev. ed. Tallahassee, Fla.: State Library of Florida, 1978.

Byrd, Beverly Pittman. *Genealogy and Local History: A Bibliography*, 5th Supplement. Tallahassee, Fla.: Department of State. Division of Library Services, 1983. [This fifth supplement is cumulative and supercedes the four previous supplements to the bibliography.]

Tip 93: As this information indicates, searching on CD-ROMs can save much time. The CDs also save a lot of space when you are working out of a home office.

GEORGIA

Davis, Robert Scott, Jr. *Research in Georgia: With a Special Emphasis Upon the Georgia Department of Archives and History.* Easley, S.C.: Southern Historical Press, 1981. Reprint 1984, 1991.

Dorsey, James E., comp. *Georgia Genealogy and Local History.* Spartanburg, S.C.: Reprint Co., 1983.

Robertson, David H. *Georgia Genealogical Research: A Practical Guide.* Stone Mountain, Ga.: by the author, 1989.

Schweitzer, George K. *Georgia Genealogical Research.* Knoxville, Tenn. : G.K. Schweitzer, 1987.

HAWAII

Kaina, Maria. *Target Your Hawaiian Genealogy and Others as Well: A Family Guide Provided by the Hawaii State Public Library System.* Honolulu, Hawaii : Hawaii State Public Library System, 1991.

ILLINOIS

Szucs, Loretto D. *Chicago and Cook County: A Guide to Research.* Salt Lake City: Ancestry, 1996.

Volkel, Lowell M., and Marjorie Smith. *How to Research a Family with Illinois Roots.* Indianapolis: Ye Olde Genealogie Shoppe, 1977.

INDIANA

Beatty, John D. *Research in Indiana.* Arlington, Va.: National Genealogical Society, 1992.

Miller, Carolynne L. *Indiana Sources for Genealogical Research in the Indiana State Library*. Indianapolis: Family History Section, Indiana Historical Society, 1984.

Robinson, Mona. *Who's Your Hoosier Ancestor? Genealogy for Beginners*. Bloomington: Indiana University Press, 1992.

Schweitzer, George K. *Indiana Genealogical Research*. Knoxville, Tenn: G.K. Schweitzer, 1996.

KENTUCKY

Hogan, Roseann Reinemuth Hogan. *Kentucky Ancestry: A Guide to Genealogical and Historical Research*. Salt Lake City: Ancestry, 1992.

Schweitzer, George K. *Kentucky Genealogical Research*. Knoxville: G. Schweitzer, 1983.

LOUISIANA

Boling, Yvette G. *A Guide to Printed Sources for Genealogical and Historical Research in the Louisiana Parishes* Jefferson, La.: Y. Boling, 1985.

MAINE

Frost, John Eldridge. *Maine Genealogy: A Bibliographical Guide*. 1977; rev. ed., Portland, Maine: Maine Historical Society, 1985.

MARYLAND

Heisey, John W. *Maryland Research Guide*. Indianapolis: Heritage House, 1986.

Meyer, Mary Keysor. *Genealogical Research in Maryland: A Guide*. 4th ed. Baltimore: Maryland Historical Society, 1992.

Schweitzer, George K. *Maryland Genealogical Research*. Knoxville, Tenn. : G.K. Schweitzer, 1991. 211 pages. [Includes descriptions of material and an indication of location of the material.]

MASSACHUSETTS

Schweitzer, George K. *Massachusetts Genealogical Research*. Knoxville: G. Schweitzer, 1990.

MICHIGAN

McGinnis, Carol. *Michigan Genealogy Sources & Resources*. Baltimore: Genealogical Publishing Co., 1987.

MINNESOTA

Porter, Robert B. *How to Trace Your Minnesota Ancestors.* Center City, Minn. : Porter Publishing Co., 1985.

Pope, Wiley R. *Tracing Your Ancestors in Minnesota : A Guide to the Sources.* 9 vols. St. Paul, Minn. : Minnesota Family Trees, 1980+ Vol. 1 is 2d ed., rev. and enl.

Warren, Paula Stuart. *Minnesota Genealogical Reference Guide.* Warren Research & Publishing: St. Paul, Minn., 1994.

Warren, Paula Stuart. *Research in Minnesota.* Arlington, Va.: National Genealogical Society, 1992.

MISSISSIPPI

Lipscomb, Anne S. and Kathleen S. Hutchison. *Tracing Your Mississippi Ancestors.* Jackson, Miss.: University Press of Mississippi, 1994.

MISSOURI

Steele, Edward E. *A Guide to Genealogical Research in St. Louis.* St. Louis: St. Louis Genealogical Society, 1992.

MONTANA

Richards, Dennis Lee. *Montana's Genealogical and Local History Records.* Detroit: Gale Research, 1981.

NEBRASKA

Nebraska: A Guide to Genealogical Research. Lincoln, Neb.: Nebraska State Genealogical Society, 1984.

Nimmo, Sylvia, and Mary Cutler. *Nebraska Local History and Genealogical Reference Guide.* Papillion, Neb.: S. Nimmo, 1987.

NEVADA

Spiros, Joyce V. Hawley. *Genealogical Guide to Arizona and Nevada.* Gallup: Verlene Publishing, 1983.

NEW HAMPSHIRE

Towle, Laird C. and Ann N. Brown. *New Hampshire Genealogical Research Guide.* 2d ed. Bowie, Md.: Heritage Books, 1983.

NEW JERSEY

Barker, Bette Marie. *Guide to Family History Sources in the New Jersey State Archives.* Trenton: New Jersey Division of Archives and Records Management, 1987.

NEW MEXICO

Spiros, Joyce V. H. *Handy Genealogical Guide to New Mexico.* Gallup: Verlene Publishing, 1981.

NEW YORK

Clint, Florence. *New York Area Key: A Guide to the Genealogical Records of the State of New York.* . . . Elizabeth, Colo.: Keyline Publishers, 1979.

Epperson, Gwenn F. *New Netherland Roots.* Baltimore: Genealogical Publishing Co., 1994.

Guzik, Estelle M., ed. *Genealogical Resources in the New York Metropolitan Area.* New York: Jewish Genealogical Society, 1989.

Schweitzer, George K. *New York Genealogical Research.* Knoxville: G. Schweitzer, 1988.

NORTH CAROLINA

Hofman, Margaret. *The Short, Short Course in the Use of North Carolina's Early County-Level Records in Genealogical Research.* Roanoke Rapids, N.C.: Margaret M. Hofmann, 1992. [Three-hole-punched for notebook use.]

_____. *An Intermediate Short, Short Course in the Use of Some North Carolina Records in Genealogical Research.* Roanoke Rapids, N.C.: Margaret M. Hofmann, 1992. [Three-hole-punched for notebook use.]

Leary, Helen F. M., editor. *North Carolina Research: Genealogy and Local History*, 2d ed. Raleigh: North Carolina Genealogical Society, 1996.

Schweitzer, George K. *North Carolina Genealogical Research.* Knoxville: G. Schweitzer, 1991.

OHIO

Bell, Carol Willsey. *Ohio Genealogical Guide.* 6th ed. Youngstown, Ohio : Bell Books, 1995. [More instructional than her *Guide to Genealogical Sources* (below), which is mostly a list of sources.]

_____. *Ohio Guide to Genealogical Sources.* Baltimore: Genealogical Publishing Co., 1988.

Ohio State Library. *County by County in Ohio Genealogy.* Columbus, Ohio : The Library, 1992.

Schweitzer, George K. *Ohio Genealogical Research.* Knoxville, Tenn.: G.K. Schweitzer, 1994.

OKLAHOMA

Blessing, Patrick J. *Oklahoma: Records and Archives.* Tulsa: University of Tulsa Publications, 1978.

O'Brien, Mary Metzger. *Oklahoma Genealogical Research.* Sand Springs, Okla. : M. O'Brien Bookshop, 1986.

OREGON

Lenzen, Connie. *Research in Oregon.* Arlington, Va.: National Genealogical Society, 1992.

Lenzen, Connie. *Oregon Guide to Genealogical Sources.* Rev. ed. Portland, Oreg.: Genealogical Forum of Oregon, 1994.

PENNSYLVANIA

Heisey, John W. *Handbook for Genealogical Research in Pennsylvania.* Indianapolis: Heritage House, 1985.

Pennsylvania Line: A Research Guide to Pennsylvania Genealogy and Local History. 4th ed. Laughlintown, Pa.: Southwest Pennsylvania Genealogical Services, 1990.

Schweitzer, George K. *Pennsylvania Genealogical Research.* Knoxville: G. Schweitzer, 1986.

Woodroofe, Helen Hutchison. *A Genealogist's Guide to Pennsylvania Records: Reprinted from the Pennsylvania Genealogical Magazine.* Philadelphia: Genealogical Society of Pennsylvania, 1995. (Special publication, The Genealogical Society of Pennsylvania ; no. 5)

RHODE ISLAND

Sperry, Kip. *Rhode Island Sources for Family Historians and Genealogists.* Logan, Utah: Everton Publishers, 1986.

SOUTH CAROLINA

Hendrix, Ge Lee Corley. *Research in South Carolina.* Arlington, Va.: National Genealogical Society, 1992.

Holcomb, Brent Howard. *A Guide to South Carolina Genealogical Research and Records.* Rev. ed. Columbia, S.C.: B. H. Holcomb, 1991.

Schweitzer, George K. *South Carolina Genealogical Research.* Knoxville: G. Schweitzer, 1985.

TENNESSEE

Bamman, Gale Williams. *Research in Tennessee.* Arlington, Va.: National Genealogical Society, 1993.

Fulcher, Richard Carlton. *Guide to County Records and Genealogical Resources in Tennessee.* Baltimore: Genealogical Publishing Co., 1987.

Schweitzer, George K. *Tennessee Genealogical Research.* Knoxville: G. Schweitzer, 1986.

TEXAS

Bockstruck, Lloyd DeWitt. *Research in Texas.* Arlington, Va.: National Genealogical Society, 1992.

Kennedy, Imogene K. and J. Leon Kennedy. *Genealogical Records in Texas.* Baltimore: Genealogical Publishing Co., 1987. Reprint 1992.

UTAH

Jaussi, Laureen, and Gloria Chaston. *Genealogical Records of Utah.* Salt Lake City: Deseret Book Co., 1974.

VERMONT

Eichholz, Alice. *Collecting Vermont Ancestors.* Montpelier, Vt.: New Trails, 1986.

VIRGINIA

McGinnis, Carol. *Virginia Genealogy: Sources & Resources.* Baltimore: Genealogical Publishing Co., 1993.

Schweitzer, George K. *Virginia Genealogical Research.* Knoxville: G. Schweitzer, 1982.

WASHINGTON

Genealogical Resources in Washington State: A Guide to Genealogical Records Held at Repositories, Government Agencies, and Archives. Olympia, Wash.: Office of the Secretary of State, Division of Archives and Records Management, 1983.

WEST VIRGINIA

McGinnis, Carol. *West Virginia Genealogy: Sources & Resources.* Baltimore: Genealogical Publishing Co., 1988.

Stinson, Helen S. *A Handbook for Genealogical Research in West Virginia.* Rev. and exp. South Charleston, W. Va.: Kanawha Valley Genealogical Society, 1991.

WISCONSIN

Danky, James P. *Genealogical Research: An Introduction to the Resources of the State Historical Society of Wisconsin,* Rev. ed. Madison: State Historical Society of Wisconsin, 1986.

Ryan, Carol Ward. *Searching for Your Wisconsin Ancestors in the Wisconsin Libraries.* 2d ed. Green Bay, Wis.: C.W. Ryan, 1988.

WYOMING

Spiros, Joyce V. H. *Genealogical Guide to Wyoming.* Gallup: Verlene Publishers, 1982.

Further Educational Opportunities

Personal Enrichment

Tip 94: I have been known to go to conferences and spend eighty percent of my time learning from vendor demonstrations rather than lectures. This will probably continue to be the case as new computer technologies are applied to genealogy.

Tip 95: Don't be lulled to sleep on the cushions of advantage, never to reach the ultimate goal. While technology is good, we need to temper its use with wisdom, or it can consume all our time with its novelty and we may never achieve our ultimate goal.

Conferences and Seminars

Each year national conferences are held by the National Genealogical Society and the Federation of Genealogical Societies. There is nothing quite as invigorating as being at a national conference with 1500 to 3000 fellow genealogists. Many of the best of the profession are invited to give lectures and provide training to others. In addition to learning from the many societies, organizations, and individual researchers at these conferences, commercial vendors are present to demonstrate a multitude of aids and research sources.

To find more information on the various conferences being held, or to buy copies of the conference syllabi, contact:

Federation of Genealogical Societies
PO Box 200940
Austin, TX 78720-0940
Phone/FAX 888-FGS-1500
Internet Home page: www.fgs.org

National Genealogical Society
4527 Seventeenth Street North
Arlington, VA 22207-2399
Phone 703-528-2612
Internet Home page: www.ngsgenealogy.org

As mentioned previously, the Utah Genealogical Association holds a yearly conference in which training is given on the major collections of the Family History Library and other aspects of foreign and domestic genealogy. They also sponsor the Salt Lake Institute of Genealogy in which the various curriculum tracks deal with not only research skills but also how to improve your professional skills. Brigham Young University (BYU) also offers correspondence courses in family history, a one-week Family History Conference, and year-round classes.

Several colleges and universities, associations, and societies, offer excellent classes taught by experienced researchers. Among the courses offered are the following:

Institutes (usually one week in length)

JANUARY

Salt Lake Institute of Genealogy, Salt Lake City, Utah. For application forms write to Salt Lake Institute of Genealogy, P.O. Box 1144, Salt Lake City, UT 84110-1144. Because UGA has the largest number of Accredited Genealogist of any genealogy organization, the Institute sponsors courses which focus on maintaining research skills as well as helping new candidates prepare for the exam. Unlike UGA's normal yearly conference, these in-depth courses of twenty-hours during the week on one topic such as foreign research or professional standards in reporting and analysis are particularly beneficial to the serious candidate.

JUNE

Samford University. Request information from Institute of Genealogy and Historical Research, Samford University, Birmingham, Alabama. Write to Director, IGHR, Samford University Library, 800 Lakeshore Drive, Birmingham, AL 35229, or phone (205) 870-2780 or FAX (205) 870-2483.

JULY

Genealogical Institute of Mid-America, Springfield, Illinois. For a brochure write Continuing Education Coordinator, University of Illinois at Springfield, Springfield, IL 62794-9243, or call (217) 786-7464.

Family History Conference

AUGUST

BYU Genealogy and Family History Conference. Write to Conferences and Workshops, Brigham Young University, 136 Harman Building, P.O. Box 21516 Provo, UT 84602-1516, or call (801) 378-4853 Fax (801) 378-6361. Many instructors at this yearly conference come from those who formulate and give the Accreditation exams. Therefore, these one-hour courses are of particular value to the candidate for accreditation.

Full Semester Classes

End of JANUARY to end of MAY
End of AUGUST to mid-DECEMBER

Monterey Peninsula College, Associates Degree Program under Family Research Studies, Office of Admissions and Records, 980 Fremont Street, Monterey, CA 93940-4799, or call (408) 646-4002

Tip 96: There are numerous tracks offered yearly and each track contains 20 classes. The basic subjects include British Isles (one year it might be England, then Wales, then Ireland, then Scotland); U.S. Research (Midwest, New England, Eastern, or Southern States); Genealogy Computing; Librarianship; Professional Support (Building a Genealogy Business, Advanced Research Techniques, Publishing Your Family History, or Genealogy Writing); Intermediate Genealogy; European Research (Germany, Scandinavian, France, or Eastern European); and Speciality Record Groups.

Tip 97: Master the law of evidence and become an expert at finding the facts, filtering the facts, and following the facts.

206

Tip 98: No matter what the job is, most people can learn to do the actual work involved, yet few become successful. Why? Most stop when the pressure is off. They never learn to manage themselves and operate under their own supervision. Successful genealogists not only do the job and manage themselves, but they motivate others.

or (408) 646-4000 or for information call (408) 373-5206.

Hartnell College, Associates Degree Program under Library Media Technology, Office of Admissions and Records, 156 Homestead Avenue, Salinas, CA 93901, or call (408) 755-6711 or (408) 373-5206.

Brigham Young University, Office of Admissions, Administration Building Building, Provo, UT 84602-1516.

Online Genealogy Courses (Distance Learning Courses)

Monterey Peninsula College offers Internet courses in Family History Studies each semester. Registration is by telephone during the two months before the classes start (June-July; November December). The first class is LIBR 60 Family Research Studies: Genealogy 1. Introduction to family history research methods using sources from 1850 to 1920. Students use the computer program Personal Ancestral File (PAF) to record, analyze data, and establish a family history archival notebook. The class is ONLINE, 3 units. Students must have access to a computer and be familiar with using the Internet. Questions about the class can be answered by calling 646-4095. These courses are offered under the Library Department and are part of either an associates degree program or a certificate program.

Home Study Classes

Brigham Young University, Department of Independent Study, 206 Harman Building, Provo, UT 84602-1516. (801) 378-2868.

National Genealogical Society Home Study Course, 4527 Seventeenth Street North, Arlington, VA 22207-2399. Phone (703) 528-2612.

Lectures on Tape

Tip 99: Although the tapes are wonderful for cross-country driving and waiting in traffic in between research trips, the lectures and corresponding visual aids given at the conferences are invaluable. Treat yourself to a conference as often as possible.

When you are unable to attend a major conference, you can still learn from the speakers by ordering the lectures on tape. Below are addresses of companies who have tape recorded national genealogy conferences in the past. Write for their catalogs if you are interested in studying in the comfort of your own home or while driving back and forth to work.

Once you have the catalogs, you can order the tapes by reference to the conference at which they were recorded. To receive an index to the various lectures offered, request a copy of the *Index to NGS and FGS Conferences and Syllabi* compiled by Joy Reisinger, C.G.R.S., and published by the National Genealogical Society and the Federation of Genealogical Societies, 1993.

Business Products, Inc., 21 Federal Blvd., Denver, CO 80219.

Infomedix, 12800 Garden Grove Blvd., Suite E, Garden Grove, CA 92643.

Tip 100: Periodicals often contain articles on how to conduct research in a particular area. They also contain information on how to access the holdings of a particular repository or how to use a specific record group.

Tip 101: Use PERSI which is available at every family history center on microfiche, to help you locate articles of interest.

Tip 102: The Genealogical Journal of the Utah Genealogical Association is an excellent source for learning to use the resources of the FHL.

Tip 103: I was once told, "A computer will not replace a professional genealogist, but a professional genealogist with a computer will replace those without one."

Tip 104: The Internet's Web pages are a great place to pick up new sources in such places as Karen Green's site for Frontier Press, Ancestry's "Home Town," and Family Tree Maker's home page.

Repeat Performance, 2911 Crabapple Lane, Hobart, IN 46342, (219) 947-1024.

Triad, PO Box 120, Toulon, IL 61483. (May be out of date.)

Periodicals

I have mentioned repeatedly the value of genealogy conferences and tapes for keeping informed. Now I would like to focus on the value of genealogical periodicals. They are valuable even if you are traveling to conferences. Some of these periodicals might be just what you need.

√ Select a good periodical covering the state you are researching.

√ Select a periodical that covers techniques:
   1) *The Genealogical Journal* published by the Utah Genealogical Association
   2) *The National Genealogical Society Quarterly*
   3) *The New England Historical and Genealogical Register*

√ Select a periodical that covers computer programs:
   1) *Genealogical Computing* (published by Ancestry)
   2) *NGS/CIG Digest* (published by the National Genealogical Society)

√ Select a periodical that is produced by vendors and covers new sources (almost all of them have some sources in them) such as:
   1) *Ancestry* (Published by Ancestry)
   2) *Heritage Quest* (published by AGLL)

√ Select a periodical covering news about genealogy in general:
   1) *The Forum* (newsletter of the Federation of Genealogical Societies)
   2) *NGS Newsletter* (newsletter of the National Genealogical Society)
   3) *NEXUS* (newsletter of the New England Historic Genealogical Society)

√ Select a periodical that covers the profession:
   1) *The APG Newsletter* (published quarterly by the Association of Professional Genealogists)
   2) *On Board* (published by the Board for Certification of Genealogists)

The *Periodical Source Index* (*PERSI*) is a very valuable search tool that enables you to find information that is hidden in thousands of genealogical magazine articles. It is a comprehensive subject index created by the Allen County Public Library in Ft.Wayne, Indiana, with more than one million entries to articles that have appeared in English-language (and French Canadian) genealogy periodicals since 1847. *PERSI* is now available from Ancestry on CD-ROM. This edition makes searching the twenty-seven printed *PERSI* volumes easier and obviously occupies much less bookshelf space the printed *PERSI* volumes. With the CD-ROM you can track down every article searched according to locality (both state and county), publication date, family surnames, and subject. The CD is available from Ancestry, 1-800-ANCESTRY(262-3787).

Final

Tip 105: New societies are springing up each year with various goals and projects. Thousands of them are compiling records that may be of benefit in your research. Start your search at www.fgs.org, which will soon link you to over 500 other societies. Watch the Internet for society Web pages and you will find information on nearly every state in the union and most foreign entities as well.

One of the hardest things to do is to accurately assess your own abilities in anything. This book was written to help you, the aspiring genealogist, along the path to a professional credential. May you find that thirty years from today you enjoy what you are doing as much as you do today. There are just a few more things I would suggest that you do before you have completed your preparations. If you truly have accomplished all the suggestions in this book, I'm sure I will see you soon on the front cover of a published volume, lecturing in a classroom, searching corners of the globe for missing ancestors, or involved in one of dozens of other genealogy related businesses. Good luck, and here's your last assignment.

1. Complete assignment 1 by adding your personal experiences to the prepared sample letter. Don't forget all your volunteer time and those hours of pure joy you spent in the library. Don't forget to include your business, computer, and report-writing classes. All these experiences will come in handy in your genealogy business.

    Now look at the blanks. Could some of the suggestions given in this chapter help you out? What do you intend to do to improve your skills?

Tip 106: Accredited genealogists contribute to the APG Newsletter and The Genealogical Journal of UGA.

2. Make a copy of the time chart in appendix C and start today to fill it out. Assume that you have been paid $350 to trace one of your ancestor's lines. How productive were you? Did you solve the problem? How many hours did it take? Could you do it faster if you did it again? Did you use your study guides prepared in the previous chapter?

Tip 107: We should all write a short report before we stop a research session. It doesn't have to be much, just what we were doing when we stopped and what we plan to do the next time we start.

3. Did you remember to write a report for the question above? Very few clients will pay you if you don't give them a report. Write your report if you haven't already done so.

4. Compare your report with the checklist found under appendix D. Indicate what you missed and try to fix the problem. Could you find a way to decrease your report-writing time? Would a template help? Ask other genealogists how they speed up their client reports.

    If you have no one to critique your work, let me hear from you regarding this last assignment. We all need peers to assess our work. You can do it! I know you can.

Tip 108: Spend your life on something that outlasts it.

Assignment 1: Practice Letter Describing Experiences

Use the following outline as a sample letter. As you fill in the blanks, it will help you to describe your personal experiences.

Date _____

My name is _____. By occupation I am a _____

My address, telephone, e-mail and FAX are _____

_____

_____

I wish to apply for a genealogy credential in the category of_____

I have attended these non-genealogical schools, colleges, universities or instructional courses.

School/College Courses	Locations	Dates in Attendance	Degrees or Certification

I read or write the following foreign languages:

Language	Read	Write

I have attended the following genealogical courses and obtained the following degrees or certificates. (Attach copies of certificates or degrees.)

Genealogy Courses or Degree Programs	Sponsoring Organizations	Lecturers	Dates

I am a member of a genealogical society and have served in the following capacities:

Genealogical and Historical Society	Offices Held

I have written or compiled for publication the following articles or books using standard bibliographical form. Please find enclosed a photocopy of the title page and a few selected pages from these publications relating to the category in which I am seeking my credential. [If you have not published, so state; publications are not required.]

I seek a credential in order to _____

My area of specialty is _____

I am available to do research (when) _____ and I have access to _____

_____

I am very interested in working on _____

_____.

I plan to work on records in my area. I have access to federal archives records in the _____
_____, to original vital records in the _____

_____, to probate and land records in the _____

to _____ in _____.

I plan to do research for hire and to serve my clients in a timely manner by _____

_____

Do you live far from another genealogist and need a peer-reviewer? Send to: Karen Clifford, AG, Genealogy Research Associates, 2600 Garden Road, Suite 224, Monterey CA 93940.

Appendix A: Certification

Even though this book focuses on accreditation, the certification program of the Board for Certification of Genealogists should at least be introduced. You can receive the Application Guide, testing materials, and a one-year subscription to the BCG's skillbuilding newsletter, *On Board*, by sending a $25 check with your request for a preliminary application. Write to:

> Board for Certification of Genealogists
> Post Office Box 14291
> Washington, D.C. 20044

You may apply for one of six certification categories, each requiring different skills. Learning these different processes builds your self-esteem as well as your abilities. (The Board is currently reviewing the certification process. Please write to the address above for information.)

The applicant has one year from the date of the Preliminary Application to submit the *Final Application.*

The *Final Application* fee, currently $150, is payable when the completed portfolio is submitted. It is the same price for all categories. A *Renewal Application* is required every five years. To change categories you are required to submit a new application. The following category descriptions are condensed from the *Application Guide* produced by the Board for Certification of Genealogists:

Certified Genealogical Record Specialist (CGRS) are researchers, librarians, teachers, writers, and compilers of source material—all of whom have important expertise in common: a sound knowledge of the records within their geographic or ethnic specialties.

CGRSs are well informed about the various types of resources relating to their geographic or ethnic specialties. Broad experience enables them to identify proper sources for any needed information. They are familiar with the handwriting used over the period of years covered by their work. They can knowledgeably interpret the records they use. They know the strengths and weaknesses of both original and secondary records in their fields, and they can design and carry out an effective search within relevant national, state, and local resources.

Certified Genealogists (CG) are those who have amply demonstrated their ability to resolve difficult lineage or identity problems, compile well-crafted family histories, and understand all facets of genealogical research and analysis.

Those who earn this seal must have a good working knowledge of geographic and historical bibliography in general and a thorough knowledge of the history, literature, and records of the area(s) in which they specialize. They must know the terms used to express relationships, occupations, and status in the time periods of the search—as well as the local laws, customs, and handwriting of various eras.

CGs exhibit a thorough knowledge of principles and materials of genealogical research and an ability to apply such knowledge to problems as they develop. They are able to differentiate between the various classes of evidence, know the weight to be given to each, select the best evidence, and draw logical conclusions.

A CG is skilled in analyzing each step of the research problem. They are able to identify and locate records that would answer a research problem. If they are not able to personally examine a set of records relating to a research problem, they can skillfully direct an agent to do so, assuming that he supplies copies of the records or thorough abstracts so there is no misunderstanding of the meaning of the document.

One of the hallmarks of the CG is to be able to prepare a well-planned, properly arranged, thoroughly documented, and sufficiently cited family history.

The CG is also able to prepare intelligent, efficient, and businesslike reports that identify the records searched and recite positive or negative results for each of the consulted sources.

Certified American Lineage Specialists (CALS) reconstruct single lines of descent and ascent and prepare papers for individuals seeking admission to hereditary and patriotic societies.

CALS are thoroughly familiar with genealogical bibliography and are able to evaluate printed work; but they do not base a lineage solely on printed books or periodicals. At no time do they use undocumented compilations as supporting evidence of a fact or relationship.

CALS know the types of records applicable to the purpose of admission to hereditary and patriotic societies. In all cases they fully record, when submitting documentation to lineage societies, the sources of the documentation.

Certified American Indian Lineage Specialists (CAILS) engage in research to determine descent from a historical Indian tribe that is native to the North American continent.

CAILS are well informed on principles of genealogical research and prepare lineages supported by evidence to prove each statement made and each link between generations. They know the types of records applicable to this purpose, how to locate them, and how to interpret them. At all times their approach is duly critical. They fully document all sources and if less-than-direct proof of any generation exists, they thoroughly discuss the evidence, pro and con.

Certified Genealogical Lecturers (CGL) give public addresses of an educational nature on specific genealogical topics or on related subjects pertinent to the tracing of family relationships. The CGL will have also passed requirements in a research category—that is, CGRS, CG, CALS, or CAILS.

Certified Genealogical Instructors (CGI) teach genealogical courses. The CGI must also meet requirements for a CG as well as show that they can plan and execute a genealogical course. They must also show that they have already taught courses successfully and list an area of specialization.

Whichever credential you ultimately apply for, you will certainly grow as you stretch beyond your normal capacities to become a recognized member of a tested and proven group of individuals.

Suggested Reading

Board for Certification of Genealogists. *Application Guide*. Falmouth, Va., 1995.

Board for Certification of Genealogists. *Education Preparation for Certification*. Falmouth, Va., 1995.

Board for Certification of Genealogists. *Roster of Genealogists Certified: Researchers, Editors, Instructors, Lecturers, Librarians, and Writers*. Falmouth, Va., 1995.

Board for Certification of Genealogists. *Which Category is Right for You?* Washington, D.C., 1996.

Mills, Elizabeth Shown, Kathleen W. Hinckley, Phyllis Brown

Miller, Marsha Hoffman Rising, and Christine Rose. "Certification: A Workshop," *From Sea to Shining Sea; Federation of Genealogical Societies and Seattle Genealogical Society*, 20-23 September 1995; Seattle, Wash., F-95.

Rose, Christine. "Preponderance of Evidence: When CAN it be used?" *Traveling Historic Trails; National Genealogical Society and Middle Tennessee Genealogical Society*, 8-11 May 1996; Nashville, Tenn., F-95. (May be ordered from Repeat Performance, 2911 Crabapple Lane, Hobart, IN 46342, session F-95.)

Stevenson, Noel C. *Genealogical Evidence: A Guide to the Standard of Proof Relating to Pedigrees, Ancestry, Heirship, and Family History*. Laguna Hills, Calif.: Aegean Park Press, 1979.

Appendix B: Hiring a Professional Genealogist

FAMILY HISTORY LIBRARY™
SALT LAKE CITY, UTAH

RESOURCE GUIDE

Hiring a Professional Genealogist

Hiring a professional genealogist can be an excellent way to discover your family roots. If you lack the time and skills for research or if you encounter a very challenging research problem, you may need the assistance of an experienced professional. These guidelines will help you find and employ a competent genealogist.

The keys to finding a good genealogist are the same for hiring other competent professionals. First, you need some general information about what genealogists do and the services they provide. This information can be found in Part I of this guide. Second, you need to know the right questions to ask and how to evaluate the responses you get. This information is found in Part II.

PART I: GENERAL INFORMATION

Services Provided by Genealogists

The services of professional genealogists fall into four major categories.

Tracing Ancestry. A professional genealogist can help trace your family lines back in time. For example, a genealogist may be able to discover who your immigrant ancestors were and where they came from. Or, a genealogist can research one of your family lines back to a specific time period or individual. This is often helpful when someone wants to join a lineage society and must prove that one of their ancestors participated in a historical event such as the Revolutionary War.

Researching Descendants. A professional genealogist may help you in descendancy research. A genealogist identifies people who descended from a particular individual. For example, you may be a descendant of Daniel Boone and want to start a family organization of his descendants to share genealogical information. A professional genealogist can help you identify the frontiersman's descendants so you can contact them.

Finding Missing People. Many people employ genealogists to find missing relatives or lost friends. Attorneys hire genealogists to search tax records, computer data bases, and other records to locate heirs to an estate. Some adopted children hire professional genealogists to help them find their birth parents.

Searching Records. To save time and avoid travel costs, you can employ a record searcher to find and review the records for you. Record searchers review only the records you instruct them to search.

Providing Other Services. Genealogists also provide a range of other services that include—

- Consulting and counseling with you about how to solve a research problem.
- Deciphering handwriting on old records.
- Translating foreign records.
- Instructing and lecturing on genealogical topics.
- Computerizing genealogical information.
- Abstracting and publishing records.

Professional Methods

Regardless of the type of research they perform, most professional genealogists follow a similar research process. Understanding this process will help you know what to expect from the genealogist you hire.

Define the Research Problem. Good genealogists first review the information you already have. They discuss your research problem with you and make sure they clearly understand what you want them to accomplish.

Develop a Research Plan. Genealogists next develop a research plan that outlines what they will do to find the information you want. Most plans consist of a prioritized list of the records the genealogist will search. Research plans can be written or verbal. Your genealogist may share the plan with you.

Conduct the Research. As they follow their research plans, genealogists go to libraries, courthouses, archives, cemeteries, and other places to search for the information. As they search, they may photocopy pertinent records or acquire official copies.

Analyze the Findings. Genealogists regularly review their research and make conclusions about what they found. They also compare their findings with other documents to confirm or disprove conclusions.

Report the Findings. Periodically, genealogists prepare reports about their research activities. The report should include photocopies or abstracts of important information. It may also include suggestions for continued research.

Prepare Forms. At your request, a genealogist can prepare forms such as pedigree charts, family group sheets, and applications to lineage societies. They may also enter information into a genealogical computer program for you.

Share Results. Genealogists can help you share the results of your research. A genealogist can contribute the findings to genealogical data banks such as

Ancestral File™, prepare articles or books, or submit names of ancestors to LDS temples.

Bill for Services. Genealogists bill for their services at agreed-upon intervals. Bills should clearly identify the time spent and expenses incurred on the project to date. Bills are often included with reports.

Genealogical Credentials

Genealogists are generally not required by law to be licensed or certified. However, they can receive credentials from several organizations. Each organization sets its own criteria for granting credentials. The reference section at the end of this guide includes two major organizations that grant credentials and offer arbitration when problems arise.

You should also consider other criteria as you make your hiring decision. Most genealogists are self-taught, and many competent genealogists do not seek credentials. Years of education, research experience, and satisfactory service to clients may be just as important as credentials.

Genealogists' Rates

Three concepts determine a genealogist's rates. First, rates charged by genealogists vary widely. Genealogists who charge higher rates do not necessarily do better research. However, some genealogists who charge lower rates may be less educated, inexperienced, and their work may be less than satisfactory. Many genealogists charge more to afford the ongoing training needed to provide better service.

Second, the nature of the work may affect rates. For example, record searching is less demanding than researching a lineage. Consequently, a record searcher may charge less than a genealogist.

Third, reputable genealogists cannot guarantee to find the specific information you need. For example, if the census taker missed your great-grandfather's house, even the best genealogist will not be able to find his name in the census.

Fee Structure. Although rates vary between genealogists, most genealogists charge an hourly rate plus expenses.

Hourly Rates. Most genealogists base their hourly rate on their education, training, skill, experience, and credentials and what the market will bear. Rates range from $10.00 per hour to as high as $100.00 per hour. The average rate charged by most competent genealogists ranges from $15.00 to $35.00 per hour. Record searchers often charge between $7.00 and $20.00.

Since rates vary, it is sometimes hard to know what warrants a higher rate. In general, genealogists may justifiably charge higher rates if they—

- Are experienced researchers in great demand.
- Have some unique research specialty, such as a knowledge of records in a foreign country or expertise concerning a particular set of records.
- Have credentials that reflect advanced skills.
- Have years of education and professional development.
- Live in a large city with a high cost of living.
- Have access to facilities with many records.

Although the majority of genealogists work independently, you may find genealogical firms in areas where large repositories of records exist. Firms usually offer a wider variety of services and expertise.

Expenses. In addition to an hourly rate, most genealogists bill for the expenses they incur. Common expenses include—

- Costs of copies of records, certificates, and other documents.
- Fees paid to other researchers to search records in distant cities.
- Field travel (auto, meals, lodging).
- Admission fees paid to courthouses, repositories, and other record facilities.
- Administrative costs for items such as postage, supplies, and secretarial services.

Payment. Methods of payment vary. Many genealogists ask their clients to pay a certain amount of money (a retainer) before work begins. The genealogist then works and bills against the retainer until it is spent. Then, another retainer is paid and work continues.

Some genealogists simply bill as they work. Others charge a daily rate or charge a flat fee per project. These payment methods are less common than the retainer system.

You can do the following to help control costs:

- Gather together as much information about your family as you reasonably can.
- Break a large project into smaller tasks and pay periodically.
- Request frequent reports and detailed billings to keep you informed.
- Clearly specify whether the genealogist can bill for additional services (cost overruns) and under what conditions it is appropriate to do so.
- Have other family members help pay costs.

Research Scope

Generally, genealogists use the first few hours of a research project to define their clients' goals, analyze the problem, and develop a research plan. This can vary considerably depending on the amount of previous research.

Be sure to give your genealogist enough start-up time on your project. Genealogists usually need at least eight to ten hours to be productive on most research projects. Simple tasks, such as performing a record search or evaluating a lineage, should take much less time.

PART II: THE HIRING PROCESS

The six steps in this section are designed to help you locate several professional genealogists, and then choose the one that best meets your needs.

Six Steps for Hiring a Genealogist

1. Determine your research needs.

2. Obtain a list of genealogists.

3. Contact <u>appropriate</u> candidates.

4. Determine which candidate is best for you.

5. Make an agreement before work begins.

Step 1: Determine Your Research Needs

Before hiring a professional genealogist, clarify your research problem and determine what you want the genealogist to do. If you define your research goals early, you are more likely to be satisfied with the results. In addition, you can often save money by gathering information that already exists.

However, if you do not have the time or interest to gather the information needed to define a research goal, you may want to skip step one. Once you have hired a genealogist, you can let the professional decide where to begin.

Do not start with a general or vague goal (example: I want to know more about my ancestors on my mother's side). Begin to clarify the problem by finding and reviewing as much existing information as possible. You may want to check—

- Pedigree charts and family group sheets.

- Family histories and traditions.

- Birth, death, and marriage certificates; obituaries; funeral programs; and so forth.

- Diaries, journals, old letters, and photocopies of family information from Bibles.

- Military records, naturalization certificates, photographs, and so forth.

After deciding what you want to learn, summarize your research problem and state how the genealogist can help you.

At this point, determine if you really need to hire someone. Maybe you can get help from friends or a genealogical society.

Step 2: Obtain a List of Genealogists

If you need to employ someone, try to determine what expertise the genealogist needs to have.

Next, obtain a list of potential genealogists. The reference section identifies lists of genealogists. You can also contact libraries, archives, or genealogical societies in your area.

Step 3: Contact Candidates

Contact several genealogists whose skills and credentials seem appropriate. If you telephone candidates, you can find out immediately if the genealogist is available and interested in working on your project. And you may also be able to gain a sense of the genealogist's competence. However, be considerate of the researcher's time. Do not expect too many ideas before the genealogist has seen your records.

Writing letters is a slower process, but many genealogists prefer written correspondence because they have time to think about the project before responding. Be sure to include your return address, phone number, and a self-addressed stamped envelope (SASE).

Discuss the following in your phone call or letter:

- Your research problem, materials, and goals.

- The genealogist's availability and interest in your project.

- The research strategies the genealogist might use.

- The genealogist's access to records required for your project.

- The reporting procedure. (You may even want to see a sample report.)

- The genealogist's areas of specialty and credentials (including language skills if needed).

- Rates and billing procedures.

Step 4: Determine Whom to Hire

After contacting several genealogists, decide which one will best meet your needs. Consider:

- Do you feel the genealogist has a good understanding of your research problem and knows how to solve it?

- Do you sense that the genealogist is really interested in your project?

- Do you feel that the genealogist has the required background and skills?
- Do the genealogist's fees seem appropriate?
- Does the genealogist have familiarity with and access to the records that are most likely to solve your research problem?

Step 5: Make an Agreement

Before the genealogist begins working on your project, be sure to make a verbal or written agreement. Verbal agreements are possible, especially when the project is small. A written agreement can be as simple as a letter stating your expectations and authorizing the genealogist to proceed, or it can be a formal written contract. Either you or the genealogist can prepare the agreement. In lieu of a formal contract, some genealogists have a list of their research methods and policies that is modified for each project and signed by the client.

Any agreement, verbal or written, should include at least the following:

- The research goal and scope of the project.
- Frequency of reports and bills.
- Content of the reports.
- What constitutes fees and expenses.
- Payment and limitations of fees.
- How cost overruns should be handled.
- What happens if one or both parties do not or cannot fulfill their part of the agreement.
- Publication rights to the research findings.
- What forms the genealogist will prepare.

Step 6: Provide Information and Fees to Start

After selecting a researcher, share the information you collected in step 1. You will avoid needless duplication by informing your genealogist of the records you found and the research that has already been done. Send good photocopies of your materials. Never give original documents or other materials for which you have no other copy.

Send whatever retainer or fees are required for the genealogist to begin working.

Stay in Contact

As you work with your genealogist, be sure to communicate often. Most problems can be avoided through good communication. However, if problems do arise, get in touch with the organization that credentialed the genealogist. Many organizations will mediate or arbitrate disagreements between the genealogists they credential and their clients.

PART III: REFERENCE SECTION

Accredited Genealogists
The Family History Library™
35 North West Temple Street
Salt Lake City, UT 84150
List provided at no charge.
The library accredits researchers conducting research in most major countries. An agreement of integrity is signed.

Certified Genealogists
Board for Certification of Genealogists
P.O. Box 14291
Washington, D.C. 20044
Cost for directory: $12.00
This organization tests and certifies researchers in various categories of services. All certified individuals must agree to a "code of ethics."

APG Directory of Professional Genealogists
The Association of Professional Genealogists
P. O. Box 40393
Denver, CO 80204-0393
Cost: $15
Available at your local library or from the Association of Professional Genealogists. Researchers listed in the directory must agree to a code of professionalism.

Directory of Professional Genealogical Researchers
Everton's Genealogical Helper,
September-October issue only
P.O. Box 368
Logan, Utah 84321

An annual list of those who pay to have their names listed. Many libraries, archives, and courthouses maintain lists of researchers who use their facilities. Lists are usually provided as a courtesy to patrons, and no attempt is made to assess credentials.

Appendix C: Research Time and Expenses Chart

Research Time and Expenses

Researchers name _____

Client	Date	Records searched	Surname searched	Time spent	Expenses: Copies, Postage, FAX, etc.

Appendix D: Checklist for Customer Report

1. Have the directions given by the client been followed closely?

2. In the report, have you been able to make transcriptions of almost illegible documents?

3. Are all documents and photos identified? For example, photos of tombstones should be identified with the name and location of the cemetery and a transcription of the tombstone.

4. In the report there should be no typographical errors or strikeovers.

5. The dates in the report and the dates on the documentation should always agree.

6. Do not submit as original documentation a family history you personally wrote.

7. Do not submit any family history without documentation from primary sources.

8. If you use secondary published genealogies make sure they are documented genealogies.

9. Give sources for all names, dates, and places mentioned in your reports.

10. Include the dates and places for all lines, not just the direct line that the paper goes through.

11. Insure all dates are in proper form: 6 Feb 1776 and not 6-2-76.

12. Submit complete references for your sources - "1870 census" or "Smith Genealogy by Jones" is not sufficient.

13. Check the original source rather than hand-copied materials from others' research.

14. Don't place superfluous documents in your report.

15. If you are submitting a "weight of evidence" or "circumstantial evidence" case, give clear explanations. In fact, have someone else read it who is completely unfamiliar with the report to see if they understand your logic.

16. Include documentation to prove each marriage for multiple-ancestor marriages.

Index